Other Books by PHIL COUSINEAU

The Hero's Journey: Joseph Campbell on His Life and Work

Deadlines: A Rhapsody on a Theme of Famous
and Infamous Last Words

The Soul of the World: A Modern Book of Hours
(with Eric Lawton)

Soul: An Archaeology: Readings from Socrates to Ray Charles

Prayers at 3 A.M.: Poems, Songs, Chants, and
Prayers for the Middle of the Night

UFOs: A Manual for the Millennium

Design Outlaws: On the Ecological Frontier
(with Christopher Zelov)

Soul Moments: Marvelous Stories of Synchronicity—Meaningful
Coincidences from a Seemingly Random World

The Art of Pilgrimage: The Seeker's Guide to Making Travel Sacred

A World Treasury of Riddles

The Soul Aflame: A Modern Book of Hours
(with Eric Lawton)

The Book of Roads: Travel Stories from
Michigan to Marrakesh

ONCE AND FUTURE MYTHS

The Power of Ancient Stories in Modern Times

PHIL COUSINEAU

Foreword by
STEPHEN LARSEN

CONARI PRESS
Berkeley, California

Conari Press books are distributed by Publishers Group West.

ISBN: 1-57324-146-6

Cover Illustration: © PhotoDisc
Book Design: Suzanne Albertson

LIBRARY OF CONGRESS CATALOGING-IN-PUBLICATION DATA

Cousineau, Phil.
Once and future myths : the power of ancient myths in modern times /
Phil Cousineau ; foreword by Stephen Larsen.
p.   cm.
Includes bibliographical references and index.
ISBN 1-57324-146-6
1. Myth. 2. Life. 3. Cousineau, Phil. I. Title.
BL304 .C69 2001
291.1'3—dc21
2001001822

Printed in the United States of America on recycled paper.

01 02 03 04   Phoenix   10 9 8 7 6 5 4 3 2 1

For Jo,
my once and future love

ONCE AND FUTURE MYTHS

The latest incarnation of Oedipus, the continued romance
of Beauty and the Beast, stands this afternoon
on the corner of 42nd Street and Fifth Avenue
waiting for the traffic light to change.

—Joseph Campbell

Perhaps if we could really listen to what the myths are
    telling us
we could hear what I heard myself saying not so long ago:
"Everybody has to be the hero of one story: his own."
I said it lightly; or rather something said it in me,
for we know more than we know, more than we
    understand.
And if it is true, what an awesome undertaking!

—P. L. Travers

Maybe true.
Maybe not true.
Better you believe.

—Old Sherpa saying

FOREWORD

by STEPHEN LARSEN, Ph.D.,

author of *A Fire in the Mind:*
The Life of Joseph Campbell and *The Mythic Imagination*

*H*uman beings ceaselessly mythologize their environments. That is why most traditional cultures have a sacred well, tree, or mountain, in which this or that event is conceived of as happening in *illo tempore*, "that time" in which the veil parted between this world and the invisible one, and something sacred took place. Around that something they will embroider a web of stories, establish a "frame of reverence" and perhaps base a culture or a way of life upon it. Thus sacred space is established, and equally, sacred time, marking *when* as well as *where* the event took place (celebrating the birth of Christ in Bethlehem each year at Christmastime).

The stories become "testaments," old or new, that choreograph the life of the community, giving it a mythic warrant, a sacred raison d'être. According to historian of religion Mircea Eliade, the profane, a temporal order, looks toward the sacred, an eternal order of things, to dignify it with greater meaning. The tracks of the encounter with the sacred in human history are found everywhere. They are synonymous with the human quest for meaning. An understanding of human culture, then, seems inseparable from what is generically called "mythology." James Joyce said, "Eternity is in love with the productions of time," and the reverse seems equally true: Mortality conducts a perennial love affair with immortality. The personal and the universal dance in and out of our lives and our dreams.

The urge to understand mythology as a discipline in and of itself began in the latter part of the nineteenth century and then broke forth riotously, as if it were some new species of life, long denied recognition, in the twentieth. The early "ethnographers" were scholars who studied the "ethnicities" (the bewildering variety of world cultures other than monolithic Euro-American) to look for patterns that might help to explain the roots of their own culture. Sir James Frazer's monumental twelve-volume *The Golden Bough* showed scholars—and the educated public—that crosscultural themes and patterns were widespread and persistent. A divine figure, the dying and reviving God of Spring and the equivalent human figure of the "Year King" (the king who "must die") permeated European and Middle Eastern history.

A perennial landscape began to be discerned, with its mythic *dramatis personae* and events. Beneath the human realm lay a spooky underworld—often equated with the land of the dead, into which all mortal beings pass and from which they make an eternal return. Existence on the human levels was to be ennobled and immortalized by heroes and their miraculous quests. The origins of things, the encounter of good and evil, the nature of destiny and the meaning of life—all are addressed in mythology.

Anthropologists began systematic studies of cultures in hope of contributing to the world of social science. The structural patterns that underlie mythic forms were investigated. Theories of the why and how of mythology began to become current in the early twentieth century. Novelists and artists realized that there were untold riches of inspiration in dusty old volumes. Consider some of the great names: European ethnographers Leo Frobenius, Lucien Levy-Bruhl, and the founder of structural anthropology, Claude Lévi-Strauss; the American anthropologists Clyde Kluckhohn and Margaret Mead.

Nor could a new generation of depth psychologists resist the mythic, for therein lay the perennial patterns that fascinate and compel the psyche: Oedipus, Narcissus, and the "hero with a thousand faces" who shows up in myriad cultural inflections. Sigmund Freud and Carl Jung found ancient myths being enacted in the dreams of common folk, and developmental psychologist Jean Piaget showed how "magical" or mythic thinking dominates the mental world of childhood. In the literary domain, James Joyce, Thomas Mann, and Robert Graves, and the poets Ezra Pound and T. S. Eliot were exploring the evocative and dramatic powers of myth. In French philosophy, a new "postmodern" school that followed the writings of Jacques Lacan and Roland Barthes (who showed that ancient myths permeate popular modern culture) emerged, and influenced academia profoundly.

But then there was the great twentieth-century mythologist Joseph Campbell, of whom depth psychologist James Hillman has said, "No one in our century, not Freud not Jung, not Thomas Mann, not Lévi-Strauss, has so brought a mythic sense of the world back into our daily consciousness."[1]

"And why should it be," asks Campbell, "that when men have looked for something solid on which to base their lives, they have chosen, not the facts in which the world abounds, but the myths of an immemorial imagination, preferring even to make life a hell for themselves and their neighbors in the name of some violent god, to accepting gracefully the bounty the world affords?" And elsewhere, "In the absence of an effective general mythology, each of us has his private, unrecognized, rudimentary, yet secretly potent pantheon of dream. The latest incarnation of Oedipus, the continued romance of Beauty and the Beast, stand this afternoon on the corner of Forty-second Street and Fifth Avenue, waiting for the traffic light to change."[2] Further, Campbell showed that when the myths are held unconsciously, as in fundamentalist Christianity or Islam, or even in secular social movements such as Nazism or Marxism, they can operate with catastrophic consequences. He seconded Jung's belief that we ignore mythology at our own peril.

Cultivated consciously, however, Campbell shows us, the mythic sensibility incomparably enriches our lives. We understand how typical human situations have been handled since time immemorial. Campbell called it "the secret opening" through which mythological understanding breathes life into psychology, and also into the creative arts and literature, music, dance, theater and film. Timeless messages are delivered in timely ways!

Surely then, Joseph Campbell has shown how contemporary culture needs a "mythic sense of the world." But the inevitable question then also arises, What then?

This leads us to the book you hold in your hand, and—this is consistent with Phil Cousineau's essential message—to a story. In May 1987 Campbell was already carrying the aesophogeal cancer that would claim his life five months later, but it had not yet been diagnosed. He was living in Hawaii in those years, but returning to New York fairly often to meet with his publishers or to accompany his wife Jean, whose Theater of the Open Eye was giving regular performances in New York. So Robin and I were delighted when Joe called us to let us know he was back in town, and asked us, "Would you like to get together?" He was his usual cordial, warm self, but I thought there was just a little edge of an unknown anxiety in his voice.

A few days later we met for dinner and watched the screening of *The Other Side of Life,* a new film on death and dying we had been working on at the Swedenborg Foundation. After the viewing, Campbell stood up in the distinguished company and said what he most liked about the film was that it opened the metaphysical perspective without proselytizing for any creed. After dinner we left to see an Open Eye presentation of a contemporary Japanese Noh play: *The Dream of Kitamura.* As the cab crossed the Brooklyn Bridge from Manhattan (the play was in Brooklyn Heights) Campbell froze us, as he was wont to do, with one of his unnervingly direct remarks: "I'm not afraid to die," he said. Then he gave us the sequel: "I just don't want to be there when it happens." He had, in fact, just given us Woody Allen.

After the laughter Joseph grew more pensive. "It's for you folks to carry on..." he said, and I immediately had one of those uncanny frissons to which the author of *Once and Future Myths* is also prone (we use them to know when a moment is, well, "momentous"). To both Robin and me it felt like there was the passing of a mantle of some kind, but to whom, and how? There was also a hollow feeling. It deepened as we saw the spooky play that night, which invoked those delicious ghostly presences that haunt Japanese folk mythology. Our good-bye that night would be our last. Joseph passed away on October 30, 1987.

So what of that mantle he was passing on? Where did Joseph Campbell's influence go, we wondered, as the twentieth century was grinding to a close? We were to find out two years later as we undertook to write *A Fire in the Mind,* Campbell's authorized biography, which would be published in 1991.

We had already seen *The Hero's Journey,* the moving documentary film on Campbell's life by Stuart Brown, William Free, and Phil Cousineau. Even though Campbell had a distinct aversion to lionization, during his latter years he had realized that he too would achieve mortality in his own lifetime. Invaluable footage of Campbell in his eighties was taken for posterity by Free, Brown, and Cousineau. The "Mythos" series made from it would come to supplement and deepen the popular "Power of Myth" series made with Bill Moyers. (The latter was one of the classics of educational television in America, attracting millions of viewers in the late '80s and '90s.) In 1990 Cousineau had created a companion book to the film out of the raw footage of Campbell's autobiographical reflections, but we had not yet met him.

Our first meeting was to be two years after Campbell's passing, in an old Victorian hotel in San Francisco. Phil and I "sized each other up," cautiously, as students and protégés of Campbell. We seemed to be rather different people. Would our biographies compete with each other? But Robin's and my task was to interview Cousineau for the book we were writing. As we began, so did a magic web of story. Joe had mentored Phil in as unique a way as he had mentored each of us— me in writing and Robin in her art. As we listened to each other's tales we were filled with a mutual and overwhelming gratitude for the mentorship. Our friendship began then, and has continued ever since.

Cousineau writes beautifully and movingly of mentoring in this book, and surely it is one of the most important mythic themes of all time: Aeneas to Odysseus, Merlin to Arthur. As we interviewed for *A Fire in the Mind* each of the uniquely creative people that Campbell had mentored, Robin and I realized that we were truly part of an intellectual and creative family. Though we had a common legacy in Campbell's approach to myth, we were very different people and had followed our own path in the forest (in one of Campbell's favorite images from the Grail literature). Perhaps Joseph Campbell was a prophet of sorts, but he failed to start an orthodox priesthood of initiates. Instead he empowered a generation of uniquely creative spirits. Poet Robert Bly, himself in turn a mythic mentor to a whole generation of creative questers, has spoken gratefully of the mentorship he received from Campbell. Also mythically inspired psychologist Jean Houston, novelist Richard Adams, filmmaker George Lucas, dancer and tai chi master Chungliang Al Huang, philosopher Sam Keen, anthropologist Joan Halifax, musicians Jerry Garcia, Mickey Hart, and David Darling, and many others were mentored in some special and personal way by Campbell. (In this family there can be no sibling rivalry because the new mantle is a rainbow garment; we don't compete with, but complement, each other's creative colors.)

What I love about Phil Cousineau's tapestry, especially as woven in this new book, is its autobiographical flavor—while somehow entwined with the wisdom of the ages. Cousineau takes personal mythology in a different direction than that taken by Sam Keen in *Your Mythic Journey,* or by Stanley Krippner and David Feinstein (who also drew inspiration from Campbell) in *Personal Mythology.* In a uniquely creative development including the mythologies of place, time, creative struggle, athletic striving, journeys, music (jazz particularly), writing, and parenting, Cousineau shows us once again that myth is "something that never was, yet always is," through the unique prism of a life lived with intelligence and compassion. And he demonstrates how myth relates to life in a wonderful variety of ways. There are quotable sections and juicy quotes from world literature throughout.

Cousineau's chapter on the mythology of time would by itself make the book worthwhile. As he presents it, sacred time and sacred space are the defining landscape of the soul. We visit the Detroit of his childhood at the same time we join him on a present-day return to the city—a quest to introduce his young son to his father's history, and a moving exploration in personal mythology. The diamond of baseball, the mythic American game, becomes a symbolic matrix for athletes to touch the hero-journey of all time—a veritable Field of Dreams. Cousineau uses these interlocking time-strands to weave together a brilliant excursus on the mythology of the city, the athletic *agon* conducted in its *stadia*, and the ways in which the psyche is fascinated and ensorcelled by such metaphors. His essays in this volume migrate from smoky San Francisco jazz cabarets to the cafés and bookstores of Paris in *illo tempore*, that timeless time when it was exploding with avant-garde writers and artists. Paris emerges, as it did for Joyce and Campbell, as the paradigmatic city of the creative soul in search of its destiny. (Campbell was there in the legendary 1920s when the city was exploding with artistic and literary creativity, a period of time which Cousineau also mythologizes as the apotheosis of the creative impulse.)

As the book unfolds we get to visit the eerie stone *moai*, the giant "gods" of Rapa Nui (Easter Island) with Cousineau, and in this section I almost felt as if I were on one of Phil's legendary guided tours. I love the textured way his narrative weaves geography and journey metaphor, soul reflections and poignant biography, along with the mythic nuggets to be found lying around everywhere in the living landscape of his prose. Indeed Phil Cousineau, through his many films and books, has helped to introduce a new genre in spiritually informed journeying (see *The Art of Pilgrimage* and *The Book of Roads*) to the modern world.

Cousineau's reverence for the landmarks of the inner journey is as great as that of the outer (see *Soul Moments: Miraculous Stories of Synchronicity and Meaningful Coincidences from a Seemingly Random World* and *Soul: An Anthology*). In these forays into the realms within, Cousineau developed the multidimensional vision that informs this book. When we encounter the world with mythic senses aroused, it invites a galvanizing response, and life becomes a mysterious and magical adventure that leads you along. Phil Cousineau has grown into a unique fulfillment of the task that Joseph Campbell laid on us in that cab: "It's for you folks to carry on. . . ." ("Take what I have given you, make it your 'bliss,' your own, and see if the universe doesn't respond. . . . Doors will open for you that you didn't even know were there"—those synchronicities Cousineau writes about so intriguingly!) Campbell, with his last words to us, was speaking to an entire creative generation yearning for inner fulfillment—and yearning to make a creative contribution to life.

This book fills me with awe for the creative fire glowing within my mythic brother and fellow scholar as he walks his creative path, with books and films that guide the soul and instill life-affirmative values. And I think of the words of mythically informed psychologist Jerome Bruner, who said that, "Not until we tell ourselves a story can we make sense of our experience." This book is woven of stories; and when we share stories a profound communication takes place. We experience the archetypal realm through a personal journey in it. *Once and Future Myths* is a remarkably intelligent and intriguing walk through the world with mythic sensibilities open and tingling. Let it guide you past the twin gateway monsters of materialism and meaninglessness, and you will find yourself on a new kind of journey that both reveals the timelessness of life and brings out the best in you: a hero's journey. Read on!

[1] In a speech delivered by Hillman at the National Arts Club of New York, on the occasion of Campbell's receiving the Gold Medal of Honor for Literature.

[2] Quoted in *A Fire in the Mind* by Stephen and Robin Larsen. Joseph Campbell, Primitive Mythology, in *The Masks of God* (New York: Viking Press, 1959), p. 545.

INTRODUCTION

The Splendid Prism
of Myth

7 t is a late autumn evening. Lamplight is glinting off the bookshelves in the living room. I know every title by heart and exactly where my father placed each book. I see the way he caresses their bindings when he takes his favorite volumes off the shelf, ancient classics such as the *Iliad, Grimm's Fairy Tales,* and *The Nibelungelied,* as well as modern ones like *Faust, Moby Dick, Huckleberry Finn,* and *The Great Gatsby.* I hear his voice as he turns off the ballgame playing on the old black and white Philco television, pours himself a shot of J & B whiskey, and grabs his favorite edition of the *Odyssey.*

"We're going to read out loud together," he insists, pausing dramatically. "As a family."

When he hears me groan, his response echoes across the decades: "Someday you'll thank me, son." I'm twelve. I have no idea what he's talking about. I want to watch *Gunsmoke* or the Tigers' game, but it's useless to argue. He's been stuck behind a desk all day at the Ford Glass House in Dearborn, Michigan, writing out a press release for some new sports car called the Mustang, and he wants to forget the corporate pressure that is bending his soul. He wants to enter a different world altogether. So we're going to *read.*

For the next few hours my father, mother, brother, sister, and I take turns reading a page apiece about the epic wanderings of the wily Greek hero, while my dad keeps a running commentary on why this family ritual is good for us. The night grows furtive; we fight to stay awake. My father can read till dawn and can't understand why we can't keep up with him. By eleven the others have trundled off to bed, and it's just the two of us. He pours another scotch for himself, sloshing it over crackling ice cubes. Then he winks at me and clinks his glass of whiskey against my cup of Vernor's ginger ale. Carefully, he reopens the book and turns to a new chapter about old heroes.

Did we read about the agony of Achilles or the courage of Hector that night? I don't remember the details, but something deep within me recalls our family voices merging together above page after page of fantastic voyages, magical transformations, and heartbreaking deaths on the battlements.

Slowly, over the course of that evening and many others like it, the nutrients of those books seeped into my bloodstream. Together, those stories have inspired my lifelong fascination with heroes and monsters, gods and goddesses, beauties and beasts, quests and explorations, distant lands and romantic adventures. That was a great gift I got from my father, but just as fine was the ritual he enforced as if he were a tribal elder.

After we completed each book on his classics list, my father found some way to bring it even more alive for us. When we finished reading Homer and Virgil, he drove us in the old Ford Falcon to the Detroit Art Museum so we could look at the Greek and Roman vases. Once we had turned the last page of Apollodorus' rendering of *Jason and the Argonauts,* he insisted on seeing the movie version at the State Wayne, our hometown theater, and after gazing at a book about ancient Rome we ventured into Detroit to see Kirk Douglas lead the slave revolt in *Spartacus.* The first summer we spent in New York City we read Melville's *Moby Dick,* then sauntered down to the Village to see John Huston's movie version. The next day we drove out to New Bedford, Massachusetts, so we could experience the old seaport that had inspired the whaler-turned-author. There on the docks we ate chowder at an old clam shack, and then, with the creaking of the ship's mast in the wind to accompany us, as if to indelibly imprint the story in the wax of memory, we read out loud from my father's favorite passages.

My father, Stanley H. Cousineau, who worked in public relations for Ford
Motor Company for thirty-three years, is seen here at the helm of Henry
Ford's original Model T, at the Ford Rotunda, Dearborn, Michigan, 1957.

One of the most exciting results of my father's synesthetic teaching
came about on the weekend we saw, at the Metropolitan Art Museum,
some old Greek pottery and sculpture depicting the original Olympic
athletes, followed by a game at Yankee Stadium. I vividly recall the fris-
son, the uncanny shiver down my back, from watching Mickey Mantle
and Roger Maris glide through the same outfield that Babe Ruth and
Joe DiMaggio had once roamed. It was the thrill of recognition com-
bined with the fascination of mystery. When I mentioned to my dad
that the way Mantle threw the ball home from deep center field
reminded me of the statue of the old Greek javelin thrower I'd seen in
the museum the day before, his eyebrows arched; he looked up from
the newspaper he was glancing at, and muttered, "*Hmm.* You thought
of that all by yourself?"

He didn't say he agreed or disagreed, but I could tell he was surprised that I had made a connection between the two. For a flickering moment he even seemed astonished that perhaps all the books and museums may have made a difference in my life.

I could tell he was proud from the smile he tried to hide behind his newspaper.

※

Of course, this is one of my own myths. I was raised on the knee of Homer, which is an Old World way to describe growing up on stories as old as stone and timeless as dreams. So I see myth everywhere, probably because I am looking for what my American Indian friends call "the long story," the timeless aspect of everything I encounter. I know the usual places to look for it, such as in the splendor of classic literature or the wisdom stories of primal people. I've memorized a litany of luminous definitions and descriptions of *myth*, such as "a sacred narrative," "the collective wisdom," "the group dream," "other people's religion," "the vehicle of profoundest metaphysical insights," "cultural DNA," even "a metaphor transparent to transcendence." I am profoundly indebted to the great scholars of mythology who have rendered such complex material into pithy sayings, and I am often startled by the beauty of their theories about its origin and function.

But in the chapters following I want to explore the aspect of myth that most fascinates me: its "once and future" nature. Myths are stories that evoke the eternal because they explore the timeless concerns of human beings—birth, death, time, good and evil, creativity and destruction. Myth resembles the god Proteus in the *Odyssey*, a shape-shifting creature who knows the secret that the lost Greek sailors long to hear—the way home. But they must learn how to get a grip on him, if only for one slippery moment, so he might surrender his hidden wisdom.

This is what I call "mythic vision." The colorful and soulful images that pervade myth allow us to step back from our experiences so that we might look closer at our personal situations and see if we can catch a glimpse of the bigger picture, the human condition. But this takes practice, much like a poet or a painter must commit to a life of deep attention and even reverence for the multitude of meaning around us. An artist friend of mine, Gregg Chadwick, calls this "pulling the moment," a way of looking deeper into experiences that inspire him. In the writing classes I teach, I refer to this mystery as the difference between the "overstory," which is the visible plot, and the "understory," which is the invisible movement of the soul of the main characters. What is mysterious about mythic stories is how they always meander back to the same place: your soul. In this sense myth is a living force, like the telluric powers that stream through the Earth. It is this mythic vision, looking for the "long story," the timeless tale, that helps us approach the deep mysteries because it insists there is always more than meets the eye. In this sense the mythic vision helps us see the stories we *really* live by, rather than the one we like to think we are living, and moreover, decide if our myths are working for or against us. If we don't become aware of both our personal myths and the cultural myths that act upon us like gravitational forces, we risk being overpowered by them.

But I am caught on the horns of a dilemma. How do I tell the truth about the immense gifts of the mythic imagination, as well as describe its bittersweet influence on my life and the life of the world? What I never learned from my father or my college professors is that myth is Janus-faced: one face turned to the ancient world of brilliantly colorful gods and goddesses, heroes and monsters; the other face turned inward, personal, soulful.

This much I know: Unless we search for ways to become aware of the myths that are unfolding in our lives we run the risk of being controlled by them. As the maverick philosopher Sam Keen has written in *Your Mythic Journey,* "We need to reinvent them from time to time.... The stories we tell of our ourselves determine who we become, who we are, what we believe."

In this book I will tell you things I myself have lived and learned about myth. No doubt, I am inspired by my father's ideas about making the world of books *real* for us, and by my friend and mentor Joseph Campbell's ardent beliefs that the myths are alive and well "on the corner of 42nd Street and 5th Avenue," and that "myths are public dreams; dreams are private myths." But in the following six chapters I explore how I've actually experienced and encountered myth: in books and museums, to be sure, but also in art, literature, movies, poetry, ballparks, playgrounds, cafés, computers, and cathedrals. In other words, this will be a mythopoetic approach to the modern world.

My other inspiration for this approach is the French philosopher Michel de Montaigne, who lived in Périgueux, the same small village in the Dordogne where my ancestor Jean-Baptiste Cousineau came from back in 1687. When I was there a few years ago exploring my roots, I picked up a volume of his sagacious *Essays* and, while reading it one afternoon in an outdoor café, discovered something that has stayed me with me ever since. Into the oak beam of the ceiling in his private library in the Dordogne, a few miles from the Lascaux caves where his ancestors carved and painted their own questions forty thousand years earlier, Montaigne carved the legendary words, *"Que scais-je?"*

"What do I know?" Montaigne asked himself. What do I really know, deep in my soul? What have I *lived?*

A few months later I returned to the Bay Area and immediately drove down to Big Sur, where I was scheduled to teach a course on "Myth, Dream, and the Movies," at Esalen Institute. As part of my preparation the first evening there, I reviewed a book by Evan S. Connell, written at Big Sur years before, and felt the tingle of literary synchronicity when I stumbled across these words: "A man's words should have the feeling of being carved in oak."

"But how did it all begin?" asks the Italian scholar Roberto Calasso in his mesmerizing study of Greek myths, *The Marriage of Cadmus and Harmony.* There is no more probing question. Whether it is the tales of Zeus and Europa, the mystery rites at Eleusis, or the origins of eros and strife, virginity and rape, comedy and tragedy, heroes and cowards, fate and necessity, the seed moment is what makes everything else possible.

At the Museum of Art in Pittsburgh, there is a twelve-foot-long narrative collage by Henri Matisse entitled, *"Les mille et une nuits" (The Thousand and One Nights.)* In this magnificent piece depicting Scheherazade and the Arabian Nights, the artist has made a cutout of a white magic lamp and set it against a mauve background, its wisps of smoke turning into flowers that drift across the increasingly dark panels, denoting the passage of night. In the upper right-hand corner of the frieze is a tribute to Scheherazade's courage and cunning while telling her soul-saving stories during those mythic nights: *"Elle vit apparaitre le matin Elle se tut dicretement"* ("When she saw the first light of dawn, she fell discreetly silent").

Mysteriously, discreet storytelling is at the heart of myth.

The Strange Melody

The word *myth* comes from the ancient Greek for "word," "tale," or "story." The clue to its deeper meaning lies in the roots of the word—just as myths are, in a word, "root" stories. Myth derives from the Greek *muthos,* which means "to murmur with closed lips, to mutter, to moan." The suggestion buried deep within the strange melody of this deceptively simple word is that there is great power and perhaps even secret knowledge in stories about the beginning of things. Among some cultures, such as the Tibeto-Burman, there is a belief that *unless the origin of something is described one should not even talk about it.* Telling a story about how things began, from babies to stars, rituals to customs, is a way of paying respect to its importance, its endurance, and in so doing every event and experience is endowed with a sacred nature.

This belief has its modern parallels with family reunions, religious ceremonies, or holidays. In the moments when we feel the atavistic urge to tell our origin stories—anecdotes about our ancestors, tales of how we met our spouses, the roots of hallowed customs at Easter, Halloween, Hanukkah, or Christmas—we participate in mythmaking. We experience the mythic vision when we thrill to the findings of distant signals from outer space that push back the origins of the universe another billion years, or become alternately disturbed and enthralled by the mapping of the human genome, or are ineffably troubled by the threat of a hydroelectric dam inundating the recently discovered paleolithic temple-caves in Portugal, whose paintings of leaping bulls and wizard-beast shamans go back more than fifty thousand years.

An obscure Scottish definition of *myth* reveals yet another layer of meaning: "to mark, to notice, to measure," and "the marrow of a bone." Out of the heather and highlands comes a helpful suggestion that myths are the stories that mark us deeply, notice the sacred dimensions, measure the depths of our souls, and cut to the marrow with their slicing images of the never-ending struggle between life and death.

In these associative ways of approaching the essence of myth, we begin to see its beauty and its power. While science revels in explaining *how* the world works, myth and poetry explain *why*. Its stories and images about creation, origins, animal powers, quests, death, and rebirth are attempts to give a sense of the movements of the soul's experience of the world. This is why myths are lies that tell the truth, unreal stories that "signify the inner meaning of life," in Alan Watts' memorable phrase. Or as Elie Wiesel writes of Hasidic legends, "Some things happen that are not true, some don't happen that are."

What the deterioration of the word *myth*—implying delusion, falsehood, or a farrago of nonsense—reveals is the ironic truth that many of our myths *are* lies in the sense that they no longer reveal the *inward* significance of things that happen in our lives. As religion journalist Don Lattin has written, "Myths are stories, and we find meaning in our lives through the stories we tell. Myths are not true or untrue— they're living or dead."

In fact, the modern world is full of living mythology. There is a wonder-cabinet of curiosities, stories, images, icons, and presences. In the past few months alone I've noted in the pages of the *New York Times* references to the American Myth of Progress; myths of love and romance in the movies; the myth of killer sharks; the mythic aspirations of George Lucas' *Star Wars* trilogy; the twisted myth of Frankenstein as mad gene-splicing scientist; the mythmaking machine of political campaigns; the crippling effects of family myths; the legendary outsider status of Marlon Brando and the Olympian influence of Wall Street insiders; the fabled genius of Leonardo da Vinci and the legendary curse on the Boston Red Sox; and a much-ballyhooed story of the pre-Christian nomadic discoveries of dinosaur bones in Asia centuries before Christ that inspired the headline, "Monster Myths Born of Fossils?" and, just the other day, "Evolution: Myth or Fact?"

Despite the brash claims of scientific materialists and religious moralists, myth still suffuses and enlivens everyday life. We've hardly banished or "progressed" past it. We've simply renamed the stories, both good and bad, the way the names of Hindu gods have changed through the centuries, though their powers remained intact, or the way ballplayers come and go from our favorite teams, while the team uniforms remain the same. The urge to go back to the beginning to understand ourselves, then tell the tale, thereby mythologizing our life and times, is irrepressible.

In this uncanny way it is thrilling to me to notice the way a few of the old stories I grew up on keep reappearing in modern guise in movie theaters, the sports pages, art galleries, or science magazines, often recalling William James' whirligigging line, "There goes the same thing I saw again before."

With the old telltale shiver of recognition, I recall a night back in the late 1980s when I found myself in an old café on Place Contrescarpe in Paris, reading an essay by Albert Camus. One line made my eyes sting with bittersweet recognition. "A man's work," he wrote, "is nothing but the slow trek to rediscover, through the detours of art, those two or three great and simple images in whose presence his heart first opened."

This work is a series of ruminations on those stories and images that first opened my heart and continue to open it again and again each time I encounter myths that renew my faith in the mystery dimension of the world. Similarly, I hope these musings will inspire you to find the guiding images that first opened your own heart.

Stories That Make Life Endurable

By the time I took my first seminar, in 1979, with my future friend and mentor, the mythologist Joseph Campbell, I had long been under the spell of myth. My subsequent work with him gave me the courage of my convictions that the old stories are indeed alive, even "once and future," as the English fabulist T. H. White regarded King Arthur. For centuries there has been a strong folk belief that Arthur never really died. Instead, he lives on in a remote cave in the mountains of Wales, waiting for the right moment to return and redeem the land. *The Once and Future King* is both a memorable book title about the medieval model for courage and chivalry and a wonderful description of the timeless power of mythic tales and mythic imagination.

Out of the galaxy of myths to choose from, the ones I explore in this book are the ones I know in oak, as Montaigne carved, the ones that haunt me. In these essays I explore myth in the way I've encountered it in the street, on the road, inside books, through dreams, by way of vigorous conversation, and presented in a montage style that blends story, anecdote, poetry, freeze frame, and musical segue.

The chapters that comprise this book emerge out of thirty years of reading myths and traveling the world over in search of their origins, as if drawn to them by magnetic forces. Their topics range from a meditation on myths about the riddle of time to the creative struggle, contemplations on the soul-guiding influence of mentors to reflections on the ancient lore about travel, a rhapsody on the theme of mythic cities, and, finally, a reverie on the mythic pull of sports.

Unfolding within each essay are many other themes recurring in myth—origins, time, play, place, rhythm, gods and heroes, love and death—discussed as eternal metaphors for the invisible webwork of these mighty forces, symbolic stories for the sacred energies that forge our fate and destiny.

The old storytellers knew this. They knew that every life is mythic, and that each of our myths, our sacred secret stories, is the outpouring of deep longing for meaning, which by some still unknown form of alchemy confers purpose to our lives. To those who go beyond appearances and seek the truth of their lives, everything is a symbol, everything a story, everything mythic, and the discovery of these things, *back at the beginning,* is an uncanny kind of coming home. This is the deep urge to seek out the living meaning of myth.

For psychologist Carl Jung, meaning was the secret opening into the realm of myth. According to his assistant, Aniela Jaffé, Jung believed that *every* attempt at meaning was a myth, in the original sense of the term: a sacred story explaining an entire world.

But can the currently accepted authorities on the way world works—science, media, technology—satisfy the human need for meaning?

I asked just this of the psychologist Rollo May at his home in Tiburon, California, the last time I saw him, shortly before his death in the spring of 1991. With a sadness in his voice that startled me, he said that for him the sign of the times was what he called the "nothing-ness," the lack of meaning in their lives that drove so many of his clients into therapy. He described this as "the cry for myth," the cry for a pattern. That *cri de coeur,* he determined, wasn't for the rose-hued glasses of nostalgia or escapism into romanticizing the past, but the *cry for meaning,* which he believed is the heart of true myth. Isn't there anywhere in modern life where people can glean that depth of mean-ing? I asked him.

"Great drama in theater, books or even movies," he replied. "Works like *Hamlet* and *MacBeth, The Great Gatsby* or *Waiting for Godot* speak straight to the heart of people and we retain them in our memory as myth." He looked out over San Francisco Bay to the city that shim-mered in the fog like Frank L. Baum's Emerald City, and talked about loneliness as being the absurd price we are paying for the "myth of progress."

"I've come to reluctantly believe Nietzsche was right," he told me. "Our powerful hunger for myth is a hunger for community. As a mat-ter of fact, after fifty years of practicing psychoanalysis I'm convinced that people go into therapy not so much for advice as for *presence,* to be in the presence of someone they trust and admire."

I asked him if he believed that was what Joseph Campbell was allud-ing to when he said, "People are always talking about looking for the meaning of life, when what they're really looking for is a *deep experi-ence* of life."

"Yes, yes, but not only deep," May responded. "Numinous."

The Nod of the Gods

Our word *numinous* has its roots in the Latin *numen,* which means "to nod or command; the presence or revelation of divine power." The psychologist Edwin Edinger illuminates the depths of meaning in the word when he writes, "An experience is numinous when it carries an excess of meaning or energy, transcending the capacity of the conscious personality to encompass or understand it. The individual is awed, overwhelmed, yet fascinated."

Now this is what beguiles me most about the guiding images of mythology. In what the ancient Celts called the "thin places" of sacred sites, and during what the Buddhists call the "eternal now," it is still possible to discover the mythic dimension, and with our senses alert to the possibility, we can witness the "nod of the gods" and delve deeper into the mystery of how stories move us from afar.

I recall Dr. May emphasizing to me how ironic the "cry for myth" was in our time, considering the plethora of myths all around us, if we only knew how to recognize them: The Myth of Paradise, the Golden Age, the Lone Pioneer, Rugged Individualism, the Age of Melancholy, the American Dream. He told me that a novel like *The Great Gatsby* is the secular myth of the solitary hero, an image of one of the culture's most sacred stories, the myth of constant self-invention and compulsive change, as well as its colossal shadow of loneliness. Gatsby's tragedy was mistaking his myth, the American Dream, for reality. The task of Nick, the narrator, at the end of the novel, is to find the myth that will illuminate some meaning in the absurd fate of his friend Gatsby. To Rollo May, this is everyone's task in the modern world, which is why he saw the novel as a modern myth. The hunger for myth, he said, is the hunger for community, and the hunger for community is the hunger for myth.

As he spoke about contemporary myths, I thought about Campbell's poetic notion that myths are masks of god through which shine the eternal truths, and the philosopher Philip Wheelwright's remark that the essence of myth is a "haunting awareness of transcendent forces peering through the cracks of the universe."

Tentatively, I asked Dr. May, "What is missing from our way of thinking?"

"A touch of infinity," he said softly, and stared out the window at the sailboats in the bay.

The Presence of Myth

Not long ago I was teaching a screenwriting class at San Francisco State University and chose to close one session with a clip from John Huston's thirty-seventh and final movie, *The Dead,* an adaptation of James Joyce's stirring short story. As I introduced the scene for my class I felt my heart pounding.

"*The Dead* is sometimes called the greatest short story in the English language," I explained to the class. "It takes place on a single night in turn-of-the-century Dublin, on the Feast of the Epiphany. There is a ritual gathering of old friends and the slow revelation of a secret that exposes the truth about the marriage of the two main characters. That is the plot, the overstory. The understory is revealed in the slow accumulation of details: a piano recital, a poetry reading, an after-dinner speech, a haunting Irish ballad, a wife's confession, and the strange report that 'snow was general all over of Ireland.' In this sense the understory is the movement of soul in the lives of these characters, described by Joyce in his book, and Huston in his film, as the strange interdependence of the living and the dead."

I turned off the classroom lights and ran the VCR, which was cued up for the last three scenes of the film. In the first scene Angelica Huston, playing the wife, Gretta, descends down the staircase of the Dublin mansion where the dinner party was held. But she hears the siren melody of an old Irish ballad, "The Lass of Aughrim," being sung as she leaves, and it seizes and transports her, a sure sign of a mythic moment. Stunningly framed by a stained glass window, like a madonna, she begins to weep. Huston intercuts the sorrowful gaze of her husband Gabriel (Donal McCann) as he watches with utter incomprehension a look he has never seen before on his wife's face.

The chance singing of the song has ignited the memory of a

long-ago romance, and it's as if a trap door has opened underneath the story. Hidden depths emerge. These are the mythic depths of anguish and passion that exist in the souls of *everyone*, including our wives, husbands, closest friends, which is why the greatest folklore, art, and literature appeals across time and space.

The final scene takes place in a bleak hotel room. Gabriel confronts his wife and she reveals that the song she just heard was once sung to her by a young lad named Michael Fury, who died of a broken heart for her when she was young. In this epiphany is the realization that there are inaccessible places in the heart and memory, even for husband and wife.

"I suppose you were in love with this Michael Fury?" Gabriel asks with an ache in his heart.

"I think he died for me," Gretta answers, then collapses onto the bed in tears.

Gabriel is utterly baffled, turns away, asking himself in the film's mournful narrative track, "Why am I feeling this riot of emotion?" He moves dreamily to the window and peers out at the "snow falling faintly through the universe," wondering whether he has ever understood his own wife or ever known the depth of love of which she is capable.

The scene dissolves like a dream to a montage of snow-covered medieval ruins.

The narrator intones, "One by one they were all becoming shades. Better pass boldly into that other world, in the full glory of some passion, than face and wither dismally with age.... His soul swooned slowly as he heard the snow falling faintly through the universe and faintly falling like the descent of their last end, upon all the living and the dead."

My heart was in my throat as the lights came flickering on in the classroom. I have long vaunted the mysteries of what the anthropologist Claude Lévi-Strauss called "participation mystique." This is the uncanny ability to write characters so thoroughly that an audience can drop into a kind of dreamtime participation in the story. But rarely have I so deeply identified with a series of characters as I did that morning, though I have read the book and seen the movie each a dozen times.

As the students stirred in their seats, adjusting their eyes to the bright lights, I was left wondering with Gabriel, *Why am I feeling this riot of emotion?*

My class of thirty students sat in stunned silence, waiting for me to speak. In the front row a young guy in a François Truffaut T-shirt and his long-lashed girlfriend squirmed in their seats, then turned painfully away from each other, like the fateful couple in the film, as if pondering in their heart of hearts the breathtaking lines about the difficulty of ever understanding their own lovers.

I watched them with tenderness, as if projected forward by the story and able to see them struggling with love and death in their various futures. Looking at their faces trying to get used to the classroom lights, I found myself reeling backward in time, recalling my first night in Dublin, December 1974, when my landlady, Mrs. McGeary, handed me

James Joyce meets with his publisher Sylvia Beach and Adrienne Monnier in Shakespeare and Company Bookstore in Paris in May 1938 to celebrate the publication of *Finnegans Wake*. The dreamlike novel took seventeen years to complete, a task that has become symbolic of the perseverance required in the arts.

a copy of Joyce's collection of short stories, *Dubliners*, saying, "Here, take it. You need to read this," and how I read until dawn, recognizing in Joyce a mentor, a kindred spirit, and more, my own destiny, closing in around my soul.

The class waited as the last minute of class ticked off and I recalled the night I helped my brother and sister clean out my father's apartment after he died. On the reading table next to the chair in which he died, I found a beautiful bound edition of Joyce's masterpiece, *Ulysses*. I picked up the book and wished we had had a chance to read it out loud together, at least had one last chance to talk about it.

The class bell rang. Still, the class did not stir. They would not move until I said something to wrap up the film. I realized that they were right where Joyce wanted his readers and Huston wanted his viewers reeling in the "riot of emotion." They were in the mythic moment.

I suddenly felt like my college professor of twenty-five years before must have when we asked him, while the Vietnam War was still raging, what he would do if *his* draft number came up.

I began tentatively, and then a great calm came over me as the words seemed to choose me. "John Huston called this movie his love letter to Ireland. Before he died he told the press that reading James Joyce when he was a young man made him want to become a writer. Joyce was only twenty-five when he wrote *The Dead*. That can either intimidate us or inspire us. Twenty-five. That's just about your age, isn't it? I found him when I was about your age. It changed everything. What he taught me was to trust the 'riot of emotion' that arises when we touch the depths. Can you *feel* it—can you feel the myth? What I'd like to urge you to do is try to get what you're feeling at this moment into your own scripts. If you haven't gotten there yet, go deeper. Then go back and go deeper yet. If you do you will find the secret opening to myth, dream, and art."

The Secret Opening

Once in a great while we are pulled into the vortex of living myth, the stories and images that open us up to the great unknown. That screening of *The Dead* was such a moment for me and, I learned later, for several young members of my class. As Joyce mythologized turn-of-the-century Dublin, connecting the ancient wanderings of Ulysses with the modern peregrinations of Leopold Bloom, so too do modern filmmakers like John Huston, who mythologized our times with filmed stories that have become part of our cultural "sacred histories." From the paleolithic caves of Lascaux to the dark movie palaces in small-town America, stories have helped define who we are and what is truly sacred.

For our purposes, stories become mythic when they evoke eternal concerns, whether on a stone tablet in the sands of ancient Sumer or on the flickering screen at your local Odeon. True myths, ancient and modern, stop time because they emerge from somewhere beyond time, which is why they are sometimes described as being written by an "anonymous hand." Myths seize the imagination because they take on questions—love and war, birth and death, good and evil—that otherwise cannot be answered. While echoed in books, music, and art, myths are also experienced in ordinary life, as everyday epiphanies.

Although I was prepared that day in the classroom to lecture on the artistic merits and screenplay structure of an important movie, I was still surprised by its mythic impact. By compressing time, space, and emotion, myth reveals the inner meaning of our lives. In his very first book, the upstart Joyce announced himself as a mythmaker, a supreme artist who could pour old wine into new bottles.

In this book I explore a few similarly modest moments from my life and the life of my times, and reflect on the way they open onto the unknown and become mythic in memory. We all tell stories and conjure images from the fragments of memory and shards of dream, which means we are all, still, myth-making creatures. Sacred stories have always been the most natural way for us to defy our isolation and boldly make connections with others as well as with our own souls.

This work is an invitation to see how marvelous ordinary life is when we rediscover it by way of the mythic imagination.

The secret is that the mythic is everywhere, but most often appears when and where it's least expected. It exists on a superficial level in the myth-making apparatus of celebrity in Washington, D.C., and in

Hollywood, but is far more significant when we notice it in the unfolding narrative of our own lives. All it takes is the willingness to look with what the painter Cézanne called "the mythic slant," the eye that considers what is eternal, timeless, soulful in every encounter. This perspective doesn't require a university degree or arcane terminology, just the desire to search beyond the world of appearances to the mythic world that surrounds us at all times. What we learned from our parents, teachers, mentors, books, or travels about Hector, Gilgamesh, Ishtar, or Tristan and Iseult is still happening, if only we open our eyes and pay closer attention to the hidden places where myth lurks.

I'm prowling after images in this book, scavenging after metaphors, in the spirit of the poet Coleridge. I see myth as the old ruins of literature. They are the last stones, the jagged outline, of the grandeur of long ago, but stones that have been placed into new buildings, reused, recycled, reimagined. I read them the way I rove around the old grounds of Glendalough, Ireland, Ephesus, Turkey, or Angkor Wat, Cambodia, that is, for the reverie, for the prods to my imagination. I recall them the way I recall my own mythic memories, such as my own rambles, when I was in my early twenties, through the gladiator quarters of the Roman Coliseum or my midnight moonlit climb to the top of the Giza pyramid—for the pleasure of the story.

In this sense, mythic memory is not unlike the way the novelist and traveler Rose Macaulay famously described her visits to the relics of dead cities and remains of lost civilizations as "the pleasure of ruins." She was referring to an Old World way of thinking that preferred contemplation to self-improvement, reverie to psychological transformation, and mythmaking to theory-developing. There is an unknown room in the soul that is constantly turning the stuff of daydreams into myths for us, helping us to get at meaning we can't get to through the front door.

And that reminds me of another story. One night a few years back I was drinking some wine with two of the great musicians of our time, Mike Pinder, the founder of the Moody Blues, and David Darling, the virtuoso cello player. We were discussing the immortals of music. I told a few Jim Morrison stories, inspired by my days of co-writing a book about the Doors; Mike regaled us with personal anecdotes about John Lennon; then David did his bluesy imitation of an encounter with Miles Davis, telling us a winsome tale that had been circulating in the clubs for years.

After Miles died, David told us in a voice that mimicked Davis' notorious growl, they say that he went up to heaven and no one saw him for awhile. One day Charles Mingus, the *amazing* jazz bassist, was wandering around heaven and bumped into the *incredible* saxophonist, John Coltrane. Well, man, while 'Trane was giving Mingus one cool tour of the place they saw this heavy dude with a long white beard, rocking in the Chair-of-Ages. Mingus couldn't believe his eyes, and sussed out 'Trane, "Who's that?" 'Trane rolled his shoulders and shook his head and said, "I don't know. But *He* thinks he's Miles."

All around us, every day in every way, we are turning the stuff of life into myth to express what defies explanation, precisely because we're only human. Myths emerge from dreams, visions, inspiration, but also from a cultural need to explain the inexplicable, such as the unearthly sounds of Miles Davis' trumpet. We can't in ordinary words, so stories emerge from "anonymous authors" to describe in symbolic terms the "divine" source of genius and suprahuman accomplishment.

We yearn for the story, the image, that sheds a little light on the mysteries, like how in the world the great trumpet player can distill from his anguished life so much ineffable beauty. Creativity belongs to the mythic realm because it involves a struggle with the gods. World folklore is rife with stories about pacts that artistic types have made with gods and devils, because the everyday mind can't seem to reconcile mortal souls with immortal acts. This helps explain the many rhapsodies on a theme from *Faust* over the past few centuries.

"So you see how the mythmaking mind works," writes P. L. Travers, "balancing, clarifying, adjusting, making events somehow correspond to the inner necessity of things." This occurs in the country of myth, she says, where opposites are reconciled, as in the urban myth of Miles Davis who thinks he's God—and God who thinks he's Miles.

The Mythic Vision

"As it was in the past, so it is now," a neighborhood priest, Father Stephen Gross, told me one day while we were discussing the need for even modern people to have a sanctuary away from the madness, a place to collect our thoughts and believe in the power of silence.

I thought of him again just the other morning. I was feeling out of sorts, numb and defeated, unable to write, converse, connect with anyone. After my ritual café session I was feeling like Sisyphus putting the shoulder to the boulder as I begrudgingly trudged back home up the steep hill where we live. Suddenly a man with a thick German accent ran across the street and grabbed my arm, shouting for help.

"That man over there is blind," he yelled. "He needs directions. He's lost."

I said of course and crossed over with him to find a tall elegant black man with salt and pepper hair leaning on his white walking stick. Very gently, he put his hand on my arm and said, "Can you help me? I need to find the stairs with all the flowers."

I knew immediately that he meant the nearby Filbert Steps, which are festooned with beautiful flower gardens that border wooden stairs rising up to Coit Tower.

"Of course, I know where they are," I told him, then hesitated, feeling rushed but needed. "I'd be happy to lead you there myself."

I led him across the street and up the Montgomery Steps, then headed toward the gardens. On the way he confided to me that he was a poet and he had come there a year before with a writing class. He had fond memories of the smell of the flowers, but had been haunted by something else he needed "to put his finger on."

"Where I come from isn't such a good city for blind people," he said, looking crestfallen. "But San Francisco is a good city for blind people." He carefully tapped his cane on the sidewalk in front of us as we walked, dipping his knees seconds before an approaching curb and pushed away the branches of overhanging trees before they would have brushed him in the face.

"There is something in the air here. I was raised here and need to come back every once in awhile just to see it, to smell it and hear it again, and feel it in my soul. It helps my poetry."

There was joy in the brief telling of his story, and in the way his face lit up as we made our way down Montgomery Street. He sounded like Nat King Cole singing to himself on a drive down Route 66, or Pablo Neruda describing the effect of cherry blossoms on his lust for life. The noon bells chimed from the nearby Shrine of Saint Francis as we arrived at the base of the steps. The sun shone brightly on the purple bougainvillea around us, and monarch butterflies flickered in the light around the red roses. A flock of parrots rainbowed the air above the steps that led to the tower.

Oddly enough, the joyous sight triggered a sudden rush of sorrow for the blind poet because he couldn't see these things, but then, as if sensing my unwarranted pity, he startled me with a few choice words.

"You know I'm not completely blind," he said, as if forgiving me. He placed his strong hand on my forearm as I led him up the steps to a wrought-iron gate. "I've just had to learn to see in new ways."

He nodded thanks to me, sensed the presence of the gate, gently pushed it open, and sat down on the bench that overlooked San Francisco Bay. The sun lit on his face like a blessing. He smiled happily for a few moments and opened his backpack and pulled out a pen and blue spiral notebook.

"What we don't look for," he said, "we'll never be able to see and never be able to tell, will we?"

Then, like the blind poet Homer, he looked out over the bay to see what he could see, and in so doing, he helped me see in new ways ever since. Not a day has gone by since that encounter when I haven't tried to see my own neighborhood with new eyes—and with gratitude.

And still the mystery turns. The mythosphere is all around us, to borrow Alexander Eliot's luminous image, in the most profound and the most ordinary of moments. We can sense it whenever an experience opens onto the unknown, as it did for our ancestors in the paleolithic caves who scattered flowers on the graves of those who had just died and told the first stories about what happens after death; or for me during my screening of *The Dead* when the spirits of all those who had ever died in my life were suddenly evoked. We can sense the mytho-sphere whenever an experience generates a deep longing in us for more lasting truths than the ephemeral ones of our own brief time. The mythic imagination, as Stephen Larsen has so beautifully written, "makes the soul talk," and helps us transform the meandering path of our everyday life into a journey of soulmaking. The mythic vision gives us the courage to find personal meaning in the here and now, through which the past plunges into the future, and affords us the sense of being utterly alive.

✳

"So we beat on, boats against the current, borne back, ceaselessly into the past," were the last words of the last novel F. Scott Fitzgerald, the past-haunted novelist, wrote before he himself was borne back along the plangent waters of time. We move back over the river of memory, seeking the stories and images that will fit the curve of our soul.

One night in the Paris of *les années folles,* the crazy years of the 1920s, a group of acolytes gathered around the Russian mystic Gurdjieff. All night they explored the loftiest of philosophical ques-tions, wrestled with the darkest issues of existence. Near dawn one of them prepared to leave for home—but was stopped by the philoso-pher. "You can't go yet," he explained, "we haven't figured out yet whether God exists."

You can't go yet. We haven't figured out yet whether, when, or where myth exists—for you. We haven't found what—if anything—endures. We haven't discovered where our meaning lies. It is not diversion or cleverness or even answers that we are seeking; it is understanding. Understanding of the stories at the heart of our lives that reveal in a way nothing else can just how it is that we choose our gods, our heroes, our destinies.

When asked why, I can only answer elliptically.

The nothing is a craving after something.

We are here to deepen the mystery.

Phil Cousineau
North Beach, San Francisco
October 2000

ONE

The Myth of
the Creative Struggle

*Late-Night Thoughts from
Sisyphus to Sinatra*

Myths are made for the imagination
to breathe life into them.

—ALBERT CAMUS, *The Myth of Sisyphus*

I am sitting in the dark at my rolltop desk and marveling for a few minutes, as I do every night, at our view of Coit Tower at the top of Telegraph Hill in San Francisco. The tower glows proudly, throwing light and mystery out over the city, making me think of the old engravings of the Pharos Lighthouse in ancient Egypt.

Moonlight pours into the room, falling onto a book that lies open on the desk, the exquisite Heritage Club edition of Ovid's *Metamorphosis* that I inherited from my father. The book still has the unmistakable smell of the well-crafted book, an odor of ink and glue that wafts forth each time it is cracked open. I pick up the book, slowly turn the pages, and feel an unexpected shock of recognition. The Hans Enri pen-and-ink drawings of the ancient gods and heroes bring back blushing memories of the first time I saw the lasciviously grinning Zeus, disguised as the swan, coiled around Leda. Once again I feel a pang of joy from simply reading off the pantheon of names in the table of contents: Daedalus and Ariadne, Actaeon and Artemis, Hades and Sisyphus. After all these years they are still powerful figures for me. I have often reread their exploits, which to me is like opening an old scrapbook full of memories of marvelous friends and family.

Each time I return to them I am surprised by how the ancient tales of sudden transformation force me to think about the strange changes in my own life.

Then I come across the story that has been a part of my own story for a long time. Just staring at the word *Sisyphus* is enough to make my shoulder ache. I can't even pronounce the old king's name without thinking about my own years of pushing the boulder up the hill. It is a living myth for me, vividly reminding me of my own youthful rebellion, my long struggle with struggle itself.

For seven long years after my post-college world travels I raged against the great dragon doubt. I had dreamed of becoming a writer since I was a boy. Other than fantasizing about playing right field for my hometown team, the Detroit Tigers, I never wanted to do anything else with my life. The problem was, as the poet Robert Bly gleefully pointed out in a poetry workshop I attended in the early 1980s, there are people who want to *be* a writer, and there are people who want to *write*.

"Which one are you?" he asked, scanning the faces in the room, busting half of us like a literary cop. In fact, I did want to write, desperately. I just couldn't. My years of voluminous reading and protracted travels had humbled and intimidated me into creative silence. I had a writing block the size of Gibraltar and twice as unmovable.

So I did what all self-respecting wannabe writers do. I read and read and read. For seven long years I painted Victorian houses around San Francisco (forty-four of them in all) during the day, and then back in my apartment in Berkeley I read until the wee hours of the morning.

Eventually I formed a little company with a friend of mine that we called "Painter's Palette," which boasted the motto, "Custom Painting for a Classic City." To keep my mind alive during the often numbingly repetitive work, I memorized reams of poetry, a litany of limericks, and a passel of French phases that I copied onto white index cards hidden in my overalls. At night, I stared at blindlingly blank paper in my old Smith-Corona typewriter. I saw myself as a paint-flecked version of the frustrated writer in *The Shining*, as demonically portrayed by Jack Nicholson. Not unlike him, I used to type hundreds of versions of the same short stories and poems, often without changing clothes after work, living on tunafish and beer.

The horrified expression on Shelley Duvall's face in the movie when she peeks at a page of her tormented husband's writing and sees the same sentence—*All work and no play makes Jack a dull boy*—repeated line after line, page after page, was a little too close for comfort when I saw it in the middle of my own enfeebling torment.

Regardless of how the writing was going, I eventually sank down onto the futon on the floor, picked up a book, and eagerly disappeared down the rabbit hole of another writer's work. During that dark stretch, I read well over a thousand books, some of them again and again, taking prodigious notes, cross-referencing them in large journals, and often writing short reviews of them. Desperate to write, but even more hungry to learn things that had just been hinted at in my wide travels, I had embarked on a kind of self-imposed Ph.D. program on the world classics. I started a novel, a movie script, an epic poem, dozens of travel stories, but all I had to show for seven years of work was the publication of two modest freelance stories in the local newspapers and a few poems in obscure journals.

No doubt about it, I was frustrated by my lack of progress, but proud of my rebellion against the dead-end life I had left behind in Detroit, as well as the traditional form of journalism I had studied in college. I reveled in my bohemian life, meaning a matchbox-sized apartment, an old car, few possessions other than books, and a life I fancied, of Joycean "silence, exile, and cunning." I even grew to accept the frequent descents into depression and submersions in melancholia.

It was worth it, I told myself; it's just part of the creative struggle.

✦

Finally, one night in the spring of 1983, during a period of increasing despair that often found me curled on the floor unable to move for hours at a time, my brother Paul called me from Pensacola, Florida. The first word out of his mouth was, "Help!" Then he laughed and added, "I've got a term paper due in my mythology class—in a week! Hey, bro,' can you help me?"

"One week?" I asked warily. "Well, what's it supposed to be about?"

"Hey, how am I supposed to know? No, just kidding. I think we're supposed to write about a myth that we think has some relevance today."

Out of the blue, I blurted, "How about Sisyphus?"

"You mean the guy who was condemned to roll the boulder up the mountain forever? What's that got to do with us?"

"Yeah, same guy. I think you'd dig his story. I recently read an essay called 'The Myth of Sisyphus' by Albert Camus, the French philosopher, and he said some things that are a helluva lot more interesting than the usual moralistic reading. Camus actually saw him as one of the first rebels, what he called 'the absurd hero,' a man who learned how to overcome his fate."

There was a long pause on the telephone. I ran my fingers through my hair, as I do when I'm nervous, and they got tangled in clots of dried beige paint.

Silence. My brother was carefully measuring my words.

"How did he do that?"

"If I remember right, Camus said that Sisyphus was paying the price for a life of passion, and had learned to accept his ordeal, learned to love the struggle."

As I spoke those words, I felt a tremendous surge of emotion. I suddenly knew I wasn't just talking about something that happened once, long ago, if at all. By chance, I realized in astonishment, I had stumbled onto a description of something permanent, eternal, in life, my own life.

"Paul, has your teacher told you how Salutius, the old Roman writer, described myth? He said myths were things that never happened, but always are."

I remember trembling with excitement as I held the telephone. The air around me felt charged, as if after one of those green-skied electrical storms back in the Michigan of our youth. The hair stood on the back of my arms and my scalp prickled. The Camus phrase I had quoted—

he "learned to love the struggle"—seemed to hover in the air like the last words of a great stage play. Not only did the ancients adeptly describe the problem; they also prescribed a way of dealing with it.

"That's great, Phil. If you can write down a few of those ideas just the way you told me, I'll do the rest."

"Write it down?" I muttered, then thought to myself, *Easy for you to say*. But before I could say something I'd regret, I felt some resolve return to my voice for the first time in a long time.

"Sure, just give me a few days."

For the next few days, I wrote down a flurry of thoughts about Sisyphus on the blank index cards I always carried with me to the painting sites. Around four o'clock, when the cold fog began blowing in from the Pacific Ocean and made it hard to hold onto our paintbrushes, I packed up and headed home, where I wrote until dawn.

By the end of the week I had a thirteen-page essay to send off to my brother. Afterward, I felt as if an enormous burden had been lifted from my shoulders.

❋

I wouldn't know it for many years, but that serendipitous call woke me up from a long, potentially dangerous slumber. Writing about Sisyphus unleashed years of pent-up creativity. His story was my story; his struggle was my struggle. In those benighted days there was tremendous pressure on me from my family, from old friends and new, to become successful, famous, productive. It's the All-American way. If you choose the contemplative life, decide to drop out for awhile, it tends to trouble the people around you. One girlfriend confided to a buddy that I was "a diamond in the rough," but she wasn't sure if she could hang around long enough to see me all polished. Another asked me, *sotto voce,* one day when I was going to grow up and get a real job.

However, I held out, stubbornly. Then one night, I got a package of old *Life* magazines in the mail from my father. Tucked inside one of them was a postcard asking me to tell him one more time exactly what it was that I was writing because his friends kept asking him what I was doing with my life. I had no idea what to tell him. How could I describe the uncanny feeling of being pulled forward by a dream, an image, a story, even my destiny, for so many years, but had somehow lost sight of it? Well, I couldn't. I sensed he was ashamed and couldn't come right out and say it. Hadn't he recently confided to my sister that he was afraid that I was throwing my whole life away? I felt like an utter failure after reading his cryptic note, and my heart sank like a stone. A stone rolling to the bottom of the hill.

The Shoulder to the Boulder

On a blistering hot day in the fall of 1995 I stood on a hillside overlooking the site of the mythical King Sisyphus' domain, the ancient citadel of Corinth. The old grounds looked as parched as I felt at the ungodly hour of high noon. I was leading a tour around Greece for the Joseph Campbell Foundation. Our Greek expert was an elderly professor named Adrianna. She found a bit of shade for us underneath a gnarled olive tree and began the session with a brilliant history of Corinth, but then delivered a surprisingly conservative version of the Sisyphus tale, tinged with a slight sense of condescension, as if telling a fairy tale to a group of schoolkids she was sure had never heard the myth before.

Adrianna may have had the best of intentions, to simply entertain the group for a few minutes in between the hotel, the ruins, and lunch, but I found her approach to be the kind that had earned mythology its reputation for being charming but irrelevant. Told like this, I thought to myself, a myth *is* a lie, irrelevant, untrue to the way people live *now*.

As I stepped forward for my turn to talk, the group shuffled around uncomfortably. A few of them took desultory photographs of the archaeologists at work in the ruins of the old citadel below. Adrianna nervously checked her watch, then clicked at it with her finger, as if to signal me that we were short on time. *Remember,* she was reminding me, *we still have half the Peloponnese to see today.*

Unwilling to be rushed, I leaned against the chained link fence that surrounds the excavations of the agora, then began by saying, "Many things change over the centuries, but the one thing that never changes is human character. That's why the old myths are still so fascinating to us today. They reveal the inner meaning of human life, what they used to call 'the workings of the soul,' the realm that defies time and space. As I see it, myths like this are metaphors for the dramas of our inward life, and the story of Sisyphus is a metaphor for *struggle* itself. On the outside, this is a tale of betrayal and retribution, but on the inside, the domain of myth, it tells us something about our *attitude* to struggle we can't seem to learn any other way."

Slowly I spun my version of the myth.

※

Sisyphus, ruler of Corinth, regarded by Homer as the wisest and most prudent in his relationships with other mortals, was also, according to other ancient sources, rather a wise guy in his relationships with the gods.

One afternoon, Sisyphus chanced upon Zeus *en flagrante delicto* with the lovely maiden Aegina, daughter of the river god Asopus. Before Sisyphus could even conjure up any judgments, he watched as the mighty god abducted the poor girl. As one might imagine, Asopus, the god of flowing water, was inconsolable over her disappearance. Asopus was so distraught he approached the king for help. Sisyphus felt compromised between his loyalty to the gods and the truth he witnessed, but the cisterns of his citadel were dry. So Sisyphus risked everything by trading a divine secret for a perennial spring, chancing retribution for an act of compassion for his own citizens.

The fury of Asopus was so great that when he learned the true source of his daughter's sorrow, he went into a rage. The rivers around Corinth roiled. The banks overflowed, nearly drowning Zeus, who was hiding from his outraged wife Hera, and who narrowly escaped by disguising himself as a large stone so the waters would run off the slope of his back.

Zeus soon discovered who had betrayed his pawky little secret, and he turned to his brother Hades for help, hoping to render Sisyphus invisible by having him hauled down to the underworld. As usual, he wanted to get rid of all the evidence of his incorrigible philandering.

Once immured in the dark underworld, Sisyphus was restless and unwilling to accept the justice of his fate. As his name in Greek suggests, he is "the crafty one" who devised a clever ruse to chain Hades, the Dark One, to his own stone throne. Strange to say, with the god of death literally enchained, the gravediggers were out of work. No one was dying in the world above. This gravely upset Ares, the god of war, whose love of igniting the desire for battle in men's hearts was now thwarted. Zeus soon learned that he had been twice scorned by the pesky Sisyphus, and he reluctantly agreed to allow Ares to rescue Hades from his humiliating predicament.

Meanwhile, Sisyphus called upon Persephone, the half-time bride of Hades, cajoling her with a mournful tale of longing for his wife Merope (who is immortalized as the seventh—and invisible—sister in the Pleiades constellation) and the need for him to fulfill his duties as a husband and father.

"Let me return to Corinth for three days," he pleaded. "I am a king. Let me arrange a funeral so my family can properly grieve."

Persephone was either duped by this clever sob story or else simply empathized with a fellow soul who had been unfairly seized and sentenced. She agreed to guide Sisyphus out of the dank caverns of the underworld and back into the overworld, where Sisyphus paid his respects to his wife and family and the people of his kingdom. But once he had escaped the underworld, and as the ancients said, smelled once more the fresh air of the living world, he had a change of heart and refused to accept the terms of parole. When Hades came calling for him to return to the underworld, instead Sisyphus chose the "sun, warm stones, and the sea" to the hall of horrors awaiting him below.

Outraged, Hades dispatched the messenger god Hermes to collar the incorrigible one and haul him before the Judges of the Dead. For his hubris and his scorn, Sisyphus was condemned to suffer the seemingly most futile and hopeless of labors. In a shadow world of skyless space and depthless time, in a place echoing with the cries of the damned, Sisyphus was given the sentence of shouldering a stone—the *very same size* as the one Zeus took as his disguise to escape the wrath of Asopus—for all eternity, up the forlorn mountain slope in Tartarus.

At that point in the story, I took a long pause, sipped from my water bottle, and then opened up my copy of the *Odyssey* and read Homer's own description:

> With both arms embracing the monstrous stone, struggling with
> hands and feet alike, he would try to push the stone upward to
> the crest of the hill, but when it was on the point of going over the
> top, the force of gravity turned it backward, and the pitiless stone
> rolled back down to the level. He then tried once more to push it
> up, straining hard, and sweat ran all down his body, and over his
> head a cloud of dust rose.

By now the group was rapt. They leaned forward to hear what would happen next, which is the point of all great stories.

This was the true vengeance of the gods, I told the group. Sisyphus was condemned for all eternity to shoulder the boulder up the mountain of hell, and all the while Hades would be watching for the look of despair that would mark the defeat of another mere mortal. But Sisyphus resolved never to allow the gods to see him defeated by despair. He silently vowed that because his fate was in his hands he could be superior to it. That is the genius of the mythic view of this complex image, that this, "the hour of consciousness" as Camus called it, is born out of the beauty that can be heard in the midst of our ordeals.

The myth of Sisyphus is a *living myth*, I concluded, because it reveals the *inner meaning* of our outer struggles. And who doesn't struggle? Who doesn't look for meaning in the everyday drama of their life? The myth personifies the notion set forth in models of drama, from Aristotle to screenwriter William Goldman, that growth comes through conflict, change from response to defeat. Moreover, it presages the marvelous thought of the Scottish poet Kathleen Raine about "the mysterious wisdom won by toil."

The Terrible Beauty

When I finished there were a few flustered looks in the group, as they were pondering the apparent doom of our hero.

"Now don't despair," I said, trying to be reassuring. "It's not as bad for Sisyphus as it may sound. Remember a living myth is inexhaustible, like great works of art or significant dreams. You don't just listen to Beethoven's symphonies *once* or look at Vermeer's paintings *once* or ponder a tantalizing dream *once*. You go back again and again. It's the same thing with the myths. If you delve into this myth you'll find something new about it—and yourself—every time. There is great pain, but also great beauty, even a rare kind of hope."

When I was a boy, I told them, going to good old Wayne St. Mary's, a Catholic school run by the blue-and-white-robed sisters of the Order of the Immaculate Conception, they used this ancient tale as a warning. "Look," said Sister Marie-Walter, "even the pagan Greeks knew better than to insult God. Look what happens when you disobey God. You have to spend the rest of eternity in the fires of hell!" It never ceased to amaze me how worked up those placid nuns could get over the prospects of eternal damnation.

I read the myth again at college, but it wasn't until my discovery of Camus' essay that its power truly touched my life. I described how it had been written at the outset of World War II, as a kind of manifesto for the absurdist movement, and that Camus saw his book as a summing up, "a lucid invitation to live and to create, in the very midst of the desert." I admitted to the group that I had read it at a time when I was, as Rollo May describes the plight of Gatsby, someone groping for a new myth that could absorb his "ceaseless failure." The problem was I didn't know it. Only after I had written about the myth and began to use it in various lectures about the creative life did I come to appreciate the strength of the myth.

I suggested that Camus' mythic vision was seeing how Sisyphus *embraced* his stone because he came to accept the consequences of his actions. As a man of passionate political convictions, he saw Sisyphus as a fearsome symbol of "futile labor," but also as a psychologically complex image of transcending the monotony and melancholy of our tasks in life.

The group didn't look convinced, but I plunged ahead.

To some, the tale of Sisyphus may be the usual dish of deceit and retribution, I said, but I'm convinced that it is far more, a fable about the acceptance of one's burden, which makes it as relevant today as it was three hundred centuries ago. At the heart of this story is an image that points to a message that is at the core of the teachings of many great wisdom teachers from Epictetus to William James. It is the moment that Sisyphus watches the boulder roll to the bottom of the hill and turns to walk back down the hill.

"That hour," I read out loud, from Camus' essay, "is like a breathing-space which returns as surely as his suffering, that is the hour of consciousness. At each of those moments when he leaves the heights and gradually sinks toward the lairs of the gods, he is superior to his fate. He is stronger than his rock."

I paused and quoted from memory Camus' observation that "the price exacted from him for his betrayal of the gods," he wrote, "was fair."

What is implied here is that there is always a price to pay for our passionate convictions, whether we are pursuing love, art, or political change. In the end what matters is our attitude toward our burden.

I asked if anyone knew how Camus had ended his essay.

"Zeus gives him a pardon?" somebody joked.

"He escaped?" someone else suggested, hopefully.

"Hades allowed his wife to have conjugal visits?"

"No, no, nothing that easy. Remember that at the time he wrote this Camus was afflicted with tuberculosis and the Nazis had occupied France. He had no illusions about the struggles of ordinary people. Still, he found a remark in Sophocles' play about Oedipus that he felt revealed the secret Greek attitude toward fate: 'Despite so many ordeals, my advanced age and the nobility of my soul make me conclude that all is well.' Camus then writes, 'That remark is sacred,' and concludes with the stunning thought that *One must imagine Sisyphus happy.*"

I paused for a few minutes and we shared some refreshments. Our Greek bus driver triumphantly showed us the trick of slicing open a watermelon so it pops open like a sprung flower, and the group drank gustily and savored the juicy fruit.

"I think everyone who has a creative urge," I tried summing up, "from poetry to gardening—can find some solace in this story. It's a great antidote to the reigning myth in our culture that there is only *one* ascent up the mountain—to marriage, money, or success. That's the kind of fairy-tale thinking that makes it difficult to accept the inevitable descents back down the mountain. And we wonder why we're afflicted with massive depression."

I wiped my brow, and took another sip from my water bottle, then pointed to the sharply rising mountain beyond the town of Corinth and suggested that the story of Sisyphus may have taken a strong hold on the imagination of the ancients because they could go outside everyday and visualize their ancient king pushing his boulder up the subterranean mountain that was a mirror image of the one in their own world.

But the story carries on, like the voice of the goddess Echo herself, I suggested, because it teaches us something every generation has to learn for itself: It's not what happens to us that matters; what matters is our *attitude* toward what happens.

At that point, Mary, one of the members of the group challenged me. "Are you suggesting that suffering is noble? I'm an artist and I'll tell you right now that suffering is no fun."

"The story doesn't ennoble suffering, it ennobles struggle," I answered carefully. "I'm not saying that suffering is noble, I'm saying that *struggle* is inevitable and those who learn to perceive it as an obstacle rather than a burden make life a lot easier for themselves. The image of Sisyphus climbing and descending, climbing and descending, seems to echo the basic oscillation of life's backward and forward movements, owing to the diffusion of energy.

"Now it may be heresy to say this in these success-obsessed times, but even *failure* is noble—if you keep going. I think that's what the story is telling us. It reminds me of the old Australian toast, 'Press on, regardless.' Or Thomas Edison's admission that he was the most successful inventor in history because he had the courage to be history's greatest failure, meaning he never allowed defeat to crush him, only to spur him on to try a different approach. I'm saying that I find that the power to resist despair allows us to keep going. That's why writing or painting or composing never gets any easier for real artists. They keep on going back up the mountain, but by different routes, different challenges."

I paused, and looked for the ghost of Sisyphus on the slopes of the distant mountain, then concluded, "What does it mean to suffer? Wasn't that the great question in the story of Job in the Old Testament? There is no final answer to that parable, as there isn't, can't be, in the myth of Sisyphus. The only answer to the constant question of life and death is *your* answer, *my* answer. Remember these stories are mythic images, attitudes not theories, and as far as I can tell, attitudes of awe and wonder."

Mary sighed and looked away. Something had been nudged inside her, an old image, maybe even her previous personal myth about the creative life.

"Having pushed the boulder up the hill for a long time," I said, "let me just say that I find a lot of unexpected comfort in this story. I don't find writing getting any easier. Who knows? Maybe it's because I push too hard. But I *have* learned something invaluable from this story— that the secret of the creative life consists in taking the next step, doing the next thing you have to do, but doing it with all your heart and soul and finding some joy in doing it."

I paused for a moment, then remembered some lines I had once written down on an index card and taped to my typewriter.

"Henry James described the task of the creative life as well as anyone ever has," I concluded. "He wrote in his exquisite short story, 'The Middle Years': 'We work in the dark—we do what we can—we give what we have. Our doubt is our passion and our passion is our task. The rest is the madness of art.'"

When I had finished, our Greek guide stunned me by clapping robustly, and not just to get us back on the bus. Her eyes positively shone with delight, and she said, "I've known that story since I was a girl, but I've never thought of it that way, you know, *psychologically.*" She paused, looking for the right words in English. Her hands brushed hair out of her eyes, and she added, "I didn't know you could do that to a story. Interpret it, I mean."

She rooted around in her purse, took out a notebook, and asked me with great earnestness, "Now tell me the name of that French philosopher again."

Metaphors We Live By

The myth of Sisyphus is more than a cautionary tale that embodies an important realization about ordeal. It is a metaphor—like the stories of Hamlet, Faust, and Quixote—for what the psychologist Robert A. Johnson calls "the evolution of consciousness." They are the spiritual descendants of Sisyphus. Quixote, the idealistic rebel, is incapable of accepting authorities he cannot see or respect, and he will not accept defeat. Hamlet, the incurable brooder, reveals our capacious ability to live in the dark underworld of anxiety and loneliness. In Faust we see the first modern man who makes peace with his shadow in his soul and does not wait for redemption by the gods, but instead redeems himself by forging his own consciousness.

Together, these modern myths are not just great literature but antidotes to the denial of struggle and the dream of unending, upward, soul-denying progress. In the rich imagery of these Sisyphean stories we find a number of immortal truths. We do have a chance to overcome ourselves, the story says, our phantoms, our persecutions. Quite possibly it may be the only way to find happiness. As the pilgrims walking to Santiago de Compostela in Spain, or the Shikoku poet's shrines in Japan will tell you, it is *only* through overcoming an ordeal that we are able to find meaning that touches our souls. Wasn't it Leonardo da Vinci who said, "Obstacles cannot crush me. Every obstacle yields stern resolve"?

I think too of René Daumal's allegorical novel *Mount Analogue*. In this story of mountain climbers on a mythical island, he writes,

You cannot stay on the summit forever; you have to come down again. So why bother in the first place? Just this: What is above knows what is below, but what is below does not know what is above. In climbing, take careful note of the difficulties along your way: for as

In Rembrandt's 1652 etching, *Faust in His Study,* he renders the moment of inspiration as an epiphany, the sudden shining forth of light in the midst of darkness.

you go up, you can observe them. Coming down, you will no longer see them, but you will know they are there if you have observed them.... There is an art of finding one's direction in the lower regions by the memory of what one saw higher up. When one can no longer see, one can at least still know.

Mythically speaking, Sisyphus tells us that to "know" means seizing our fate from the zealous and jealous gods and goddesses—though all hell may break loose, as rendered in the image of Hades flinging off his chains after being freed by his brother Ares. His story may have ancient echoes of the sun's rising and falling, and may even be an echo of a much older tale about the soul breaking free of the cold clutches of death itself. It could be the model for the urban joke about knowing when you're in midlife: You've climbed to the top of the ladder and found it's against the wrong wall!

But for me the power of the image is that it captures the timeless moment when all of us who are trying to break free from the chains of "Death" (read: Depression, Melancholy, Hate, Negativity, Defeatism, Jealousy) have struggled to reach the top of the hill and felt that moment of elation of dropping our burden at our feet.

Read metaphorically, the stone is the potentially crushing weight of being unable or unwilling to leave behind our troubles, our resentments, our grief. The stone is heavy because we won't let go of it. The sorrow of Sisyphus is the weight of our melancholy and the resentful attitude toward our burden on the descent into our soul.

As part of the wisdom literature of the world, the myth of Sisyphus tells us that our descent into darkness, the inevitable realms of pain and disappointment, holds out the possibility of rapture, happiness, if we understand the crucial difference between suffering and struggling.

"We shall descend, descend, everlastingly descend," wrote Jules Verne at the end of his mythic novel *Twenty Thousand Leagues under the Sea*. The question is, What will we see when we reach the bottom of the sea of life? Will we have the courage to rise again?

"He who fears he shall suffer has already suffered," said Montaigne. The reason the myths and literature are full of suffering is that we are still searching for a way to understand it, deal with it, learn from it, grow with it. The emphasis on entertainment and escape is an avoidance of the descent and confrontation with mortality that our soul longs for. What the great wisdom tells us is not to fear suffering, but to be afraid of meaningless suffering.

"Although the world is full of suffering," Helen Keller said, "it is full also of the overcoming of it." The Buddhists say, "When the heart is big enough, it will absorb (and eliminate) suffering as a river absorbs salt." To understand how, it helps to look at the dark with new light.

The Mystery of *Duende*

In 1938, the Spanish poet and playwright Federico García Lorca delivered a spellbinding lecture in Havana. His topic was the ancient gypsy idea of *duende*, the mysterious dark spirit of the Earth that he believed infused the souls of poets, imbued the hearts of bullfighters with courage, and injected the "black sounds" of the very ground of Spain into the flying fingers of guitar players. At the heart of his talk was an unforgettable image.

Years ago, an eighty-year-old flamenco woman won first place at a dance contest in Jerez de la Frontera. She was competing against beautiful women and young girls with waists supple as water, but all she did was raise her arms, throw back her head, and stamp her foot on the floor. In that gathering of muses and angels—beautiful forms and beautiful smiles—who could have won but her moribund *duende*, sweeping the ground with its wings of rusty knives.

Once. The old flamenco dancer stamped her foot once on the dance floor. But she stamped with the authority of the *lived* life. She had lived through dark times and she had loved and she had survived. "A mysterious power which everyone senses and no philosopher explains," as Goethe described the core of Paganini's genius.

The image resounds.

The mythic imagination is an "endarkenment," bringing us down from our inflations and flights of ego, connecting us, like *duende*, to the dark and nourishing powers of the Earth and our own souls. Myths are the original soul stories, showing us, as my mentor Joseph Campbell used to say, how to live "with joyful participation in the sorrows of the world."

The Ultimate Struggle

During World War II the Austrian psychologist Viktor E. Frankl and his wife were imprisoned at the Auschwitz concentration camp. Like all incarcerated couples they were separated the moment they entered the grounds. For the entire four years of his imprisonment Frankl did not know his wife's fate, but he thought about her constantly, fantasized and dreamed about her, talked to her and wrote imaginary letters to her. He writes in his ambrosial memoir, *Man's Search for Meaning,*

> What was really needed was a fundamental change in our attitude toward life. We had to learn that it did not really matter what we expected from life, but rather what life expected from us.... Life ultimately means taking the responsibility to find the right answers to its problems and to fulfill the tasks which it constantly sets for each individual. These tasks, and therefore the meaning of life, differ from man to man, and from moment to moment.... No man and no destiny can be compared with any other man or any other destiny....
>
> When a man finds that it is his destiny to suffer, he will have to accept his suffering as his task; his single and unique task. He will have to acknowledge the fact that even in suffering he is unique and alone in the universe. No one can relieve him of his suffering or suffer in his place. His unique opportunity lies in the way he bears his burden.... The way in which a man accepts his fate and all the suffering it entails, the way in which he takes up his cross, gives him ample opportunity—even under the most difficult circumstances—to add a deeper meaning to his life.

One morning, Frankl was assigned to work in a trench. Something happened that helped him endure what he called the "ghastly moments" of camp life. We never know when and where the epiphany will come.

> The dawn was gray around us; gray was the sky above; gray the snow in the pale light of dawn; gray the rags in which my fellow prisoners

were clad, and gray their faces. I was again conversing silently with my wife, or perhaps I was struggling to find the *reason* for my sufferings, my slow dying. In a last violent protest against the hopelessness of imminent death, I sensed my spirit piercing through the enveloping gloom. I felt it transcend that hopeless, meaningless world, and from somewhere I heard a victorious "Yes" in answer to my question of the existence of an ultimate purpose. At that moment a light was lit in the distant farmhouse, which stood on the horizon as if painted there, in the midst of the miserable gray of a dawning morning in Bavaria. *"Et lux in tenebris lucet"*—and the light shineth in the darkness. For hours I stood hacking at the icy ground. The guard passed by, insulting me, and once again I communed with my beloved. More and more I felt that she was present, that she was with me; I had the feeling that I was able to touch her, able to stretch out my hand and grasp hers. The feeling was very strong: she was *there*. Then, at that very moment, a bird flew down silently and perched just in front of me, on the heap of soil which I had dug up from the ditch, and looked steadily at me.

As Northrop Frye noted in *The Educated Imagination,* "There's nothing new in literature that isn't the old reshaped." I see in Frankl's account of his descent into hell of Nazi internment a modern parallel with the ancient story of Sisyphus, not in the literal plot or depth of horror, but in the richness of psychological insight. With courage and clarity, Frankl describes not only what happened "on the bottom of the abyss which is laid open by the concentration camp," but what *happens,* from one generation to the next, from the slaughtering fields of Troy to the burning villages of Kosovo. Like the unknown authors behind the original myth of Sisyphus, Frankl shows us that the will to transcend one's circumstances can be the difference between life and death, literally and symbolically, and in so doing creates the terrible beauty of a modern myth.

Instead of ennobling suffering, ancient and modern myths *illuminate struggle* by telling stories about the mysteries of change. This distinction needs to be made in every generation, or there can be tragic confusion between the two. It came home to me in dramatic fashion in the winter of 1988, at the end of a long day in an editing room. My close friend Yasha Aginsky and the director Judy Montelle and I were watching the rough cut of her film about the surviving members of the Abraham Lincoln Brigade from the Spanish Civil War. For the umpteenth time we were searching for the "through line"—the dramatic thread that would help us finish, and maybe even give us a title we had been looking for for months.

The spools of film wound around the old editing table. When we reached the interview with Ruth Davidow, a nurse during the war, she said something that suddenly revealed the soul of our film. Speaking of her involvement in the war with the Sandinistas in Nicaragua, after being involved in so many other fights against fascism, Ruth looked heavenward, as if pleading with the gods, and asked plaintively, "I said, here we go again. Someone up there don't like me! But then I thought, wait, life is a constant struggle. There is no other way."

Ruth smiled mischievously and we knew at that moment we had our through line and eventually our title: *Forever Activists: Stories from the Abraham Lincoln Brigade.*

A few years later, I was watching *Hasten Slowly,* a stirring documentary about one of my favorite author-adventurers, Laurens van der Post, whom I had long admired for bringing worldwide attention to the plight of the Bushmen of the Kalahari. I was so struck by something he said I had to pause the VCR and rewind it.

"The Bushmen storytellers talk about two kinds of hunger," van der Post remarked. "They say there is physical hunger, then what they call *the great hunger.* That is the hunger for meaning. There is only one thing that is truly insufferable, and that is a life without meaning.... There is nothing wrong with the search for happiness. But there is something greater—meaning—which transfigures all. When you have meaning you are content, you belong."

Elsewhere, van der Post has written, "Art, poetry and music are matters of survival. They are guardians and makers of the unbroken chain of what's oldest and first in the human spirit."

They do this by reconnecting us to soul.

The Healing Forces of Myth

In the early 1990s I came across an essay in *The New Yorker* that deeply influenced my view of the relationship among art, history, and politics. The article was written by Lawrence Weschler and focused on the early round of hearings of the Yugoslav War Crimes Tribunal in The Hague, Netherlands. This was the first such session since the Nuremberg Trials after World War II. In admirably even-handed prose Weschler describes a lunch with an Italian judge, Antonio Cassese, who had been serving as the court president for two years. Cassese coolly revealed for Weschler "some of the more gruesome stories that [had] crossed his desk, grisly accounts of torture, rape, mutilation, especially those of Dusko Tadic, one of the most notorious war criminals."

Weschler writes, "I asked Judge Cassese how, regularly obliged to gaze into such an appalling abyss, he had kept from going mad himself."

The judge's answer astonishes.

"Ah," he said with a smile. "You see, as often as possible I make my way over to the Mauritshuis museum, in the center of town, so as to spend a little time with the Vermeers."

Weschler was deeply moved by the inspired choice the judge had made in dealing with his duty to daily gaze into the face of evil. Coincidentally, Weschler had been making his own pilgrimages to see the Vermeers at the Mauritshuis museum, as well as the Rijksmuseum in Amsterdam, and had discovered some remarkable parallels between Vermeer's era and ours. In seventeenth-century Delft, where the painter created his luminous portraits, life wasn't as peaceful as might be expected from the serenity achieved in his work. Instead, it was a time riddled with war and natural calamity, including a fire that nearly destroyed his hometown. As the Dutch empire expanded around the world, life in Holland was devastated by social unrest, and Vermeer himself was tormented by the financial woes of raising twelve children on his meager earnings as a painter.

To explain the trial judge's intuitive use of painting as a healing balm, Weschler cited the epigraph by Andrew Foyle in Edward Snow's definitive study of Vermeer:

> In ways that I do not pretend to understand fully, painting deals with the only issues that seem to me to count in our benighted time— freedom, autonomy, fairness, love.

The Name of the Stone

On the wall next to my writing desk I have hung an oak-framed print of Vincent van Gogh's *Haystacks*. It represents one of my fonder family memories. What makes the print special is that it was a gift from van Gogh's nephew to my father after my dad escorted him on a V.I.P. tour around the fabled Ford museums and factories of Detroit in the early1960s. As if illustrating the current Myth of the Web of Life, in which everything is connected to everything else, and everyone is within "six degrees of separation," the print provides a unusual link to an artist whose life and work have been profoundly important to me.

For me the print is a mythic image because it symbolizes the origins of a significant ritual in our family. Around the time of my father's meeting with van Gogh's nephew, he also came to know the son of the painter Auguste Renoir as well. My father relished telling us of his encounters with these men, acting like a field soldier returning from battle and describing how the generals had touched his lapel one cold morning. Soon after he began to disappear after dinner nearly every evening into the cool confines of the basement. There he would spend hours cutting clippings out of art magazines and pasting them into scrapbooks for himself—and me. For three years running my birthday presents were scrapbooks filled with magazine clippings of famous painters, mostly van Gogh and Renoir.

My eyes rove over the painting's golden slumbered fields. Once again, I feel the rare sense of serenity this painting has always given me, all the more moving because of van Gogh's lifelong struggle with poverty, physical pain, and social exile. Favorite passages from his collected letters to his brother crowd my mind. One favorite line comes from a description of a painting he'd done of a ploughed field that shone violet under a yellow sky and yellow sun: "So there is every moment something that moves one intensely."

I gaze at the furrowed road in the painting for several minutes. What was my father trying to tell me? Curiosity washes over me like a waterfall. This canvas is painted with almost ineffable affection for someone in such pain, and the courage it took to render so stupefies me. Then I recall the plaintiveness in the voice of a letter Vincent wrote to his brother Theo while describing a small cottage at the end of a road: "I am trying to get at something utterly heartbroken."

Gazing deeply at the painting, I am convinced that my father, stuck in the modern mythic world of "men in gray flannel suits," was describing his own deep identification not simply and sentimentally with artists in agony, but with artists who transcend their pain with the courage to create beauty in an often grim world.

This ability is what I think of as "the name of the stone."

In the myth of Sisyphus, the stone that Zeus transformed himself into is *exactly* the same size as the stone that Sisyphus is fated to push uphill through all eternity. In the poetic picture language of myth, Sisyphus' decision to risk the wrath of the gods is in exact proportion to his burden. The beauty of the soulful imagery is that Sisyphus transforms fate into destiny when he realizes that the weight of that burden will be measured on the scale of his attitude toward it.

Sisyphus in London

We've all met modern versions of Sisyphus. My first encounter with him was in the spring of 1975, in London. The struggle I witnessed there has haunted me ever since.

I had been working for several months for the Park Lane Cleaning Services to earn my passage to Greece and Israel and Egypt. Cleaning flats was an alternately fascinating and humiliating way to pay for continuing travels, but it did pay better than the demolition work I had already tried. Besides, I could work as many hours as I could handle, as many as ninety a week.

After four months of mopping floors, making beds, and polishing silver, my bags were packed for Cairo and only one last job remained. Fortunately, out of all my clients, who included the goalie for the Chelsea football team, the conductor for the National Philharmonic, a dentist working undercover for Scotland Yard, and a famous madam, the Harringtons were my favorite. They were an unusual bohemian couple for the Notting Hill Gate neighborhood they lived in. Mr. Harrington was a professor of economics and history at the University of London, an ex-M5 agent, and a brilliant classical pianist. Mrs. Harrington was an English literature teacher. For sixteen weeks I had gone to their flat every Sunday morning and been greeted with a cup of tea, chocolate biscuits, and the family wooden cleaning kit. I would set to work vacuuming, watering plants, and scrubbing floors, while Mr. Harrington would play Mozart's sublime *21st Piano Concerto* on the grand Steinway in his private library of several thousand books and dozens of exotic works of art from their travels through India, Africa, and Asia.

Those mornings were my introduction to the glories of Mozart, the genteel life, and the devotion of two cultured people. I was mesmerized by the way they treated each other with respect and deference, trading anecdotes from their week, and asking each other for hints to the answers to the London *Times* crossword puzzles.

On that last Sunday morning, I heard the horses clopping in Hyde Park as I pushed the buzzer of the intercom on their apartment building door. Where I had always heard the opening chords of the piano concerto, this morning I heard a raucous charivari of sounds, as if piano movers were moving the piano across the room.

"Yes, yes, whoever is it?" came Mrs. Harrington's voice over the intercom. Her voice was troubled, constricted.

"It's Phil—"

"*What?* Didn't the agency ring you to tell you we canceled?"

"No, sorry. I didn't call in this morning."

The Burghers of Calais, by Rodin, in the gardens near the Parliament Buildings, London. A modern Sisyphean image of freedom wrested out of bondage and beauty out of struggle.

"Oh, my, my." The intercom went dead, then her voice came back on. "I suppose you might as well come up, since you came across town. But you mustn't stay long."

The door buzzed and I stepped inside to the vestibule of the apartment building, but rather than wait for the open-cage lift to descend, I bounded up the three flights of stairs to their apartment, passing a neighbor in her dressing gown, who muttered to me as I passed, "The woman is an absolute angel to put up with that man. The way he carries on. It's just not done!"

Mrs. Harrington was waiting for me, adjusting her headband, and the brown corduroy overalls she always wore on Sunday when we cleaned. She took my jacket and hung it for me on their antique coat rack.

"There's something you must know," she began.

I tried to wave her off, as if to say, *Don't worry,* but it was too late.

Her face was carved in agony; tears misted her eyes. In her trembling hand was a glass of sherry.

"Mr. Harrington doesn't know you're coming—"

"Emma, Emma, love. Where are you, my dear?" cried Mr. Harrington in a scotch-slushed voice from the library. His footsteps shuffled across the well-worn wooden floor. "Who goes there, love?"

He appeared, drunk as a fiddler. Up went his arms in a wassailing greeting, spilling his whiskey all over the floor.

"Phil, Phil, my lad," he slurred. "How good of you to come. I was afraid you would forget to come around to our commodious abode on your final day in London before your peregrinations around the Mediterranean. *Bienvenu, mon vieux.*"

I was stunned. Mr. Harrington had always been the paragon of reserve and genteel behavior, as far as I knew.

Mrs. Harrington seized me by the arm and dragged me inside and past her husband. She whispered to me, "Just an hour, then away with you. Please." She was humiliated, and just this side of terrified. She pulled her black woolen sweater tightly around her, and I had the startling image of her as the uncertain Persephone accompanying Hades down into the underworld.

"No work for you today, lad—" Mr. Harrington cried out. Underneath the jolly facade, though, I detected a strain of grief I'd never seen before.

"Desmond, please, love, *I* can use the help, even if you can't."

She dragged me away from him and into the kitchen and began to talk uneasily as she loaded me up with her well-burnished wooden box of cleaning equipment. "Since you're here, I want you to understand because I know you are fond of each other. Tomorrow he will be positively shattered that you saw him like this, but he will have to deal with it." She led me into their bedroom and began picking up his scattered clothes. "Meantime, you should know our *arrangement.*"

I began making their bed, and my ears reddened as I heard her stress the word *arrangement,* which struck me as doubly odd because this morning I could still feel the heat of their bodies on the bedsheets and pillows, smell the Glenlivet in the open bottle on the bedside stand, hear the dripping of the shower in the nearby bathroom.

"I told him donkey's years ago that I would leave him if he did. But he insisted on a compromise." Her voice caught. "So during the school year," she said, as she hung up their clothes, "he swears to me that he will not touch a single drop of alcohol. But during the school holidays—like Easter this week—he can drink, if he must."

She pulled her hair back with her hand and sighed, then took a furtive drink from a flask. I tried to appear busy by brushing the velour curtains with a Victorian lint brush.

"We usually hole up here in the apartment all alone until the holidays are over," she continued, "hermetically sealed away from the world, as it were, for these binges of his. It is just too difficult to explain his struggle to people if we go out. No one would understand. Everyone would misinterpret—"

"What about you, Mrs. Harrington?" I interjected.

"Oh, my word. Not to worry," she sighed. "I drink to keep the poor man company. Although I detest the whole business." Years later, I thought of her when I came across Nietzsche's line that "a labyrinthine man never seeks truth, only his Ariadne."

Suddenly we heard the professor's stumbling steps, then the crash of a vase, followed by a hiss of curses, and moments later, the long slow burble of liquor over ice cubes.

"Are you mad at him?" I asked, not knowing what else to say.

"No, don't be daft," she snapped. "Look, I'm terribly sorry. I'm not angry with him for drinking himself silly," she said. "I actually admire him for *not* drinking the rest of the time. You must understand what prodigious self-control he displays for months on end, and what courage it must take to keep his demons at bay all that time, all the while eyeing the liquor cabinet."

We moved down the hallway, dusting the family photographs on the wall, and I asked whether he'd ever broken down while university was in session.

"Once. Twelve years ago. He was to teach a class on the War. A lecture on Rommel's campaign with Montgomery in North Africa, I believe. He got dreadfully pissed before the class and tried in vain to lecture. They tell me it was frightful. He could hardly speak a word. The students were mortified, really, for they adored him. The poor dear was warned by the university, which promptly put the fear of God into him."

Again, there was an ominous silence and worry about what would happen next.

"Anything else I can do for you? Mrs. Harrington?" I asked, anxious to leave.

We began to put the cleaning equipment away into storage.

"Actually, it's not the drinking that bothers me as much as what he's still hiding from me after forty-four years of marriage. Whatever it was that he experienced during the war—well, he refuses to talk about the whole ghastly business. All he ever says is, 'It's all quite hush-hush, love.'"

She spun away from me in tears, leaving me alone in the shadowy hallway. I stepped tentatively into the library to say good-bye to Mr. Harrington. He looked up from the piano bench, where he was slumped over trying to find some sheet music. Shakily, he got up and approached me and surprised me by handing me a crisp five-pound note, a half-day's wages for me in those days.

"Here, here, take this, lad," he said, warmly. "Have a drink on me in Cairo, will you? Then keep going. See the world now while you can. You have the right idea. The girlfriend at home can wait. See the world, but see it *smart*. Careful of the con artists along the road and all the louche travelers, especially the Germans. They're the ones to worry about, the lost souls who pretend to be sophisticated. And *read, read, read,* lad, as you go. Don't be ignorant. You've been blessed with strapping good health and *time*—so here, take this and this and this," he said, piling a number of travel books onto the table next to me. I fingered the leather bindings of his first editions of Lawrence Durrell, Freya Stark, and T. E. Lawrence.

"Oh, and one last thing before you go," he added.

"Whatever you like, sir."

"I would like you to polish the Steinway before you take your leave."

His voice was mellow, tender, hinting at sorrow and apology.

I nodded and returned with the box of supplies whose handle was worn down by years of use and slipped like a leather glove onto my hand. The soft light of noon now dappled the dark black wood of the piano. I took a clean cloth and the wood polish and removed the sheet music from the top of the piano. The lemony odor filled the room like the memory of a lost world.

Slowly, deliberately, I spread the polish in long, interlocking spirals, like the carved spirals in an ancient megalithic tomb, then, playfully, in swirling round dots and slanted beams, like the notes on the sheet music that were before me now.

Carefully, I brought the wood to a bright sheen and I could see Mr. Harrington's face gleaming in it, his glass of scotch absolutely still in his hand, his eyes filled with tears.

He sat down on the bench, placing his drink reluctantly on the piano top in front of him. He stared desolately for some moments, then with considerable effort he raised his hands above the eighty-eight keys to his life. They hung in the air like a matador's hands holding his cape high, daring the bull to charge. On his face was one of the strangest expressions I've ever seen in my life. It was as if he was peering at the ghost of Mozart glaring at him from the sheet music, admonishing him for his disrespect.

Then, he rubbed his eyes, and slowly his hands descended to the keys. Tenderly, he began to play, and out floated the first few sublime notes. The unfathomably beautiful music lifted across the room. I watched the professor play with utter affection, and something he had confided to me months before slowly came back to me.

"I would like to die with the word *Mozart* on my lips," he said, "like Mahler did."

I closed my eyes as the music seemed to hum in my swirling fingertips, and the loneliness of the hour turned inside out with something like joy enveloping the room.

I left him that way, a half-hour later, in a Mozart reverie, and never saw him again.

However, I've thought of him often. For the past twenty-five years it has been a ritual of mine to play Mozart's *21st Piano Concerto* on my stereo every Sunday morning. With the first trilling of piano notes I am transported back to London and the sight of Mr. Harrington at his beloved Steinway, mustering up his courage, filling his aching heart with joy. His show of bravado that cold London morning all those years ago helped me understand that Sisyphus lives on. He lives on every time a struggling soul spurns despair and accepts the inevitable struggle of his or her life, and in so doing, creates what Camus unforgettably called "the hour of consciousness."

Where many have seen grim retribution in Sisyphus trials, I see dogged resolution; where others have seen fatalism, I see silent joy. There is a celebration of freedom interwoven into this ancient tale, the celebration of having connived the burden of one's fate right into one's own hands.

"I see that man going back down," Camus wrote, "with a heavy yet measured step toward the torment of which he will never know the end." Yet, by forging dignity out of his struggle he learned to say, like Sophocles' Oedipus, "Despite my ordeal, all is well."

In mysterious ways like these I have slowly learned that you have to practice happiness, the way Mr. Harrington practiced Mozart. Every morning you go back to the bottom of the hill and start all over, one note at a time.

If Sisyphus Could Sing

As exalting as the myth of Sisyphus might be, it can be a disturbing metaphor for courage, rebellion, or the creative struggle, even the loneliness that haunts the American dream.

Unless we delve still deeper.

It's after midnight. I look up at Coit Tower the very moment that the lights flicker off. It's time for my late-night walk around the neighborhood. I shuffle down the hill to Caffe Italia and order an espresso. While mulling over my manuscript I notice a young Italian couple, dressed to the nines, arguing outside on the sidewalk, tussling about what all young lovers argue about moments after the bars close. She is looking for love; he is looking at seduction. She's not convinced, and is going home alone. He's not defeated so easily, and smoothly grabs a half-dozen roses from the passing flowergirl who's working late tonight and slips her a fiver. But his date has already hailed a cab and is gone in a fingersnap, leaving him standing in the cold fog, flowers wilting in hand.

Dazed and disappointed, loverboy shuffles into the cafe and walks straight to the jukebox. In a thick accent, he asks the owners, Giuseppe and Daniella, "Got any classical music, you know, Sinatra?"

"An Italian café without Sinatra, you gotta be kidding me?" says Giuseppe, throwing me a "what are you gonna do" look.

The thwarted lover slips a fistful of dollar bills into the jukebox, takes off his Armani coat, and sits down at a table next to the window. Staring out at the mournful fog, he listens to the lovelorn saloon singer crooning his back-from-the-edge-of-the-abyss ballads. For the next hour The Voice, as he's often called in the neighborhood, spins out that old black magic called love: "Saturday Night Is the Loneliest Night," "Autumn Leaves," "Only the Lonely," "In the Wee Small Hours," and the young Italian gazes outside, his heart breaking, slowly sipping his espresso, listening to the silky sounds. Eventually, he starts tapping his foot, snapping his fingers, as the moody hits keep on coming: "I Thought about You," "All or Nothing at All," and "Summer Wind." I recall the words of the great music critic Murray Kempton, after Sinatra died: "He was just this little guy telling his story." Three-verse stories, Kempton called the songs, that reflected an undying belief in eternal love, no matter how heartbroken you are.

By the time the jukebox plays the inevitable last selection, "One for the Road," a smile is curling over the face of the smitten lover. When the last piano bar notes have faded, he throws his coat over his shoulder and strides out, inexplicably stronger, into the fogbound night.

The Healing Game

No doubt music is a healing force, even a "healing game," in the words of the great bluesman John Lee Hooker. But once in a blue moon we can see evidence for its strength as myth as well. The night with the café jukebox is a prime example for me of the often-surprising sudden appearance of myth in ordinary life. It also illustrates what can happen

According to the ancients, Apollo graced Orpheus with a lyre, which
he used to enchant wild beasts and make stones and trees moves.

when myths collide. That night showed me how the myth of love and
romance can go bump in the night when it slams up against the great
American myth of loneliness. But as often happens in myth, the question and the answer are found within the same image, the same story.

When in doubt, go back, back to the beginning, say the Old Ones in
the myths.

That is what I did when I got home the night around the café jukebox. Acting on sheer instinct I opened up my father's battered old copy
of Homer's *Odyssey,* and sure enough, I discovered that Sisyphus had
not been totally abandoned by the gods. He was granted one grand

As Sisyphus in the ancient underworld found solace in the sweet
sounds of Orpheus' flute, so too we are helped in mysterious
ways by the power of mythic music, whether in the records of
Miles Davis or the notes of the anonymous saxophonist playing
on the lonely street corner or fire escape.

consolation. As he labored with his stone, he could hear exquisite
music from the flute of Orpheus.

In his inimitable poetry, Homer wrote, "Poor Sisyphus could hear
the charming sounds that ravished his ear."

Imagine the implications of that line. The divine detail is subtly placed. This is no mere coincidence. What it reveals to me is that we can more easily bear our burden if we listen closely for the music of life all around us, the music that is there for the listening, for the solace, for the triumph over our troubles.

For as long as we know music has healed mind, body, and soul. In our own time singers from Billie Holliday to Judy Garland, Ray Charles to Elvis Presley, have often worked in the old tradition of the wounded healer. Their voices soothe the savage beast of modern life. During the past fifty years one of the most effective antidotes to the corrosive burns of lonely urban life has been the tenderly tough voice of Frank Sinatra. His story is an American saga. It begins with the myth of the Italian immigrant, is encrusted with the legends of his beginnings on the road and with Tommy Dorsey, inflamed with the reputed connections to the mythic Mafia, and is even, as journalist Pete Hamill writes, inflicted with "the sorry narrative of the Fall," the fall from grace and subsequent resurrection.

All of these elements are there in The Voice. As music was the ultimate consolation for him, so it has been for millions of listeners, the voice of reassurance that if he could turn suicidal despair around, so can we.

The myth of Sinatra, like the myth of Sisyphus, is elegiac. It is the soulfully persuasive story of coming back from the dead, as Sinatra did after his disastrous marriage to Ava Gardner and his subsequent bouts with suicidal depression, with music that signals the triumph over fate of heartbreak. In this music, as in great blues, there isn't the slightest pretense of conquering pain and sorrow forever, like you get in escapist movies or confectionery pop songs. Instead, you hear the voice of conviction that the only road back from heartache is to love again.

The mythic message from Sisyphus to Sinatra is that only love can conquer death. Sisyphus risked everything for the love of his wife, of fresh air and light and warm sand, and for his citizens, so they could drink fresh water. Sinatra risked everything to go back into his pain because he believed that music was the best healer, the most sacred thing in his life, the only way to turn pain into beauty.

That Old Black Magic

After the smitten lover left the café that night, I remember approaching the jukebox with something like amused reverence. I have heard memorable concerts at some of the greatest venues in the world, from Paris and Vienna to London, the Baths of Caracalla, the Met in New York. But rarely have I felt the *tangibility* of music as I did that night in my local café listening to Sinatra's bluesy soulfulness.

So I slipped my own dollar into the jukebox and listened once again to Sinatra's healing game song, "Only the Lonely," his "Slide on over the couch" cry from the heart from a tender tough guy to his girlfriend. I heard the song as if for the first time, this time as the voice that had tamed the dark shadows along a lonely avenue, a voice to answer the emptiness when there are no words left, only music to express the movement in the heart called courage that will help us back up the hill of love and life one more time.

The existential myth of Sinatra may be the soundtrack for urban loneliness; some say his is the voice of the century, but its power lies in its storytelling as well as its power of music. The isolation of life in our cities has been a generally agreed upon price for the myth of individualism that rules the culture, but it needed a story, a voice. As singer Julius LaRosa told the *New York Times* after Sinatra's death in 1998, "Sinatra was able to turn a 32-bar song into a three-act play." With what rock star Bono called "swagger and attitude," Sinatra did more than give urban life a voice, he mythologized it, made our loneliness and our struggle seem sacred, and triumph possible. The source of that conviction may be found in something Sinatra once said about his early influences, the main one being the old family standup Philco radio. "The music on the radio was our religion," he said, "it was even shaped like a cathedral." In tribute, Bruce Springsteen once described Sinatra's music as "synonymous with black tie, the good life, the best booze, women, sophistication, [but] his blues voice was always the sound of hard luck and men late at night with the last $10 in their pockets and trying to figure a way out."

"Don't despair," Sinatra replied to Bill Zehme when asked about dealing with defeat. "You have to scrape bottom to appreciate life and start living again." Talking to journalist A. E. Hotchner in 1955, he said, "Me. I did it. I'm my own worst enemy. My singing went downhill and I went downhill with it. . . . The only thing that can hurt you is yourself."

In other words, he made music out of the struggle that is at the heart of life.

It may be a lonesome old town, we may feel blues in the night, but there is some old black magic in the dark that we can turn into light.

The secret is the way you wear your hat, which must be done by lowering one shoulder and raising the other, as if to say you've been to hell and back and you can take on any burden the world wants to throw at you.

At Sinatra's eightieth birthday party, Springsteen gave him a mythic tribute from the stage: "On behalf of all New Jersey, Frank, I want to say that, brother, you sang our soul."

The myth endures. Music saves our soul. "To sing," writes Joan Baez, "is to love and affirm, to fly and to soar. . ." and indeed, "Beauty exists, but must be hunted for and found."

Many Stories Deep

The world is in utter darkness without stories. We need the courage of the heartbroken man at the top of the mountain to turn and go back down and turn his sorrow into joy. We need to hear the music he heard. We need his stories.

We are like wandering Aesop who discovers he must tell his stories night after night if he wants food or shelter. There is only one way to survive his never-ending travels, and that is to transform everything he sees into a story so soul-satisfying for his hosts that they will gladly feed him and give him a bed. So he learns to turn the enigmas of the day into the fables of the night. Some strangers just bring news and gossip from the down the road; the storyteller dares to bring more.

We are like the pilgrims in *The Canterbury Tales* who are reminded by the innkeeper at the Tabard Inn to tell one story on the way to the cathedral and another on the way home. He has seen and heard travel-

The Greek fabulist Aesop depicted by the Spanish painter
Velázquez (1599–1660) as an itinerant storyteller bearing an old
leather-bound book from which he will read his fables and so
earn his bed and bread for the evening.

ers come and go for years. He knows that the journey is incomplete,
not even a bona fide pilgrimage, without the stories that try to glean
meaning from the chaotic incidents along the way.

But not just stories will do. The soul demands more.

"Don't be satisfied with the myths that come before you," said the Sufi poet Rumi seven centuries ago. "Unfold your own myths."

By that I believe the poet meant to retell them in our own words, mold their lyrics to our own will and purpose—as one music critic described the genius of Sinatra—find what is intimate and personal and meaningful in them.

If we do, we may learn that the eternal struggle from the depths toward the heights "is enough to fill a man's heart," as Camus concluded, gloriously.

Out of the struggle with ourselves, from the fire in our souls, comes the thing that never existed before—the music, the art, the words that make life endurable, and more, creative and sublime.

TWO

The Myth of Time

From the Valley of the Kings to Silicon Valley

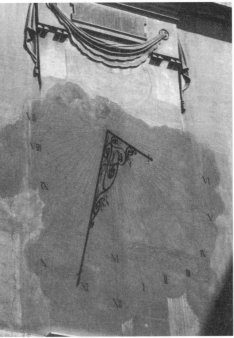

For it is important to underline this fact,
that it is, above all, by analyzing the attitude of
modern man toward Time that we can penetrate
the disguises of his mythological behavior.

—MIRCEA ELIADE, *The Sacred and the Profane*

I have been haunted all my life by a strange dream. I am wandering through a dark castle at night and hear a peculiar sound that compels me to descend ancient stone steps to a shadow-strewn room where three bent figures beckon me. I step closer and see three old crones at a cobwebbed spinning wheel shaped like a wispy clock. One of the crones spins golden thread, another measures it and weaves it into hands for the clock, the third stands poised with scissors ready to sever the timely threads. I gaze at them, realizing they are the Three Fates deciding how much time will be allotted to some unsuspecting soul.

Watching, I wonder, *What am I doing here?*

Then an icy voice whispers in my ear, *What were you waiting for?*

Again and again, for the last thirty years, I have been alternately stricken and blessed with this dream. Always the same question that feels like something between an accusation and a challenge; always the same sensation that wizened hands are trying to squeeze the air out of my lungs as the ambiguous words hover in the air.

"Why are you squandering your time?" the mournful voice is asking me. "When are you going to get on with your life?"

In the silence between the sleepstrange tones I hear a chorus of voices that have merged into one over time: my father, my track coach, the parish priest, Basho, Blake, Emerson and Thoreau, Neruda and Kerouac, and countless others who live inside me. A medley of bittersweet sources of instigation and inspiration, all contributing to the lifelong battle with time in my soul.

These dreams are no mere random firings of the synapses. The primordial scene with the tenuous thread of time is my soul talking in images. What I am trying to do is see and listen, and do as the psychologist Rollo May advises: "Identify with that which haunts you, not in order to fight it, but to take it into yourself; for it must represent some rejected element in you." So I try to savor the image, like I would an image from a work of art, letting it simmer in my imagination, and allowing the meaning to unfold.

The dream of the Three Fates represents my life, rife with all its glorious threads that turn to knots in my soul. It expresses the vital force within me that is trying to remind me of something recently forgotten, something crucial. Yet, because the dream tends to appear to me during periods of massive anxiety, I wonder if it is the cockamamie voice of conscience that I hear in the dream or the voice of a god? Whatever the source, it feels crucial that I understand it, whether it is pressing on me like a mental hairshirt to work harder, or as a gentle nudge reminding me to revel in the gift of my very life.

Moreover, the harsh truth revealed by the dream is that time itself is the heart of my personal myth. It tells me how difficult it is for me to live the life I believe I am supposed to be leading. Where that imperious "supposed to" comes from I don't know, but in my more optimistic moods it feels like a sense of destiny, the force behind my character, what the Greeks called the *daimon*. I listen, waiting, as the dream says, trying to learn how to use the time that has been allotted to me, trying to unravel the knots that tie me up like Gulliver in Lilliputia.

I'm only too aware of the noble sentiments from the East exhorting me to live in the moment, "the miracle of the present moment," as the Vietnamese monk Thich Nhat Hanh calls it. But I'm pulled in two different directions: into the past by my fascination for history, and toward the future by my interest in *what's next*, from my own next projects to the next innovations from Silicon Valley. I feel caught, like a character in an Italo Calvino short story, between two myths, attempting to make time go backward and forward simultaneously, while rejoicing in the vertigo that I try to use like adrenaline.

For thirty years now, since my college days when I worked the night shift in a Detroit factory, I've lived under a regimen of four or five hours of sleep a night, as if a character right out of a Greek tragedy who is relentlessly driven by Ananke, the goddess of need and necessity, who also was a spinner of the thread of fate. I've come to recognize this as one of the plot lines of my own personal myth. As with all true myths, the story has a ferocious drive to it. It compels me to believe I need to steal time, borrow moments, stretch my hours, dilate my days, whenever and wherever possible, and because of this daily practice I often have the sense of having already led several lives. But still the great dragon doubt breathes fire down my neck, reminding me that life is too short to be merely marking time. While stealthily borrowing from Peter to pay Paul, as my Grandma Dora used to say, I've hoped I was *making* time where there was little or none before, a task formerly reserved for gods alone.

But because of my lifelong accelerated pace I have always run the risk of being just one more guy caught up in the crank-it-up, take-no-prisoners, racing-to-relax times, the trying-not-to-get-ticketed-by-the-cosmic-cops-in-the-speed-trap times. Often, I have fretted over whether time is living me rather than me living time. The sudden swings between memorable time and forgettable time can be wrenching; the difference between lost time and found time can change your life.

So it's been imperative for me to try to practice the art of slowing down, recalling with affection Thoreau's dictum, "When in doubt, move slowly." Every day I try being as alert as possible to the miracle of the world around me. The hard work allows me the extra time for my family, music, a ballgame, a walk in the woods, a languorous meal, time to travel, but unless I slow down and *savor* the time the experiences have no clarity, no depth, no meaning, and hauntingly enough, there may not be any memory of them at all.

"It's a question of balance," as the Moody Blues sang back in the time warp of the1960s. It's also a question of myth.

"Where did the time go?" we say with rapscallion laughter after a great conversation, good party, gentle lovemaking. We also ask where it went at the end of our days, and with raking pathos if we really don't know.

"So little done, so much to do," bemoaned Cecil Rhodes on his deathbed.

"Bring back my youth," cried John Walcott in his final hours.

"But I have so little time," said composer Alban Berg.

Time is the soul of myth, as myth is the heart of time.

The Clock on the Wall

There is an old legend from the Salish Indians of North America about the trickster character Mink, in which we hear echoes of a situation that is curiously contemporary. In this wisdom tale we find a potent image that speaks directly to the soul's deep concern for time.

Long ago the People lived in accord with the rhythms of the sun and the moon, the stars and the tides, day and night, light and darkness. Then strangers from a faraway land appeared. The People called them their European guests. Of all their curious customs and possessions there was one that neither the trickster Mink nor the People had ever thought about before: an odd and seemingly useless thing the guests called Time. But soon Mink learned it was great medicine, it had wondrous power.

Mink decided he had to get some for himself.

One night he broke into the house of the strangers and discovered that they stored their Time in a gleaming box. Mink thought that the noise from the magic box sounded like woodpeckers in the forest, and that the two thin arrows on its face that moved around and around looked like birds circling around and around without ever really going anywhere. But he was impressed with the reverence the Guests gave the box and the way they looked at it throughout the day and night. Carefully, Mink tucked the ticking box under his arm and snuck away.

Now for the first time the People had Time. But it proved to be a nettlesome gift. Mink found himself mesmerized by the moving arrows inside the box and became forgetful about when he was supposed to do things he knew before by second nature. Now Mink checked out the clock before he did anything, just like his Guests. He even decided he should wear a turnkey around his neck so he would always be ready to wind up the machine and keep it ticking.

No sooner did Mink learn to tell Time than he no longer had any for himself. He spent so much time looking at the clock, he could never find the spare moments to fish or hunt or play like he used to do. Instead of being free to wake up and sleep when it was natural, Mink began to rely on the clock to tell him when to rise and when to rest. Soon he began to work more and more and rest less and less.

Lo and behold, as the wise commentator, Joseph Bruchac, has noted, "Because Mink stole Time, it now owned him and the People. It has been that way every since. Time owns us the way we used to own the Sun."

Stolen Moments

In this Salish legend we have in miniature the once and future force of myth. Ironically, its timelessness holds the key to the wonder of the way some stories and images continue to provide a *living mythology*, which resembles a running stream of stories as it moves from one generation to the next. Compressed into the mythic image of Mink is a tale rich with the psychological insight that we steal time at our own peril. Condensed into the image of mechanical time is anxiety built up over centuries about something precious that is lost when human beings began to rely on mechanical clocks. Not only did we lose the ability to live according to the natural rhythms of the sun and the seasons, we began

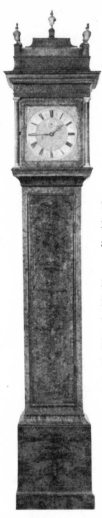

A seventeenth-century English grandfather clock echoes the ancient notion of Time as an elder, as further reflected in the colloquial expression "Father Time," a reference to the god Kronos or Saturn, the devourer of time.

to lose the ability to live *beyond* time. I believe part of the technological fury behind the gadgets and gimmicks of our time is economic, but another part is mythological: the upswelling of an atavistic urge to fight against the anonymity of Saturn's swinging scythe and live as timelessly as presumably our ancestors did.

If there is a secret opening into the realm of the mythic imagination, it is there, on the clock smuggled into the New World by the ironically named Guests, with our hand on the curious new contraption that promises power and advantage. Stealing time, it appears, is no new thing; rather, it may be a universal temptation. If we could only find a few "stolen moments," we tell ourselves, we could do the things that would change our lives for the better. If only…

Our modern myth of time, our newly minted model, our emerging story, tries to convince us that the old American myth (courtesy of Ben Franklin) that "time is money" must be inverted to "money is time." If only we make enough money, the reasoning goes, we will have enough time. But instead of reaping what we've sown and harvesting time, we find ourselves staring in disbelief at the blight of busyness.

In his indispensable book *Time and the Soul*, the philosopher Jacob Needleman calls this kind of thinking and living "time sickness" or "time-famine." Hardly a day goes by without hearing the mythical Mink's nighttime cry of "stolen time." But as Needleman asks with no little astonishment, "What *really* stole the time?" Even if the thief of time is technology, the question remains: What are the new machines supposed to liberate us *for?*

In the long run, the biggest question of all is not "What is time?" but "How do we *use* our time?" That is the philosophical prod to the well-lived life and the ice pick of terror in the hearts of those who fear that their time is not *really* theirs.

Which is why we live in an ironic age where the wisdom is written on the subway walls: *The faster I go the further behind I get.*

How fast is fast enough? How soon is soon enough?

If we live by the clock, we die by the clock.

Maybe we have become compulsive about time because we really don't know what time it is anymore. We don't know which story about time to believe, which myth to live by, which god to worship: the god of speed and efficiency or the god of slowness and contemplation.

Where Did the Time Go?

"No time to talk. Gotta go."

"Only got a second. On the run. I'll drink it on the fly."

"Gotta pump it up. Make it a double. In a to-go-go-go-cup."

"It'll keep me from sleeping? You're kidding, right? I can sleep in the grave."

"I'm here for my *edge*. An edge is an edge is an edge. Give me a double."

"24/7: That's what it's about, dude. We're just revving it up."

"You're either in the game or you're out of the game. How fast can you move?"

"Forget time is money; speed is money. Are you ready for prime time?"

"Like the song says, I got, got, got, got no time. No, no, no, no, no, no time."

"I lived in a tiny village in Thailand where time stopped, and I've always wanted to go back—but I don't have the time to go."

"Time? You mean the magazine? That's the only time anymore."

"Rest? There is no rest. This is life. It ain't no movie."

These lines aren't deletions from an early draft of *Through the Looking-Glass,* though there is a frenetic echo of time-haunted Lewis Carroll. They are what I call my "overhears," comments gathered just over the last month in the cafés, parks, and bookstores that are spread around my old Italian neighborhood of North Beach in San Francisco like so many coffee grounds scattered around an espresso machine. The subtext of all these one-liners is that life is moving at warp speed now, with the even more subversive implication that things aren't *real* unless they're *fast.*

"I'm busy," everyone is saying in the way we once heard "I'm rich."

"Wake me up when it's over," I heard the *barista* Tony Angeleri at Caffé Puccini say just the other night from behind the espresso machine. "It seems like only yesterday these cafés were an escape from the madness of the rest of the city, places where people went to get away from it all. Don't get me wrong. I still love it here. But café life is just becoming a way to get revved up for the next thing. I feel like I'm just here to serve up *an edge* for them."

For decades cafés like these have been an oasis for the locals to relax in and have animated conversations or linger over the newspaper after a game of bocce. Now most of the old-timers have retired to the suburbs, the humming of laptop computers has replaced the bell-ringing sounds of the old pinball machines, and a strong espresso is widely regarded as just a hip way to keep up with the caffeinated times.

Years ago, I heard Allen Ginsberg at the nearby, legendary Caffé Trieste shouting lines across the room from his newly minted "Plutonium Ode" to the raffish Gregory Corso, and then hovered nearby, notebook in hand, as they argued the merits and demerits about the politics of the piece. In surreal David Mamet theatrical contrast, just the other night at Caffé Puccini I heard two young stockbrokers shouting stock prices across the room to each other—on their cell phones. Shortly afterward, I watched in disbelief as a man stood on the curb in front of the café talking to himself on a nearly invisible headset, presumably to a business contact. He looked like a lunatic, but without the charm of someone who knew something privately marvelous.

Everywhere technology is seducing us to think we have no choice but to save a moment here, save an hour there, and so, finally be happy. But I don't think we're trying to save time at all; I think we're trying to stop it. I suspect we're terrified of it, because for most people time is more synonymous with death than ever before.

Once upon a time, people showed their awe and reverence for time itself by staging elaborate rituals for the moments it is most manifest—birth, initiation, and death. Now our most visual evidence of our concern about the profound passing of time is an obsession over time*pieces*, flamboyant watches and state-of-the-art gadgetry, that signal to everyone we can't afford to miss a single nanosecond.

"We try to abolish time," wrote the mythologist D. M. Dooling, "because our relation with it has become simply one of fear. It is chasing us to destroy us, we seem to think; we must stay young, we must not allow old age to have any real place in society, and we must not wait for anything but take quickly what we can get before it is too late.... What is it we are trying to abolish?... What is disappearing?"

The real moment, the presence of the present.

Once upon a time it was said, "I think, therefore I am." Now we say, "I am busy, therefore I am." So advertising firms use mythic scare tactics such as "Speed is God, and Time is the Devil," or "Time is running out!" On the sports reports, the stock pages, the love doctor radio shows, and the real estate updates, we hear the gospel message, "Timing is everything."

Connie Martinez, a consultant in Silicon Valley, is in the center of the time vortex. Through e-mail correspondence we pick up on a topic we've spoken about several times over dinner in the Bay Area—the mythic speed of modern life.

"24/7" is a slang phrase meaning "all the time" that has been used for a few years in the Valley. You now see and hear it everywhere. It reflects the dominant view that you must be accessible every hour and every day of the year. This is a place that can work and play around the clock; a place that does not really think about the sacrifices it is making, but rather the time that it may be wasting not inventing or creating or bringing a product to market.

"When I first started giving speeches about the Valley a few years ago," Connie said, "I would speak to its three-pronged competitive advantage—quality, innovation, and speed. I finally dropped quality because it did not seem to fit. Speed and innovation clearly dominated and quality actually created an inverted pull away from speed. Silicon Valley actually creates the products or tools of speed addiction. The technology that speeds up our communication is the drug itself."

When I ask her what the future looks like in terms of the livability of Silicon Valley, she says, "I see it getting worse before it gets better because our addiction to speed is constantly rewarded in all that we do. The speed-mongers win—and win big."

The Mythic Choice

The problem with time is timelessness. In the sixteenth century, the Zen Master Xiangyan felt compelled to tell his disciples an elusive and enigmatic koan to help them stop their wandering minds.

> Suppose someone is up in a tree, holding onto a branch by his teeth, his hands without a grip on a limb, his feet without a toehold on the trunk. Someone under the tree asks about the meaning of Zen. If he does not answer, he is avoiding the question; but if he does answer, he loses his life. At just such a time, what would you reply?

"Thus, Xiangyan's man in the tree has to let go of his precarious grip with his teeth," writes scholar Thomas Cleary. The koan is that he must give up his purely intellectual fixations, his "hang-ups" we might say, to realize the nature of Zen, yet not allow his detachment, his "letting go," to turn himself into a spiritual escapist.

The living meaning of the koan, as with many myths in the wisdom story traditions, is that the task of life is to know when to hold on and when to let go; that time is to be measured in intensity, not quantity; by the heart as much as by the clock.

The old myths emphasize the quality of time; the new myth stresses the quantity. The old wisdom stories emphasized the relationship of time to the soul; the rapidly emerging myth stresses the benefits of *speed*. Speed rules the day like a god from a lofty throne. We need go no further than the theme of time to illustrate the presence and power of myth in the modern world. Speed alone is the both the result and the response to the increasing complexity of the times.

We live at the rate of a runaway train, at the mercy of the myth of speed, which states subversively and mercilessly that those who don't keep up fall behind, perhaps forever. The myth has its origins in the dream of the Industrial Age and a literally mechanistic belief called "Taylorism." Frederic Taylor is the father of "scientific time management," the genius or culprit, depending on your politics, who brought stopwatches into the workplace. He is noteworthy for having announced, "We don't want the man to do any thinking." Taylor was also the first to look at work scientifically, but he ended up reducing it to little more than slavery, creating the sense everywhere he went that the greatest shortage of all is the shortage of *time*. Taylor's biographer, Robert Kanigel, illuminates the paradox that continues to plague us: "Each day we reap the material benefits of the cult of workplace efficiency that [Taylor] championed; yet we chafe—we scream, we howl, we protest—at the psychic chains in which it grips us."

James Gleick's book *Faster: Life at Full Speed* challenges our sacred myth of technological progress and our desperate faith in time-saving devices.

> We believe that we possess too little of it [time]: that is a myth we now live by. What is true is that we are awash in things, in information, in news, in the old rubble and shiny new toys of our complex civilization, and—strange, perhaps—stuff means speed. The wave patterns of all these facts and choices flow and crash about us at a heightened frequency. We live in a buzz.

Faster charts this killer pace. Acceleration, its author breathlessly points out, is the password of the day, constant connectedness the goal, speed the ideal. Rather frenetically, he cites as the poet laureate of his new cult of time a copywriter for an early watch company who wrote, "We declare that the splendor of the world has been enriched by a new beauty: the beauty of speed."

"We have become a quick-reflexed, multitasking, channel-flipping, fast-forwarding species," he writes, "with time-saving devices and strategies with the aim of finding a little time to do what we previously didn't have time for."

The latest in the long litany of paradoxes of time is that the more we save it the more we dread losing it.

> It's no coincidence that the paint has worn off DOOR CLOSE buttons in elevators across the country...and that seven million watches are made every year from cheap Swatches to $85,000 "precision chronometers" while...people fret more not less about giving up the very leisure time we worked for to make more money to pay for the gadgets we bought to save us time.

Time is indeed one of the myths we are living by, but one we always have always lived by, as evidenced by the myriad gods who have personified it, the myths that have recounted its origins, and the proverbs that have condensed centuries of convictions about it. Deep fascination with time is no new thing. It is the most enduring and impenetrable of mysteries. We can never know it. We can only imagine it, which takes us back to the homeland of myth, the place where we can linger and be amazed at how differently other cultures have visualized time and lived accordingly.

What is new is the way we increasingly define ourselves not in terms of money, clothes, cars, houses, jobs, but in time. As one movie producer confided to me recently, "There are only two kinds of people anymore: fast and slow. You have a choice. No, wait, actually, you don't...." Or the stockbroker who snarled to a companion while waiting in line for a movie, "The future ain't what it used to be. I used to be able to *control* it. Know what I mean, babe?"

Then, a strange, puckish expression came over him.

Speed.com

In the summer of 2000, at the University of Santa Clara in the heart of Silicon Valley, a conference was held, aptly called "Speed.com." The moderator began with a kind of micro-parable. An innocent snail was robbed by two turtles. The investigating fox asked the poor snail what happened. "I don't know," he sighed. "It all happened so fast."

As if on cue, the audience roared on the stressed word *fast*, which of course was the point of the whole weekend.

The renegade philosopher Sam Keen delivered the keynote address, which he dubbed, "Slaying the Speed Demon." He began by contrasting the conversations he had been involved at dinner parties over the last few decades. In the '60s, he said, we talked about revolution, in the '70s we discussed consciousness, in the '80s it was real estate, and in the '90s investment. Now, he said, everybody talks about their computers and Palm Pilots and new software.

"We're going faster and faster," he added, "but we're not really going anywhere."

The audience snickered. The reason, he said, is that we are paralyzed by "the myth of speed" that tells us we will fall behind if we slow down. It is a myth that creates more and more access to information, what Keen calls "The New Messiah," but it also creates burnout.

A woman in the audience remarked in decidedly Faustian overtones, "I've sold my soul to make lots of money, but I'm out of here in three more years. I can't sell my soul any longer. I want *out*. Everybody wants out. They all say they want to go live on a farm."

The nearly packed auditorium mumbled sympathetically.

"No," said Keen, correcting her, "they want half-time. They want to work at a human pace."

Everybody wants in, but few know *why*.

Everybody wants out, but few know *how*.

"Ultimately," Keen concluded at the end of the evening, "it's a mythic matter."

In his mythic vision that means a change of story. If our souls are contorting under the pressure of speed like the faces of those test pilots in their rocket-sleds, we must rediscover the way of sacred time, the belief that time is a gift, not a commodity. It means slowing down, stopping time, taking our time, simmering, as Keen's mentor Howard Thurman used to recommend, and remember the old invocation of the Romans: *Festina lente,* Hasten slowly.

The old myth said, "Time and the tides wait for no one." The founding myth of our culture said, "Time is money." The streamlined myth says, "Speed is God—and we are its hapless converts."

This is one of the new riddles about time, but it may be helpful to know the old ones, because it's in the nature of riddles that they reappear with every generation. They may hold a clue to the old enigmas.

"So are you going to live by Kronos, clock time, or Kairos, sacred time?" Keen challenged the audience in Santa Clara. "Ask yourself, by what time do *I* really live?"

Then he picked up a cheap plastic wall clock he had positioned in front of his podium and stamped his foot on it, dramatically crushing it to pieces.

The Salish Indians would have been proud.

Stunned but delighted, the audience cheered wildly.

And this is the point about the unfolding myth of time. The clock is ticking so fast we don't know how to stop it, but apparently many of us would love to crush it or at least slow it down. This doesn't herald the Luddite cry for abolishing clocks or modern technology. Who wants to live in a world without penicillin, heart transplants, e-mail, recorded music, even cars? What it does mean is that in the marvel-a-minute world of the high-tech age we are finding it harder to see the *meaning* in the way technology is changing the way we live, in the words, the way the clock is ticking.

Every technological innovation shouts the news of greater computer speed, quicker connections, and a more efficient life. But as one of the other speakers asked, "So what?" If the mad rush for more and more innovations to save time is an illusion, what's the point? Is every advance of technology really progress? The recent scourge of radio stations—a digital device that traps fractions of seconds out of talk show conversations in order to sell more commercials—is metaphorical for the surreal ways we are saving time without knowing what to do with it.

"Half our life," said Will Rogers, "is spent trying to find something to do with the time we have rushed through life trying to save."

The other half is spent in the fear of failing, where we are frightened to death that all our hard work is, in the end, wasted time.

***

After the conference I rode home on the train, lulled by the clacketing sounds of wheels on rails and the words of the conference. The ones that resounded most for me were among the last, a *cri de coeur* that was heard when one of the participants at the conference joked that he had been recently ill for five years and feared getting better because he'd have to go back to work. Going back to work, he said, meant reentering a world that might have passed him by.

As I stared out the window of the rumbling train I recalled Keen's concluding the evening by asking us, "What time is it for you, now? By what time do you live?"

Instantaneously, my mind made a movie jump-cut to an afternoon a few years ago when I was shuffling around an antique market in São Paulo, Brazil. While marveling over some old conquistador armor I overheard a breathtaking tale. An American tourist was haggling over an antique sword with the vendor and walked away in a huff, sighing, "I guess it just wasn't my time to have it."

His friend chortled and said, "What do you know about the right time?"

Then he proceeded to tell a chilling tale. "Hey, let me tell you what. If it's your time, it's your time. I saw this program the other day. A guy and his brother crashed in Mexico fifty miles from anywhere. Terrible, right? But you know what? It's not their time. They crashed three hundred yards from *the best hiker in the world* who discovered them alive and offered to get help. She hikes fifty miles in three days, finds a plane and a pilot, and flies straight back to the crash site. Can you believe it?"

The storyteller holds up the top of a plastic cup to resemble the topography of the mountains. "Did you hear what I said? The hiker flew *straight* to those brothers in a place *this big* in a 100,000-square-mile national park and jungle." He makes a tiny fingernail mark in the top of the paper cup to dramatize what a speck in the forest the hikers must have been. "Let me tell you this—it wasn't their time. If it's your time, there's nothin' you can do."

Of course, he is talking about fate, his myth of time. It is an ancient belief about time, a myth with surprising staying power. But I also hear a powerful metaphor at work here: *It wasn't their time,* the man said.

If it wasn't theirs, whose was it? I wondered as they got up to leave, chortling at the weird fortune of the tourists. Then I thought, *Yes, they are on to something,* the modern terror that most of us don't own our own time, no matter how expensive our watches are. But if isn't our time, whose is it?

✸

"So what's *my* myth of time?" I wondered as the lights blurred along the railroad tracks and the train whistle moaned across the night.

Strangely and wonderfully, as if peering into an old carnival kinescope, a series of images began to unreel in my mind, images I hadn't thought of for years. I saw my own hand punching the grimy time clock at the factory in Detroit where I labored during my college years, vowing that I would never again live by the clock. I saw my fingers wrapped in masking tape and clenching sandpaper as I sanded the windowsill of a musty old Victorian house, and nine layers of different colored paint appeared under my fingertips, the last evidence of lost worlds. I saw the long talonlike roots of the *kapok* trees slowly strangling the thousand-year-old temples at Angkor Wat. I saw the special watch with raised numbers that a friend gave to Helen Keller so that she could "touch the time." I saw my father's face when I left Detroit at the callow age of twenty-three to drive across country and begin my new life in California, and heard his voice as he shook my hand, telling me not to worry about when we'd see each other again: "Son, you have all the time in the world."

I close my eyes to throttle the surge of images, and realize with a shiver of recognition what an impact those words have had on my life for the past twenty-five years. It has meant a life in search of timelessness, a life of reveling in the past, exulting in the future, and wondering why it is hard to live in the present moment.

In this, I am a man of my times, of all times, a soul in wonder about the inscrutable mystery of time itself. I am trying to understand the power of these mythic images, and trying to remember the truth of the words the monk whispered in my ear as we walked together in the cloister of his monastery so long ago: "If you miss the moment, you miss your life."

The God with a Thousand Faces

In her book, *Time: Rhythm and Repose,* the Swiss psychologist Marie-Louise von Franz described the gap in our understanding of time: "Even our seemingly self-evident concepts of past, present, and future do not seem to be universal."

Primal people, she writes, originally conceived of time as a deity, synonymous with existence itself and the ultimate divine mystery, a gift from the gods indistinguishable from the powers themselves. Time flowed like the river of life; it issued forth like a cosmic breath. "Only in modern Western physics has time become part of a mathematical framework," she writes. The Western genius for rational explanation has wrought a world of technological marvels, but the penchant for objective observation has also placed us *outside* the very time that obsesses us.

Fortunately, there is a bewildering melange of myths that can remind us that there is more to time than the oddly mechanical ticking of the clock; that, in fact, there is a sacred dimension to time that has been all but forgotten in the mad schemes to save it, stretch it, or worse, kill it.

The Roman god Janus embodies the notion of mythic time or the soul of time, and simultaneously personifies thresholds and exits, beginnings and endings, youth and old age, ancient chaos and hope for a new order.

In the Western Christian tradition, time is linear, with a set beginning and forecasted ending. In Islam, time and space are equally sacred, and each year, each month, is holy. The Greeks had nine gods of time, including Oceanos, the god of the river that girdled the globe, who gave rise, like the waters, to the image of time as a river. They honored Kronos, father of Zeus, god of ultimate time, symbolizing both life and death, alternately depicted as devourer of all things and benevolent measurer of the sands of time. They also imagined one of the subtlest gods of all, Kairos, the god of lucky chance and synchronicity, depicted as a winged god poised on a razor's edge and holding the scales of fate with one hand and reaching toward the scales with the other. The mythic implication is that if the god's fingertip touches the

The Greeks regarded time so mythically they represented it with nine different gods. In this frieze in Tragir, Dalmatia, Kairos, the god of synchronicity, is shown as a winged being poised on a razor's edge and gripping the Scales of Fate. If encountered, the ancient injunction was to "grab him swiftly," suggesting that one seize the moment and so turn fate into destiny.

scale he is influencing fate—taking destiny into his own hands, as the saying goes. Kairos is one of several deities who personified numinous moments of time, such as the winged goddess Nike, who personified the split second that decides battles or games, similar to the Roman Fortuna, goddess of good and bad luck.

Across the Mediterranean, in the Valley of the Kings of ancient Egypt, there are innumerable tombs with ceiling paintings of Nut, goddess of the night sky and symbol of the passing of time. She was believed to swallow the sun each evening, digest it in the darkness of her stomach through the night, and spit it up over the horizon in the morning. In northern Europe, the Vikings envisioned the three Norns, goddesses who wove the threads of the past, present, and future together in the skein of life. Indonesians believe they live in the midst of "rubber time." In India there is a belief in endless cycles of creation and destruction, endless cycles to infinity in a "triple rhythm of creation, duration and destruction [that] repeats in immense cycles forever and ever," according to von Franz, and the Dance of Shiva represents the "cosmic cycles in time, of creation and destruction, birth and death."

According to Evan T. Pritchard, in his world of the Micmac tribes of southern Canada and the northeastern United States, time is measured by experience and the rhythms of the nature, and "things take as long as they take. As a matter of (startling) fact, 'There is no word for time in the Micmac language nor in most Algonquin tongues. You can't say it.'" Instead, Pritchard writes, you can inquire, "When is it?" but your answer may be in images, not numbers. "Where is it now?" the Micmac people will ask about the sun. So the myth of Indian Time is no myth in the pejorative sense. He reveals that he knows Algonquin people who have never worn watches, which are believed to remind you of the demands others may have over you and dim the light of real time. The fact that there are no words for *hour, minute,* or *second* in Micmac, but one for *now—neegeh—*emphasizes the here and now and reminds tribal people of the sacred need to connect with the marvel of the moment.

Comparably, the Hopi Indians do not have separate words for our three stages of time—past, present, and future—only words for what is manifest or objective and what is coming into being, perceptions that are purely subjective. The Aztecs imagined a sun god who laid down the measures of time and who demanded to be appeased by human sacrifice to empower his daily journey across the sky.

"As to 'Mexican time,'" reports my friend, the Silicon Valley consultant Connie Martinez, "having been married to a Latino for ten years, I think they view time as a gift, not an obligation. You get to where you are going when you are ready to give that gift—your gift of time. I come from the Scandinavian culture, which views time as an obligation and would not consider wasting someone else's time when a meeting time is agreed upon. So a Scandinavian will be five minutes early to an appointment or a gathering. But a Latino will honor the need to take his or her time along the way, thus arriving when other deserving 'tugs' have been met, usually up to two hours past the generally agreed upon time. Personally, it drove me crazy."

In ancient China, calendars and clocks may have been zealously guarded by emperors, but divination was commonly practiced in temples and was used to determine what the gods wanted you to do. Rather than interpret events sequentially, the Chinese tended to ask, "What likes to happen together in a meaningful manner? What tends to happen together in time? What likes to happen together?" Von Franz points out in her book, *On Divination and Synchronicity*, that there are two fundamental ways of looking at time: timeless or eternal time and cyclic time. "Sometimes," she warns, "they overlap or interfere."

The Chinese appear to be "preoccupied with the chance aspect of events," according to von Franz. This is symbolized by the *I Ching*, the Book of Changes, which reflects an ancient belief that while time cannot be measured in all its mysterious depths, an awareness of change allows us to "see" time in its different aspects, past, present, and future. In contrast, the Wheel of Salvation in Buddhist doctrine represents "the dynamic teaching of the Eightfold Path, set in motion by Buddha and rolling on and on in the world. Gradually increasing man's consciousness, it finally helps him to overcome all time-bound existence and to awake to a timeless state."

Similarly, His Holiness the Dalai Lama states in a 1990 *Parabola* magazine interview that "time is understood or conceived only in relation to a phenomenon or a process.... If there is no change, then one cannot conceive of time in the first place.... It hasn't so much to do with awareness of impermanence, but rather with a very instinctive nature of humans, which is that we lack contentment. When we enjoy something, we feel it has gone very fast. We are not satisfied, we want more. When we do not desire a particular experience, then that situation seems very long."

The Vikings had the mythopoetic notions of ax-time, sword-time, wind-time, and wolf-time. Who can compete with that Beowulfian imagery, other than the Irish, specifically the Aran Islanders? The Irish author and playwright J. W. Synge observed they had no idea of time by the hour, just shadow-time, as it were, their only gauge of time available on sunny days, less reliable on cloudy ones. The measure of how the islanders passed time also fascinated Synge, which wasn't by the clock either, but by the story. This sensibility was an essential aspect of the Celtic Twilight that he shared with his mentor and friend, W. B. Yeats, who wrote of his fellow Irish in *Mythologies*, "We gave ourselves up in old times to mythology, and saw the gods everywhere."

Regarding the "rumor of Irish Time," the contemporary Irish musicologist and record producer P. J. Curtis writes to me that there is indeed such a thing.

> We live both within and without Time. The past is present, the present is the Past. When my late father would speak of the Famine Time it was as if he was personally there and living through the horrors of it with his ancestors who had done so.
>
> [My ancestors'] lives were governed by the sure flow of the days and seasons, which were marked by rituals such as Lughnasa, Mid Summer, Mid Winter. Our attitude to Time and the passing of it would be akin to that of the Moroccans, where the feeling is, "Let Time happen. It has nothing to do with us." It is as if we know that we cannot push against the flow of time and so we flow with it and inside it. We cannot shape it or make it, we can only use or abuse it, which we do with relish, as we know deep down it makes fools and dust of us all. But we are sometimes disdainful of it, and this gives us the ability to see the past as being very present in the now. Our music and storytelling has that "timeless" quality to it, a sort of hypnotic "spiraling" within its linear flow like a snake or a torque. I say, Let Time go its own way—and good luck to it.

His poetic musings echo the rapscallion observation of his fellow Irishman, John O'Donoghue, who is fond of saying, "Time is eternity living dangerously." But to see such things, he says, we need the light of the soul, which he likens to Rembrandt's lantern that shines forth an uncanny presence from the divine world.

In a conversation with me at his home in Portland, Oregon, the journalist John Nance movingly described to me the way that the Tasaday tribe in the Philippines "tell" time. After having visited them more than twenty times, he is convinced that "they refer to the different times of day by using the sunlight as it hits the rocky face of the cave, or by holding their open hand at an angle similar to the slant of the rays of the sun, indicating morning, noon, afternoon, night."

In other words, they hold time not in a Palm Pilot, but in the palm of their hands.

Is this not the oldest dream of all?

The Hands on the Clock

We need not look only to old stories preserved in amber or listen to modern mystics to see the mythic imagination at work for images of time. Who among us doesn't remember watching the clock during our schooldays, hoping against hope that it would move faster and bring on the bell that announced recess, break, or the end of the day, so we could escape and pursue our secret passions? Or just plain play? Who among us has not watched the seconds and hours, then weeks, months, and years go by, since then, and been driven to sign a Faustian pact or two with the gods and demons of time in the ardent belief that hard work is really just a way to buy time, make a down payment on the Myth of Leisure when we will finally get to live?

What were you waiting for? ask the Fates in my private dream, my personal myth, which in many ways echoes the public myth that fuels the frenzy ad campaigns that urge us to move a little faster, buy a little more, because *time is running out.*

"Myth reveals the very hands on the clock of our existence," said the philosopher Nietzsche. It may also reveal their absence, as in Ingmar Bergman's unnerving image of the clock with no hands in his god-haunted story, *Wild Strawberries.* We need only look as far as the watch

A venerable old clock shop in Cork, Ireland, reveals an oddly moving collection of images of broken time, lost time, time that is longing to be fixed.

on our wrist, the clock on our wall, the calendar in our briefcase, the Filofax on our desk, the blinking digits on our Palm Pilots reminding us to check messages on our phones, which will remind us to pick up the e-mail on our computers. Everything everywhere reminding us that the clock is ticking, that we're falling further and further behind, sexy semaphores signaling that we better hurry up. If these mythological and spiritual reckonings seem quaint, consider Einstein's whimsical definition of relativity as two minutes that seem forever with a dull person—compared to two minutes that go by in a fingersnap with a beautiful woman.

The mathematician, philosopher, and author of *The Nature of Time,* Gerald J. Whitrow, was fond of passing on a story about the Russian poet Samuel Marshak's visit to London before the First World War. In his imperfect but earnest English, Marshak asked a man in the street, "Please, sir, what is time?"

The passer-by was stymied, "That's a big question. Why ask me?"

Metaphorically speaking, from whom we ask the time helps form our entire worldview. The myth of time we are living helps determine our quality of life. One way to determine our personal myth of time is to simply ask ourselves how we really decide how to spend our time. Do I believe in immortality and that I have all the time in the world? Is my schedule dictated by the brutal reality of paying the bills to support my family? Do I do things for the sake of appearance, to help my career or social standing, instead of something that deeply concerns me? Or have the sublime photographs from the Hubble Space Telescope made all questions of time and space frightfully relative?

Consider the glorious vision seen through modern telescopes that has helped us reimagine not just the universe but time itself, allowing us to see back in time as we witness starlight that has long since gone. If Saturn's hourglass doesn't convince us about the transience of all things, then certainly the humbling pictures from deep space must.

In *A Brief History of Time* Stephen Hawking asked, "Which came first, the chicken or the egg? Did the universe have a beginning, and if so, what happened before then? Where did the universe come from, and where is it going?" For Hawking the issue of origins and time are inseparable; yet he presses the question further about what time really is by asking what, after all is said and done, is *real*.

Maybe imaginary time is really the real time and that which we call real time is just a figment of our imaginations. In real time, the universe has a beginning and an end. But in imaginary time, there are no singularities or boundaries. So maybe what we call imaginary time is really more basic and what we call real time is just an idea that we invent to help us describe what we think the universe is like.

"Consider a world," suggests Alan Lightman in his delightful book, *Einstein's Dream,*

in which cause and effect are erratic. Sometimes the first precedes the second, sometimes the second the first. Or perhaps cause lies forever in the past while effect in the future, but future and past are intertwined....

In this acausal world, scientists are helpless. Predictions become post-dictions. Their equations become justifications, their logic, illogic.... In this world, artists are joyous. Unpredictability is the life of their paintings, their music, their novels. They delight in events not forecasted, happenings without explanation, retrospective....

Some people attempt to quantify time, to parse time, to dissect time. They are turned to stone.

The Reenchantment of Time

The reenchantment of time calls for a few tricks of perspective, which the most imaginative scientists and artists provide for us. The cosmologist Edward Packard offers such a gift in his playful book *Imagining the Universe,* when he challenges us to imagine that a million years of time is the equivalent of a single mile, then picture the distance between the building of the Giza Pyramid and our own era as only a few feet, while the Big Bang is only a Little Whimper away at some thirty thousand miles.

The poet Percy Shelley challenged the notion that time is a mournful reminder of our mortality. In his immortal poem "Ozymandias," Shelley questions the importance of archaeological ruins as a prod to "remembering the past, of the immortality the dead gain through memorials and the memory of the living," actually suggesting the "fruitlessness of memorials."

Ozymandias was the Greek name of the third pharaoh of Dynasty XIX, Ramesses II, who ruled Egypt for sixty-six years beginning in 1279 B.C.E. Shelley was inspired by a fragment of a sculpture based on the ancient ruler that he glimpsed one day at the British Museum, and his knowledge of the original inscription on the colossal seated statue, which originally stood sixty-six feet high and weighed in at a thousand tons: "I am Ozmandias, King of Kings. If anyone wishes to know how great I am, let him surpass one of my works." His irony-laced meditation on the "ravages of time" may outlast the statue itself:

> I met a traveler from an antique land
>
> Who said: "Two vast and trunkless legs of stone
>
> Stand in the desert. Near them, on the sand,
>
> Half sunk, a shattered visage lies, whose frown,
>
> And wrinkled lip, and sneer of cold command,
>
> Tell that its sculptor well those passions read
>
> Which yet survive, stamped on these lifeless things,
>
> The hand that mockt them and the heart that fed;
>
> And on the pedestal these words appear
>
> 'My name is Ozymandias, king of kings.
>
> Look on my works, ye Mighty, and despair!'
>
> Nothing beside remains. Round the decay
>
> Of that colossal wreck, boundless and bare
>
> The lone and level sands stretch far away."

As Robert Alden Rubin has commented in his anthology, *Poetry Outloud,* the anonymous sculptor attempted to carve something that would overwhelm and outlast the works depicting mere mortals, "but it appears as if Time gets the last laugh." His fascination, as for most contemplative people before the modern focus on innovation, was the mystery of endurance.

So fundamental is the question of time that every age and every culture must imagine it in the imagery of the day, "breathe new life into it," as Camus described the demand on the mythic imagination. In our time we honor Bill Gates, Michael Jordan, and Steven Spielberg as godlike for their ability to save time or speed it up, seemingly stop it midair, or freeze-frame it. We make heroes out of scientists like Jane Goodall, who offered us a virtual time machine to the dawn of humanity by revealing that our DNA is 99 percent the same as that of chimpanzees, or paleontologist Stephen Jay Gould, who described the 440 million-year-old Burgess Shale fossils in such a way that time seems to dissolve before our very eyes. I think too of J. L. B. Smith, the most famous scientist in the world during the 1930s because of his discovery of the fossil of a 400 million-year-old coelacanth, widely believed at the time to be the longed-for "missing link" in evolutionary theory.

The power of the well-chosen myth of time lies in its ability to reveal a numinous perspective on all the time that has gone before us. This is what the new Rose Planetarium in New York City has done with its "Cosmological Walk" where every step you take up the winding ramp into the museum is the equivalent of 50 million years of evolutionary time. This is what the Irish bard Van Morrison means when he sings, "Precious time is slipping away."

Killing Time

Since 1996, when I first visited Cambodia, every time I hear the phrase "killing time" I think of Tuol Sleng, the bloodstained former school in the heart of the capital, Phnom Penh. Where once the laughter of children had rung out there is now a museum that reveals the grisly evidence of what happens when the mythic urge turns demonic.

For more than a century, scholars have described the apparently universal "nostalgia for paradise." This desire has been manifested in countless cultures with sacred architecture, ceremonies, rituals, and symbolic language. The yearning for paradise can also be evoked with, as Mircea Eliade writes, "talk of 'chaos,' of 'disorder,' of the 'dark ages' into which 'our world' is subsiding." This is precisely the kind of language that Pol Pot and the Khmer Rouge resorted to when they tried to establish a paradise here on Earth. To do that they tried to kill time, literally. This meant attempting to start the world all over again. So on April 17, 1975, they emptied the capital and sent millions of urban people out into the fields to begin a new day, a new universe, a new order. All that was left was to annihilate the old one, which is how the notorious "killing fields" came to pass. Two and a half million people out of a population of 6 million were executed by the Khmer Rouge over the next three years.

The long colonnade at Angkor Wat, representing a melanchotic timelessness in a land that tried to abolish time altogether.

Tuol Sleng is the evidence of the transmogrification of simple schoolrooms into chambers of horror. In room after room, there are now only the dark stains of torture victims.

The final room on exhibit contains photographs of another kind of horror altogether: funeral pyres of clocks, watches, calendars: the symbolic killing of time.

"As if you could kill time without injuring eternity," said Henry David Thoreau.

Years afterward, the only possible time in which to remember what was never meant to be recalled, the Cambodian poet and playwright U Sam Oeur wrote of the near eradication of his sense of self in his poem, "The Kingdom of Hell":

> I'll be nowhere,
>
> I'll have no night,
>
> I'll have no day anymore:
>
> I shall be a man without identity.

The poet needed many years and much spiritual practice before he could fulfill his "sacred vow" to his father and offer alms to his spirit at the temple of Angkor Wat, and in so doing "lift the curse" and restore his own identity, his own soul.

Who has the courage today to take a vow to redeem their own lost time, to take a vow that the rest of our time will be sacred? Who has the strength to unfold their own life-affirming myth of time?

The Clock of the Long Now

To appreciate time at this depth we have to change our story, become more conscious, as inventor Stewart Brand has recently written, of our very myth of time. Brand belongs to a group called The Clock of the Long Now Foundation, which is designing an instrument, a colossal mechanical clock, intended to keep perfect time for the next ten thousand years in a remote spot somewhere in the American desert. They fully expect it to become a pilgrimage destination, say in the year 3000.

The notion behind the construction of an American Stonehenge, according to Brand, is to help develop an aesthetic of slowness and commitment toward more meaningful time. He is convinced that the acceleration of modern life has devolved into a "pathologically short attention span," and believes the clock, which he sees as part mechanism and part myth, will "teach us to take the long view and to accept our long-term responsibilities, but in terms of decades and centuries."

One of his colleagues, Danny Hillis, who was one of the pioneers behind high-speed supercomputers, hopes that future pilgrims will regard their clock as a symbol of "the moment when they took responsibility for the future. When they stopped believing in just now." His original e-mail proposal to friends was to plan for "one bong per century, and every millennium, the cuckoo comes out." The cuckoo concept has been abandoned, but the land has been acquired, in Nevada, and plans proceed apace for installation in the near future.

Besides holding the potential to be a brilliant piece of conceptual art and mechanical wizardry, the project serves as a marvelous metaphor for the new perspective that is needed to help us cope with the acceleration of modern life. "The long now" is a Western version of the Buddhist notion of the "miracle of the moment" that has long been the goal of the spiritual life. The fear is that we'll forget where the clock is ten thousand or so years from now. It is sobering to note, as the International Time Capsule Society at Atlanta's Oglethorpe University reminds us, that 90 percent of time capsules are never recovered.

The Riddle of Time

"How do you stop time?" my son asked me recently, unable to stop giggling.

"With a stopwatch!" he said before I could blurt out the wrong answer.

Later in the day I could still hear his silly laughter, and like a radio jingle the riddle kept reprising itself in my mind, but with a tricksterish twist. Slowly, the riddle transmuted into: "How do you stop a stopwatch that cannot really stop time?"

For the next several days I thought about it, because in its own way I saw it as a modern koan for our dilemma about time. That was the moment I recalled the philosopher Jacob Needleman's agile response to the conundrum:

The answer to the question of time, the soul's answer to the question of time, is not anything in words or ideas. Time is incomprehensible to the mind that asks about it, *our* mind. *The soul's answer to the problem of time is the experience of timeless being.* There is no other answer.

Uncannily, the truly creative response to the anguishing question of time is no mere answer, but a mythic image. It is comprised of fragments of the old myth of Kairos, the winged god of time and chance, teetering on a razor's edge, his forefinger on the scales of fate and destiny; the relative vision of a scientist who conceived of his world-changing idea while on a speeding train; the sacred vision of a poet pretending he was illiterate; and the conviction of a timebound philosopher that *timeless experience* is our one and only answer to the riddle of time.

Timelessness.

How do we become timeless? Build a time machine? Take off our watches?

Gandhi gave us a clue when he said, "There is more to life than just increasing its speed." Tennessee Williams remarked, "Snatching the eternal out of the desperately fleeting is the great magic tragic of human existence." This is how we beguile time, by seizing life, moment by moment.

The truth of these nuggets of wisdom comes home to us every time we *savor* our time or practice some form of timeless activity. It can be listening to music, aimless walking in nature, lingering over meals, or relishing the chores in our gardens. In these activities past, present, and future imply each other, and our hours have a strange and wonderful elasticity rather than a tortured elongation. Our minds wander freely and our souls soar because we are, finally, *playing with time.* This finally makes life worthwhile, which is why one of our greatest philosophers, Heraclitus of Ephesus, imagined time as a child playing at a board game. The sublime message in this immortal image is that within play is contemplative time, which is indispensable for happiness.

The once and future myth is that we are running out of time. It's as old as the fear that the blood-red sun needs to be appeased with human sacrifices or it will die out, and as new as the slogan, "Keep Up—or Die," or the factoid, "Fact: Almost everything you learn today will be obsolete in twelve months."

The only way to stop the juggernaut is to stop running, and start thinking of time as music that we don't want to stop the flow of, or a gift with which we have been graced.

The Gift of Time

In late November 1999, I received an exultant phone call from my film-making partner Gary Rhine telling me that our trip to the World Parliament of Religions conference in Cape Town, South Africa, had finally been confirmed. I was elated. It was important to me to be part of a project that would take eight American Indian spiritual leaders to the parliament so they could describe their ongoing struggle for religious freedom to a gathering of sympathetic people from around the world.

"I have to confirm our flight soon," Gary told me. "Do you want to extend your stay, maybe go on one of the safaris that are being offered at a discount rate to parliament participants?"

It was just the kind of call that makes life worthwhile, an offer of important work coupled with a chance for some adventure.

But then, the haranguing voices of time-guilt cried out, *You don't have the time, you don't have the money, you don't have the patience to work it all out....* It was the all-too-familiar mantra from the Cult of Busy, dully reminding me about my endless deadlines, obligations, commitments. Time began to press in on me like the Clashing Rocks around Jason's ship as he tried to sail into the Black Sea. The word *busy* pounded in my temples like a gavel.

As if in response, something the novelist Graham Greene once wrote came back to me: "There always comes a moment in time when a door opens and lets in the future." This was such a moment. A door in my soul swung open and in rushed the future.

I asked Gary about our projected itinerary. He said that the return flight was routed through Miami, near where my ninety-six-year-old Grandfather Horace lives. As Gary's voice reverberated across the phone lines I remembered the cry of the old crones once again, *What were you waiting for?*

This was one of those incandescent moments in which the dark future comes to light. I knew that no matter what my current time and money problems were, no matter how tired I was of the constant travel over the last few years, something new and vital was waiting for me on this journey. The film project was important, but news had also recently reached me that my grandfather's health was worsening by the day, which was a more important reason to go. I had to see him one last time, and if possible take my son and Jo to meet him.

I could do it if I only I could figure out how to use my time.

The vision came like a hologram, complete, compressed.

The notion of a lack of time crumbled like Keen's clock.

❋

In early December, I traveled with Gary and Huston Smith, the renowned historian of religion, and our friends, the Indian leaders, to Cape Town, to help film the conference of the World Parliament of Religions. A week later, I ventured to Namibia, formerly German South Africa, for my only real break all year, a safari to the Etosha game park. It was the fulfillment of a lifelong dream to spend time searching the horizon for magnificent animals, thrill to the great beauty of the landscape. While there I thought of how long the elephants, impalas, cheetahs, and lions had moved across these same migration trails to the northwest part of the park where the water holes awaited them. One of the unexpected joys was learning from Ingo, our safari guide, how to "rest my eyes" by simply contemplating the faraway African horizon for hours at a time as we drove around the game park. One afternoon Ingo regaled us with tales of the Bushmen in nearby Botswana, with whom he had lived for years, a tribe believed to be living in more or less the same conditions for the last forty thousand years. That night, I dreamed about camping out near "the oldest road in the world," in nearby Tanzania, the seventy-foot-long track containing the earliest known footprints, dating back almost 3.8 million years, and hearing the footsteps of our ancestors.

Two days later I stood under the stars on the sands of Cocoa Beach in Florida with Jo and our son Jack. Through sheer good fortune, there was a space shuttle launch at nearby Cape Canaveral scheduled for our first night there. Providentially, it rained, and the shuttle was postponed, which allowed us to spend more time with my grandfather. After two emotional but illuminating visits with him and my stepgrandmother, we drove back to our motel in a slashing rain and dashed into our room for news on the NASA television channel about the launch.

Finally, after two postponements it was a go. With two minutes until countdown I turned grumpy and in my search for the sublime simply dashed outside with our crying three-year-old boy in my arms, forgetting to put his shoes on. But I was beside myself and not thinking, not wanting to take any chance that we would miss the launch.

Outside, the clouds were parting and the moon was spectacularly full. Astonishingly, there was a crowd of a few hundred people who had driven there from all over the southern states. All faces watched the skies over Cape Canaveral two miles away, and from a distance I heard some youngsters mimic the classic countdown, "Ten, nine, eight, seven...."

This is to say, at that divinely inspired moment I was haunted by time. Standing there in the cold breeze and bright moonlight my sense of things splintered. It was intensified by the voices I had heard at my Grandfather Horace's small condo on the lake near Orlando. For two days I had been trying to stage the probably one and only meeting with my son and his great-grandfather. Jo enjoyed getting my step-grandmother Bernadette's version of their life together, and my aunt and two cousins and two of their children all stopped by join in the reunion. The time was full of urgency, embarrassment, relief, agony, restlessness, love, compassion. I couldn't help staring at his shriveled body, his wobbling hands. He was a proverbial shell of his old self. Where was the hard-nosed ex-railwayman, gold miner, dynamiter, factory worker, watchmaker I had seen only a few years before? Where were the stories I was hoping would unlock the final mysteries of my family? Why couldn't I have some time alone with him to get the truth?

His spirit was nearly gone, that much was clear, but the spirits of the four sons who died before him were in the room, and I needed to make peace with them. There was another ghost, the three-year-old son he accidentally ran over with his car, the spirit of my son in the future, as I imagined him looking at the photographs of all of us together, twenty, thirty, forty years from now. Horace had somehow managed to straddle the century, but it meant outliving four sons and his first wife.

Now riddled with prostate cancer and a golf ball-sized tumor behind his right eye, my grandfather struggled to stay awake in his overstuffed chair, coming in and out of consciousness, but also, I felt, in retreat from years of grief. One time he emerged and whispered to me how "terrible" it was that Stanley, my father, and my uncles Roland and Dave had all died so young, and as he wept I thought of my Grandmother Olive, dead at forty-four, then caught myself gnarled in grief when my own three-year-old began to dance goofily in front of him. My grandfather leaned over and said to me with rare affection in his heavily accented French-Canadian voice, "He is so full of life. *That's good, that's good, that's good.*"

Full of life, he says of my little boy as he himself lay dying, and me wondering as our thoughts reeled across the century, *Where did the time go?* For him, my father and uncles and aunt? Where is time now for my son? And for me, in search of lost time, like Jimmy Durante in search of the lost chord, the one he heard in childhood that inspired him to become a singer?

⁂

The next day, as the countdown reaches the legendary "liftoff" stage, Jack starts crying, pleading to be taken back into the hotel, terrified of the pounding of the surf and the strange crowd and the rumbling of the Earth beneath us, the sky over Canaveral turned a blazing white

The Uroboros, the alchemical serpent swallowing its own tail, is an ancient symbol for infinity, an early intuition of what modern physicists now call "the bending of time."

and yellow, as if a distant sun were exploding overhead. Seconds later what appeared to me to be not a spaceship but simply an elongated ball of orange fire moved as if in slow motion in a beautiful parabola across the distant beach and out to sea.

This was the first time in my life I could feel the joy of the *bending* of time and space, as if a rubber ball had been bounced onto the fabric of the universe, as Hawking describes in his famous illustration of the time/space continuum. Not only am I struck by the great stretch of time I am witnessing, from antediluvian Africa to Florida's future-glimpsing space program in two days. But to dent the fabric and stretch even further, for a fugitive moment, I sense my father grasping my shoulder at the Ford Pavilion at the1964 World's Fair in New York, and saying, "That is the future," then recall how only a few hours before my grandfather had described to me the moment when his father, my Grandfather Charlemagne, took him by horse and buggy to Vernor, Ontario, to show him the first automobile that had ever driven into town.

❋

Rather than level off like any of the hundreds of airplanes I've seen take off, the *Discovery* continued in an impossibly beautiful rising on its journey into outer space to fix the Hubble Space Telescope, dropping its booster rockets into the ocean below, continuing on at fifteen hundred miles an hour until it was a pinprick in the fabric of time and space.

Call it grace, call it coincidence, call it a chance for connections, but I learned a week later when it landed that it had traveled what was for me the numinous total of 3.8 million miles in its orbits around the Earth, coincidentally the same number of years between us and the first footsteps across the savanna that I had thought about so often while in Africa.

On the beach my throat catches with emotion as I huddle with Jo and Jack underneath our blanket. I hold on tightly to my son, who is frightened by the entire moment, the rumbling of the surf on the beach below us and the shattering explosion of the shuttle, but perhaps, I fear, my own ardent enthusiasm that he witness the moment.

Far above us, the *Discovery* thrusts into space, a safe sight for Jack now. He watches intently, sniffling, racked with a cough, but gazing in wonder at the splendid sight of the shuttle as it rises higher and higher into the moonlit sky.

❋

Lately, my son has been beginning many sentences with the charming, "When I was a boy. . . ." I realize he is mimicking me in those moments. I try to compare his life to mine, especially in my attempts to make his dead grandfather a real character to him. "When I was a boy I was a space-guy," he says, and I ask him when that would have been. "Oh, uh, in 1932," he says, arbitrarily, but chillingly coincidental since it was the year my mother and Jo's mother were both born. I can sense his throat straining for the voice, his mind reaching for the words, his soul for a story, to begin to form. Not unlike my grandfather at the other end of the life spectrum, flailing for dates and words, for myth and meaning.

There on the beach, watching the *Discovery* disappear into the darkness of space, I believe that I can finally answer the old crones in my dream: I was waiting for this moment, I want to tell them, I was waiting for time's stop so I could know the great continuity between my great-grandfather, my grandfather, my father, myself, and my son.

Walking back to the room I suddenly remember something my Uncle Dave told me the last time I saw him, ironically at my Grandfather Horace's condo. We were talking about what a shame it was that my father had died so young, especially with so many things he still wanted to do.

My uncle rolled his eyes, like my father and my grandfather used to do, and crooked his head to the side as if looking for a new angle to what he wanted to tell me. He had made the same gesture minutes after I had delivered the eulogy at my father's funeral, slowly measuring his thoughts, before saying to me in the midst of my sorrow, "Time heals all things." But saying it as if the words had never been said before.

Standing on the beach, I smiled at the memory and thought to myself, *Maybe that's what my father meant about having all the time in the world,* then stopped in my tracks, shifted my now-sleeping son to the other arm, and looked back over my shoulder up into the night sky.

The flaming orange streak of space shuttle was now a glowing ball of fire climbing the ladder of heaven, finding its way into orbit, defying time, defying space, working its way into our memory, waking us from time's fury by giving us the gift of the long now when the world opens out into the unknown and calls for us to follow so we might finally know the august secret of life.

The present moment is time's own home, the place we travel so far to find.

THREE

The Mythic Power
of Mentorship

From Odysseus to Zorba

Dad, what can you do when
you have to be a man?

—JAMES DEAN, *Rebel Without a Cause*

For several agonizing days after the April 1999 massacre at Columbine High School in Littleton, Colorado, I tuned into late-night television and scoured morning newspapers to try to understand teenage boys who have been drawn down into the vortex of violence.

Speaking of the Trench Coat Mafia being armed like an adolescent SWAT team, Littleton's Sheriff Stone said mournfully, "They were kids with automatic rifles." A headline on the *Los Angeles Times* op-ed page screamed, "These Kids Are Really Failed Adults." A letter to the editor of the *New York Times* admonished the world that tragedies like this happen because young "souls purposefully crushed learn that their lives aren't so valuable." An essay in the *San Francisco Chronicle* compared the two young gunboys to the angry outcasts in slasher movies exacting their "bloody weirdo revenge." Lance Morrow, in his *Time* magazine column, wrote, "For Trench Coat Mafia members no less than ethnic cleansers, hatred becomes an object of intense study, a major, a creed. There is pleasure in it, in being on the outs with society.... Here is tribalism pure and deadly."

In interviews with the national press, the Columbine High School kids who witnessed the killings spoke in a haze that reminded me of shell-shocked victims during wartime. One teenaged boy said he couldn't agree with what his classmates did, but could understand them because they were "outcasts from society and because nobody really liked them." Another boy said, "They hated everybody." One young girl simply sobbed and expressed the feelings of kids everywhere: "School should be a safe place."

Hauntingly enough, a common refrain heard from high school kids across the country over the next several months was that there is a general physical absence of adults in their lives, *so what do you expect?* Some students bitterly referred to the bullies, jocks, and cliques who ridiculed the killers and mercilessly taunted them by mocking their clothes, their hair, their masculinity. Another complaint was the lack of teachers or counselors at school who really listened to them. One teen, seething with anger, told a camera crew, "Nobody cares, nobody listens. How can they? They're never around." The friends huddled around him stared at the camera in icy silence.

Finally, when the first photographs of the young killers were shown, I saw something in their eyes that I couldn't fathom, until I heard that one of them had combustibly described himself in a school essay as a "shotgun shell." In other words, ready to explode. The revelation prompted the press to ask the boy's English teacher whether she hadn't been alarmed at the reference. She replied that she simply regarded the boy as the son of a military man, and wrote off the self-reference as a kind of twisted poetic image about the boy's own future in the military.

Is this what one of the boys meant in his suicide note that hissed with anger about "too much peer pressure, too little adult protection"?

The words chill; the images grind. The charges by the teenagers are unnerving, but some commentators suggested an even worse scenario.

"They went berserk," wrote Philip Gourevitch in *The New Yorker*, "and although their suicide-attack was savagely premeditated, it was dumbfoundingly meaningless: a perfect waste."

Meaningless? A perfect waste?

Surely not; surely we can learn from the carnage, if only we find a pattern. Only then will we find the meaning that will save our children from killing themselves—and one another. If the past is prelude, the ritual of ridicule will lead to the catharsis of rage. Perhaps the most perturbing of all the students comments was, "They were just trying to cope." Somewhere these kids had heard that alcohol, drugs, cigarettes, promiscuous sex, and rage were "coping mechanisms." Somewhere they had come to believe that retaliation was natural, inevitable. Looking for some insight, I turned to the work of Michael Meade, the storyteller and activist, who has written brilliantly about the undealt-with rage of young men in our culture.

In his groundbreaking book, *Men and the Water of Life*, I read, "The collapse of traditional cultures, the loss of shared myths and rituals that enfold the individual into the group, and the spread of modern industrial societies are producing generations of unbonded children and adults who are not initiated to the purpose and meaning of their own lives." Further on, Meade writes, "News reports of murderous child-soldiers, drive-by shootings, increased racism and intolerance, the spread of child abuse, and the steady increase in the rape of women in the very centers of the culture are bulletins from the child-men whose bodies grow apace while their psyches remain outside the touch and blessings of human community."

His words cut like a razor. For years, Meade has explored the problem of the child-man, the uninitiated, purposeless teenaged boy with raging testosterone, who has little or no experience of what Meade's friend, the poet Robert Bly, has long called "the shoulder-to-shoulder" relationship with older men he trusts. Turning to Bly's recent work, *The Sibling Society*, I found a passage I had underlined with yellow marker only weeks before: "To go from a boy to a man is a very long road, which needs the help of older men ... but older men are working overtime on Wall Street or retiring to Florida, so they're generally not around in our culture.... Young girls abandoned by their father may go into depression, but young men will burn your city down." Bly attributes the behavior to "the deepening rage of the unparented," a generation whose neocortexes are being short-circuited by television and shoot-'em-up movies and video games, what he deems to be the

"Thalidomide" of our time, all of which combine to produce a "society of half-adults."

What I see in the world around me is that *boys learn it.* Boys learn to hate. Rather than being hard-wired for it, boys who are angry, humiliated, and isolated and live in a culture that glorifies violence, romanticizes guns, and rewards vengeance will learn to hate—and hate hard.

But while some boys learn it, others don't. Some learn another way to handle the inevitably strong feelings of adolescence.

"What then shall we do?" asked the Russian novelist Leo Tolstoy when he was caught in the grip of a spiritual crisis and felt utterly lost.

What then shall we do, when confronted with the limitations of our control over the poisonous atmosphere of media violence that our children are breathing in? How do we break the cycle of ridicule and revenge?

The Crisis in Mentoring

A few days after the terrible violence I received a packet in the mail from a friend and fellow filmmaker, Gail Evenari, who is currently working on a television documentary about heroes. Inside was a fiery essay by the Berkeley cultural historian, Theodore Roszak, written in response to the Littleton killings. Roszak pulls no punches in his charge that the media's use of euphemistic descriptions of those responsible for the recent spate of killings reflects mass cultural denial about the core problem:

> When are we going to start telling the truth about violence in our schools?
>
> They are all boys. If girls are involved, their role is that of victims. This is not a problem of "kids," "children," "teenagers," or "students." Global terms like these only mask the fact that we are dealing with a problem that is specifically and solely male. Violence among the young is as gendered as violence in the world at large....
>
> What the gunplay in our schools reveals is a crisis in male mentoring. As the Littleton killings tragically proved, men—men specif-

ically—have failed wretchedly to help some troubled boys find a more humane model of manhood than Adolf Hitler.

The phrase "male mentoring" resounded in me like the pounding of an old Irish drum. But at the same time a terrible sorrow welled up in me for young men who feel abandoned, hopeless, and angry. I set Roszak's essay down and thought back to my own late teens, and was seized by one of those feelings of *There but for the grace of God go I* that can happen when you safely pass by a car crash.

When I was seventeen my mother took me by the arm and walked me out into the backyard, and beyond into the empty fields behind our house, and told me that she was filing for divorce from my father. "You're going to be the man of the house now," she cried. Her decision triggered an ugly and violent year as he fought her to the bitter end, refusing to leave the house, then paying only meager child support for my younger brother. Looking back, I see how stunned he was, how desperately he tried to make amends. But it was too little, too late. By that time, I was full of rage, angry at both of them, and there was only one way I knew of dealing with it: *to keep moving.* I was angry at everyone from my parents to the priests at our church, one of whom, I discovered, was clandestinely dating one of my classmates at night and then lecturing us during the day about the evils of premarital sex. I was enraged at the government about the undeclared war in Vietnam that would soon devour some of my classmates. Worse, I was corrosively depressed, as if my soul was rusting from within. I lived the last year of high school in icy silence, barely speaking even to my best buddies.

We know now what can happen to teenaged boys who are angry and silent. It is the isolated ones who snap. I think back to those times and wonder why I didn't "go off," as the kids say now.

Perhaps it is because for the next few years I didn't sit still long enough to do myself or anyone else any harm. I ran track and played basketball, but that doesn't describe the half of it. A kind of mania overtook me. Outside of my team training I was also running to and from school, running in ice storms and electrical storms, playing ball after practice and games with dead balls on snowy driveways until the street lights went out—or the hometown newspaper office opened.

Providentially, halfway through my junior year, I was offered a job at our weekly newspaper, the *Wayne Dispatch*. They needed a sports-writer and a photographer. Coincidentally, I had just received an electric typewriter from my father so I could quickly type up my stories hours after covering them, and when word got out around the family about my need for a professional camera, my Aunt Barb intervened and supplied me with my uncle's Yashica 125. In her infinite wisdom, she also continually encouraged me to show her my work when it appeared in local newspapers, encouraged me to take the camera with me on all my trips. Hers was a tender guidance during these trying times, and she became a close confidante during my college years when I nearly dropped out.

Looking back, I can see now that the unlikely combination of sports and the arts, plus adults who gave a damn, saved me. I can see now that . I was like those feckless Inuit teenagers whom their elders describe as *aqunnaaki*, "between two skins." I wasn't a boy any longer, but wasn't yet a man. It is a tenuous place to be. Your life can go many ways. There are no guarantees, not with the best genes, the deepest pockets, the best breaks. The teen years are flashpoint years. It is the time when someone with the choice words, the timing for the pat on the back, the knack for challenging, can make a lifelong difference. If it happens, it's as if invisible hands step in to help.

It is the moment of the mentor.

The Power of Mentors

We never spoke about mentors when I was young. We had teachers, coaches, and role models. The era wasn't so self-conscious about high-falutin' labels and aspirations of transformation. But there is a moment that does stand out for me when the word suddenly constelled a life-time of relationships with mentors, both living and dead.

One evening, in the fall of 1984, I used the last seventeen dollars to my name to drive nearly the length of California, from San Francisco to La Jolla, to the home of a psychiatrist named Stuart Brown so that I

A contemplative Joseph Campbell with producer Stuart Brown, during a break in the filming of the documentary, *The Hero's Journey*, in Honolulu, Hawaii.

might meet the famous scholar of mythology, Joseph Campbell. I pulled into the driveway running on vapors, as we used to say on the streets of Detroit. Getting out of the car, I took a deep breath of the ocean air and strode up to the front door hoping against hope for a writing job on Brown's documentary film project about Campbell.

For a decade I had admired Campbell's work, culminating in some courses called "Myth, Dream, and the Movies"—largely inspired by his work—that I had been teaching with various friends at the American Film Institute and Esalen Institute. At the time Brown's project was on the rocks. He and his film partners were looking for someone to come in and rework the footage, and as he put it to me, "make it a little more relevant and artistic."

After dinner, we sat around the fireplace with our shot glasses full of Glenlivet, Joe's favorite scotch, and talked about a multitude of subjects until well past midnight. I remember the sound of the surf pounding against the nearby breakwater, the shouts of the surfers down on the beach, Bach's cello suites on the stereo, and Campbell's glee when I shared my course outlines with him.

"Now that's just *marvelous,*" he said. "It gives me great pride to see all of you young people making this work your own."

I was over the moon, as my grandmother used to say, to meet someone whose work I admired, and with the caliber of conversation. Our talks careened from American Indians to the Upanishads, John Steinbeck to Bill Moyers. One element of Campbell's conversation stood out as if in bas-relief even to his impressive scholarly references. It was the way he honored his teachers. Without fail he praised a favorite professor, author, or coach when he discussed each important juncture of his life, giving them more credit than anyone I had ever encountered. He mentioned his boyhood neighbor and teacher, Elmer Gregor, Heinrich Zimmer at Columbia, Ananda K. Coomaraswamy during his early writing years, Maya Deren, who introduced him to the world of avant-garde film in the early '50s, even Sylvia Beach during the Paris years, who personally introduced him to the mythic undertones of her friend James Joyce's work, *Ulysses.*

"A little push and everything can change," he said when we spoke about his favorite city and the great artists he encountered there like Joyce and Picasso. The world of 1920s Paris had changed his life, and encouraged him to break away from the conventional life of the scholar when he returned home to the States in 1929. When he finally began his own teaching career, he told us, he had the great fortune to study under the Indologist, Heinrich Zimmer.

"Oh, I owe that man everything," Campbell said exuberantly. "He taught me how to read a symbol. At lunch one time he spoke for two hours about the mythic importance of an *egg!* The symbolic life— that's what it's all about."

Innocently, I asked Campbell what difference a teacher can make. Immediately, he warmed to the theme.

"Oh, now there's something I really want to talk about," he said. Stuart filled his glass and Joe was off to the races.

"You know when I was growing up the educational system was just *terrible!* The teachers of my time weren't teaching, they were indoctrinating. After a year of studying medieval literature at the Sorbonne in Paris I was thunderstruck when I realized I still couldn't order a simple cup of coffee at a café. My studies were in Provençal French and completely useless for the life I was actually living. That's when it got into me: You either find a mentor or you go it alone, which is possible, but *very* tricky, even dangerous. Now Heinrich Zimmer, my teacher at Columbia, there was a real mentor. James Joyce was a mentor to me, through his books, and Picasso and Klee, through their art. After awhile I went my own way. But there were critical points in my life where my mentors set me on my course."

I looked over at Stuart, and he was beaming with delight. This was what he had dreamed of capturing on film, and that evening's extemporized symposium did indeed set the stage for the revival of his film.

"How is a mentor different from other kinds of teachers?" I asked Joe, tentatively.

"Oh, I'm glad you asked," he replied with an Irish cop's twinkle in his eyes. "The teacher just gives you *information*," he said with disdain, "generally without a clue about the difference between it and wisdom. The guru is supposed to embody wisdom, the spiritual life, but too often he just asks you to put his picture around your neck and be just like him. It works in India, but they've had six thousand years to work out that relationship. Now the mentor is the one who helps you find your own way. But you have to be open; you have to ask questions; you can't pretend to have all the answers. That takes guts, real guts."

For the next three years, as I worked on the film, I kept up a steady relationship with Campbell through letters, phone calls, and late-night gatherings in the Redwood Room of the Clift Hotel in San Francisco, whenever he was in town for a lecture or book party.

Our exchanges at the hotel especially reminded me of the old Arabic saying, "A subtle conversation, ah, that is the Garden of Eden!" The saying captures the thrilling exchange of ideas that went on between us because of his impassioned responses to my questions about myth and literature, and because he drew ideas out of me I never knew were there. We spoke about the parallels between the classical myths that had moved him and the modern myths that moved my generation, and he encouraged me to find as many parallels as possible, in movies, art, dreams, and literature. To a young man on the cusp of the great adventure of his life, those conversations were indeed redolent of paradise.

O Sing for Me, Muse

When the Greek hero Odysseus left his palace in Ithaka to voyage across the "wine-dark sea" to Troy to fight for the return of Helen, he had only recently become a father. In the very first line of the epic poem, Odysseus is singled out as different in character and wisdom by the epithet polytropic. He is the man of "many turns," signaling that this is one hero who doesn't just bluster and blunder his way through a problem, but looks at all sides.

The *Odyssey* is a fascinating book to me for many reasons. The very title has come down the centuries to us as a word that describes *a courageous journey that changes everything*. It is an epic poem of epic ambition. Three parallel journeys and three initiations unfold in the course of the story. Each of them is uncannily relevant to our own war-torn times: a son's search for his father, a woman's devotion in keeping together house and home, a father's longing for home. Through it all a goddess' wisdom oversees their ordeals.

I imagine Odysseus in the weeks of preparation before departing for Troy with his twelve men in their black-tarred ship, anguishing not only over the upcoming war, but because he has to leave his infant son, Telemachus. I think of Odysseus as stricken with grief with the knowledge that he will not be able to protect his boy from the palace intrigues. The wily hero knows what will happen when he leaves. There will be pretenders to his throne, suitors to his wife, plots to harm his boy. I see him dispatching a court messenger to summon his old friends, Mentes and Mentor, to Ithaka, and asking the elders to fend off the suitors and guide his son until he returns.

With a shudder of surprise we vaguely recall these names, especially that of Mentor, and sense their function and purpose even twenty-five centuries after they were described by "wise-browed" Homer, as translator Richard Lattimore describes the immortal poet. While

Mentes is simply the name that the goddess Athena assumes on her first visit to Telemachus, Mentor is the Ithakan friend that Odysseus trusts with his household. He is the personification of loyalty and the wisest of counsels, but he is also to be more than a teacher as the story unfolds. His true role is as soul-guide through the underworld for the prince.

I fill in the long narrative blanks of the poem by seeing Mentor, the wise counsel, helping Penelope raise Telemachus in a world riddled with treachery. In this role, the ancient Greek wisdom for guiding young people through the ordeal of adolescence is suggested by his very name. For the word *mentor* comes from the Greek root *men*—to think, remember, counsel—and the Indo-European word *mens*, for "mind." Mentor is the "mind-maker." By his very nature he will help the son of his friend to "make up his own mind," even "re-mind" the youth of his destiny, which is so easy to forget but so crucial to the Greek concept of character. This is evident in the key scene of the *Iliad*, where Andromache pleads with her husband, Hector, not to fight Achilles. His steadfast decision to face his mortal enemy and his reply echo across time from the battlements of Troy: "No man escapes his destiny."

Another divine detail is enfolded here. The name *Telemachus*, from the Greek words *telos* and *machia*, can be translated as "the end of fighting." Implicitly, it is Mentor's task to take the "war" out of the prince's soul, or at least help him direct the urge, cultivate it, so he is the master, not the victim, of his own martial urges. By the end of the story he transforms the struggle for war urge into a struggle for peace in the kingdom.

Significantly, we first encounter Mentor early on, in Book Two, commonly called the "Telemachy," when he speaks in defense of the now twenty-year-old Telemachus at a gathering of the Assembly. There he is confronted by the mob of crass suitors of Penelope, the wife of Odysseus, whom they believe to be dead. No one has heard from the king in twenty long years. The suitors have taken over his palace and are plotting to exile or slay Telemachus and convince his mother to marry, so that one of them might seize the throne. The house of Odysseus threatens to fall.

Mentor "rises to speak and praises the wisdom of the young man," but the "suitors harangue him and the Assembly disperses without further action."

One of the suitors mocks him, "Mentor, reckless words, wild in your wits, what a thing you have said, urging them to stop us." The trusted counsel is chided for being naive to try and stop the plundering of the palace.

Then, just as mysterious as his initial appearance, Mentor all but disappears until the end of the book. All his other appearances are mysteriously masked, with the gray-eyed goddess Athena appearing "in the likeness of Mentor." His presence is baffling, but critical. Though described as Mentor, friend and advisor to the great king, appearing to all the world as the personification of loyalty, presumably a white-bearded, slightly hunched, and quietly dignified mortal man, he is actually she, the goddess Athena, the guiding force of the entire epic.

The "doubling" is bafflingly brilliant.

The mythic ventriloquism reveals a mentor's true function. On Telemachus' voyage of initiation to Sparta and sandy Pylos, where he sets forth to learn the truth about his missing father from Nestor and Menelaus, he needs both the outer strength of the male consort and the inner wisdom of the goddess. Through it all, Athena secretly guides him, as she aided his father at Troy and during his long wanderings, on his rite of passage from the feckless boy she first discovers "sitting there, unhappy among the suitors, a boy, daydreaming." It is Athena who inspires the search by infusing a "new spirit in him, a new dream of his father, clearer now," guiding him to become "thoughtful" Telemachus, the one who has learned to make up his own mind and is worthy of his famous father.

The gray-eyed goddess had been the protector of heroes throughout the Trojan War, and now she "drifts an enchantment of grace," in Homer's elegant phrase, upon the barely twenty-year-old Telemachus. First, disguised as Mentor she exhorts him, "Go seek your father," and helps him prepare a boat, even taking on his "likeness" to guide his crew and him on his voyage of initiation into manhood.

During the mythic moments at the royal courts, again in the guise of Mentor, Athena encourages him to speak with winged words, and assures the young prince that he has been cared for by the gods all his life. Slowly, the unsure prince finds the words to describe his sorrow over ever seeing his father again. "That which I hope for could never happen to me, not even if the gods willed it." As Mentor, she chastens his sophomoric self-doubt, saying, "Telemachus, what a thing to say! However far a man may have strayed, a friendly god could bring him safely home, and that with ease."

Emboldened, he voyages on to Pylos, where, as Jean Houston writes in her marvelous work, *The Hero and the Goddess,* "The gracious Menelaus puts him at his ease by contrasting his treasures with his sorrows." There, Telemachus' disenchantment deepens as he hears more stories about the terrible fate of the Greek heroes after the defeat of Troy. At this point, with the young prince weeping over the fate of his father, the Helen of the ten thousand ships appears and serves the magic potion nepenthe, "banisher of sorrows." Slowly, the potion performs its magic, for it "had the power of robbing grief and anger of their sting and banishing all painful memories." Jean Houston points out that it is here that the equally potent brew of storytelling is drunk, for Helen "guides them into another mood to discover pleasure through storytelling." Together, Helen and Menelaus weave conflicting accounts of the war, then of the long meanderings at sea, where the king encountered Proteus, the Old Man of the Sea, who, when finally tied down, revealed the secret passage home for the last survivors.

Taking the mythic hint, trusting his own hunches (his inner wisdom), Telemachus insists on returning home, and hears the words all young lads long to hear from their mentors: "I like the way you talk, dear lad: one can see you have the right blood in your veins."

With those words, his ritual education has been completed. Athena/Mentor, Nestor, and Menelaus have all helped guide him through the labyrinth of confusing news about his father. Telemachus sets for home, evading the suitors' murderous plans, and arrives at Ithaka for the grand reunion with his father. Together, while Penelope sleeps, father and son rid the palace of the suitors in a ritually cleansing massacre. The triple-adventure ends with a new peace forged by the reunited father and son, and Athena once again disguised as Mentor forges a truce, signaling a rebirth of the world at Ithaka.

Those are the bare bones of Mentor's presence in the epic, and yet this doesn't begin to explain the complexity of his mythic image or the marvelous set of implications the story has for us today. My reading of this enigmatic business is that young men on the verge of manhood do indeed need the presence and counsel of wiser, older men if they are to know the ways of the outer world. But according to these mythic laws of psychological balance, they also need the presence, the in-forming words of a wise woman, even the power of the goddess, if they are to know the ways of the inner world, their own hearts and souls.

Athena personifies self-counsel. The magical appearances of the goddess in the *Odyssey* may be a folk recollection of the early matriarchal structure of Greek society, but its essential mythic truth still rings true: The origin of wisdom is a convergence of sacred male and female power.

This is further illuminated by the perspicacious author and teacher Valerie Andrews, who reminds us that mentorship worked differently for women in ages past. "What comes to mind immediately," she told me in a recent conversation,

> are the Penelope-like disciplines or crafts like weaving, gardening, cooking, and sewing—not flashy stuff, not apprenticing as Atalanta did to the hunters on the mountainside, or Athena did to her father in the skills of statecraft (it was her compassion that saved the city). Let's not forget, either, the mentorship of the priestesses, those women trained as temple virgins to sleep with men "to take the war out of them," or the knowledge of the body that was passed on in the sacred mating rituals and the harem.
>
> Going back two thousand years, women got their training in less formal terms—in daily life, without some articulated goal. They didn't go to the agora and hang out with Socrates or Alcibiades, or asked to be groomed for public life. They got their mentorship, in

Michelangelo's painting of *Delphica*, one of the Sybilline Oracles, on the ceiling of the Sistine Chapel, Rome, Italy. According to tradition, she was one of twelve sibyls or prophetesses of classical legend who had seats or shrines in Greece, Italy, Babylonia, and Egypt. Their oracular wisdom was consulted by emperors, senators, soldiers, and peasants alike.

large part, through *ritual*—the ritual of the bath, the ritual of the corn, the ritual of herbs and healing, and they were trained to do ordinary things, according to a sacred purpose. It was a more minute passing of the knowledge, a kind of daily saturation in the sacred wisdom of everyday life.

The goddess Athena is the personification of these womanly qualities, as well as the protector, challenger, teacher of tools, pottery, weaving, and the arts, and counselor to heroes. The maverick scholar Robert Graves makes the intriguing claim that she did not know the names of her own parents. He writes in *The Greek Myths* that she loathed the rumor that Poseidon was her father, so she *made up her own mind* to be born, as we commonly think of her, out of the forehead of Zeus. The mythic implication is that this may be why she is sensitive to the needs of Telemachus, the most notorious fatherless child in Ithaka. More than advisor, she is the reconciliator between Zeus and the Furies, Nous and Ananke, and is symbolic of the act of taking counsel with oneself, the need for quiet contemplation, the very urge to self-knowledge, mediation, conflict resolution, the divine help and guidance that has always been prayed for in times that cry out for a new peace to be forged.

The Wisdom in the Wound

One more divine detail. It occurs in the epic's depiction of the roots of Odysseus' own character. He has often been called the most human and recognizable of classical heroes, the mortal who brings back the news of the gods. His foresight in caring for his son's soul, his choosing a mortal life over immortality, indicate a special depth of wisdom, a quality that sets him apart, and has helped carve out his special stature in world literature. The question is how? How did Odysseus become so wise? How does anyone grow and learn, spiritually as well as intellectually?

Robert Graves suggests that the clue to the essential character of Odysseus, curiously enough, lurks in the Roman version of his name, *Ulysses,* which derives from the Latin words for "wound" and "thigh." The "wounded thigh" is a mythic reference to the hero being gored by a boar when he was a young lad, a common wound for classical heroes, from the Irish Diarmuid to the Fisher King, generally signifying a loss of emotion, feeling, or generativity. Since the king is always associated with the land itself, if the king is infertile, the land goes to waste; hence the Waste Land.

However, what is unique about Odysseus is that he is not mortally wounded. He survives. His wound heals. He scars. Symbolically, as James Hillman interprets it, he is "self-healed." In the secret language of myth this means "soulful." Odysseus is the rare man who is self-disciplined and does not maunder around in pain or indulge in self-pity. In the poet John Keats' sense, his world is a world of "soul-making"; he is not born soulful, but forges his soulful character through a combination of wit, wiles, heart, compassion, and a recognition that he is constantly blessed by the gods. This "in-sight" comes down to us through poetic associations in the French word *blessure*, meaning "wound," as well as the origin of our word *bless*. In our wounds are our blessings.

Perhaps that is why Odysseus does not hide his scar, nor brandish it. It isn't even mentioned until the final scenes of the book, when the long saga is coming to an end and he has returned at long last to his palace in Ithaka. As his old servant bathes him, according to the custom allotted to strangers, he is recognized for who he really is, by his scar, as we are by those who know us most intimately.

The dovetailing of these divine details reveals to me a sacred and timeless psychology. The young prince Telemachus is advised by Mentor/Athena to set forth on a dangerous journey to find news of his father. Thus encouraged, he sallies forth to the palaces of Nestor and Menelaus to try to find out what happened to long-lost Odysseus. Besides his courtly edification, the son learns that the fighting at Troy has already entered the realm of legend, with his father's exploits at the heart of it, which is meant to be a noble lesson in the importance of his own and his father's life as an unfolding story.

So it is today. The true mentor, the soul guide, sends his or her pupil in search of the story that will reach the heart, not an easy thing during the difficult, sometimes gawky adolescent years. Without the story—or the *wrong* story—young people are agonizingly alone. Armed with the story that signals the "absurd good news," to borrow from Chesterton, our youth finally know they are not alone.

There Are No Accidents in Myth

The ancient tale works as a parable for us today. Too often, young men are abandoned when their fathers go off to "war" and have neglected to leave a mentor behind who embodies both male and female wisdom. The culture is awash in abandoned princes in palaces teeming with impostors to the throne, older men more concerned with seduction and power than with fatherhood and true leadership.

What is it about this adventure that moves us so many centuries later?

I believe it is that Mentor, the mind-maker, is a character who continues to show us how to help young people "make up their own minds," and more, lend a guiding hand to the Telemachus who lives in all young souls, especially those whose fathers are long gone, gone to war, lost at sea.

Perhaps those young people who are flailing are trying to "end the fighting" in their souls. I think too of Campbell's aside to me during our filming at his home in Hawaii in 1985 that young men are "testosterone machines" who desperately need sports to grease their young engines, harness their energies, and learn to take the fight outside. One of his favorite jokes about himself was that the street wisdom he grew up with on the Irish streets of the Bronx was along the lines of, "Is this a private fight or can anyone join in?"

Yet, the power of the mentor is different than that of most coaches or drill instructors, who try to channel the aggression in ways they see fit. The mentor's job is to help young men bring an end to the war in their *souls,* as we see in the marvelous etymology of Telemachus, and to help bring about peace, as we learn at the end of the *Odyssey.* This means teaching by presence and example the ability to transform the impulse for fighting and war into the peaceful, spiritual, creative arenas of our life; to turn our battlefields into palaces. While the instructor or teacher is interested in social education, the mentor is attentive to the soul, the inner life.

One of the strengths of myth is its poetic presentation of life-and-death questions and the opportunity for us to reflect on them. The mentor myth as slyly depicted here reveals the sacred function of teaching adolescent boys—initiation through the dark night of the soul. The stories and images offer an uncanny source of assurance that there are indeed what the Sufis call "the invisible hands," the mythic forces, personified as gods and goddesses who are overseeing their difficult journey through the symbolic land of death, that treacherous territory between youth and maturity.

Without the stories and images, it is all too easy to literalize the land of death.

The myths *re-mind* us of the power of symbolic thinking, as when they tell us, in *The Arabian Nights,* that "where you fall, there is your gold."

Teenaged Boys Without a Cause

One of the once and future aspects of myth that fascinates me most is the *Aha!* factor that goes along with the recognition of continuity. I fondly recall lecturing about the *Odyssey* in 1990 on the Seabourn Spirit cruise ship as we actually sailed through the same waters that Odysseus was lost in for ten years. As part of my talk I read Homer's description of how the Greeks painted the hulls of their ships with black tar before embarking for Troy, as an example of the vivid details of the book.

Hours later, I was walking with my brother Paul along the docks of Lesbos, where we had docked for a day excursion, and there before our very eyes were a half-dozen Greek sailors painting the hulls of their fishing boats with black tar, for the same reason their ancestors did, to seal them from seawater. Time dilated for a moment; myth lived.

Similarly, I recall the thrill of recognizing "the ancient future" the first time I saw a James Dean movie. It was a screening of *East of Eden* at the art deco Michigan Theater in Ann Arbor, sometime in the late

1960s. Dean was wild, brooding, zestful, melancholic, petulant, and fearless. He reminded me of the sulking Achilles, yet he also personified a decade of defiance. In other words, he was a myth in the making.

More than anything, James Dean was the young prophet of romantic alienation. In the 1950s he portrayed rebellious but sensitive teenagers who were among the first to suggest that there was a vicious crack in the mirror of American life. His films, as Joan Mellen writes in *Big Bad Wolves,* attracted "the young of the fifties... immediately transformed him into a cult figure, because he evoked their own submerged pain, the sense of being stifled and smothered by values not their own. He represents an entire generation of struggling. Dean raged. He refused to conform to someone else's idea of right and wrong."

Elia Kazan's film *East of Eden* (1955) is a feverdream rendition of John Steinbeck's tale of two teenaged American brothers at war with each other and with their father on a lettuce farm in the Central Valley of California shortly before World War I. In this thinly veiled allegory of Cain and Abel, James Dean's portrayal of Cal is one of "beautiful desperation," as Pauline Kael ironically described it at the time. His tormented face belies the pain of emotional separation from his father, played by Raymond Massey and depicted as the iconically monstrous postwar father. Yet, as Mellen writes, "A man needs his father's help; Cal, an existential hero, is willing to ask for it, explaining, 'Man has a choice and the choice is what makes him a man.'" What is striking about the role and the portrayal is how utterly, utterly lost Cal is. He is unconnected and disturbed at every level of his life, with no interest in the outside world, few friends, and an estranged family. The echoes with the isolated Telemachus are searing, including the violence. But when the desperate Cal finally cries out, in the midst of Kazan's Greek-Gothic direction, "I gotta know who I am. I gotta know," an ominous new sensibility is enshrined: the mentor-less young man who will go it alone.

In Dean's second film, *Rebel Without a Cause* (1955), he plays Jim, a troubled and alienated teenager, but one who this time is both tough and tender. Along with his girlfriend, Judy (Natalie Wood), and closest buddy, Plato (Sal Mineo), Jim is arrested by police and driven to Juvenile Hall in Los Angeles. Dean confesses to an officer that his parents might love him, but they never talk to him, never listen, never offer advice he can use. Using the sometimes unsettling language of myth, he says that his mother eats his pathetic father alive, and that he wishes he could have one day in his life when he didn't feel ashamed or confused.

Later on, after relentless bullying at school that eerily foreshadows the recent taunting tactics in our besieged schools, Jim is wounded in a knife fight. He returns home in the dead of night and flops down into bed. The camera catches him lying in a crucified Christ pose, hands over head, as if tied, legs twisting in torment, bleeding from the chest.

Suddenly the lights in his room flicker on and his father appears, played by Jim Backus, wearing an apron. The brooding Dean rises to his elbows and mumbles, "Dad, can I ask you something?"

"Sure, Jimbo, shoot!"

"Suppose you had to do something. Had to go someplace and do this thing that ... you knew was very dangerous, but it was a matter of honor. And you had to prove it. What would you do?"

Backus as the befuddled 1950s father recoils, responding with the same confusion he used when he acted as the voice of the cartoon character Mr. Magoo, asking, "Is that some kind of trick question?"

When he realizes it is no trick question, that his son is asking about some kind of dangerous challenge, he pauses and says tentatively, "Well, you've got to consider all the pros and cons. I'll get some paper and we'll make a list. And then if we're still stuck we'll get some advice."

Dean squirms, unable to bear the sight of his feminized father, then leaps out of bed and pleads with his him, "Dad, what can you do when you have to be a man?"

Instead of responding to the earnestness, his father acts embarrassed by the outpouring of emotion. He tries to fob off his son by saying, "In ten years you'll look back on this and wish—"

Enraged by the hemming and hawing, the personification of teen confusion bolts from the room and the house and 1950s American complacency.

What the young Dean is asking for is what all teenaged boys have always asked for—encouragement to do the right thing. He wants to save his honor, but he also wants to survive. But at the precise moment he needs straight talk, his father stammers, and retreats from his responsibility.

The movie critic David Thomson suggests that the movie title *Rebel Without a Cause* is misleading. This teen definitely has a cause, which is why so many of his generation (and mine) idolized him. Jim was our existential hero, revealing the crack in the cultural facade in his own tortured face. He reveals his "cause" when he wants to do the right thing, when he wants to turn himself into the police after the car race in which one of the rival gang members dies, but his parents panic, or when Jim is furious with his mother for wanting to flee and his father for not standing up for him. Alone, he flees, and not until the final scene of the film is he reunited with them, but only after his friend Plato has been killed.

The mythic significance of the movie lies in the way it laminates the loneliness of the young American postwar male like a movie poster, and prefigures the recent violence that stems from the same dangerous dynamic of ridicule and revenge. Jim Stark is the loneliest teen in the world in the opening scene of the movie, gutter-drunk, an outcast, self-destructive, but soulfully hungry for friends and desperate for love. He is not the loner who likes isolation; he is the loner who doesn't fit, yet. He is a great soul in a soulless world, what all young teenaged boys romanticize their natural plight to be. He not only personified the "cult of cool" for the '50s and '60s generations, but a kind of rebel whose "causes are impossible to define." One hint comes in the mansion scene when Jim holds Judy close to him and whispers, "I'm not going to be lonely anymore; not me or you."

Natalie Wood, playing Judy, dreamily describes her ideal of a new kind of strong man to Dean's Jim, as "one who can be gentle and sweet, like you are...who doesn't run away...being Plato's friend—that's being strong."

Danny Peary, in his fine book *Cult Movies*, points out that director Nicholas Ray's teenaged characters "are hopelessly confused, seeking advice, and getting no answers." This futility is the source of the volcanic fury in the movie and the ongoing emotional reactions it still elicits out of its audiences, partially due to the crude but powerful shot of the movie where Dean, doomed to die himself in real life less than two months later, is finally embraced by his father, who assures him he will now stand by him, and hugged by his girlfriend, symbolizing the healing that has begun.

✸

The classical Greek prince Telemachus and the '50s L.A. teenage rebel Jim Stark represent two ends of the spectrum of mentored young men. On one side is the endangered son of a great hero who is bullied and taunted by the suitors, but is also watched over by the gods and guided through the most dangerous passage of life—the transit between youth and adulthood. On the other side is the uninitiated son of confused parents whom no one is watching and who must devise his own death-defying initiation rites, create his own "family," and in his treacherous passage save his soul with "love."

Not only did James Dean indelibly put a human face on what sociologist Philip Slater famously called "the pursuit of loneliness," but he revealed to us, by virtue of its agonizing absence from his two most famous roles, the issue of mentorship. Forty-plus years after his death by "slow-suicide," the question remains: Will modern teenagers go it alone—or shoulder to shoulder with a wise mentor across the threshold of adulthood?

The Mentors Around the Table

In the early 1990s, I was working with Danny Sugarman, friend and biographer of Jim Morrison of the rock group the Doors, on a movie script for director Oliver Stone about Danny's own colorful life in Hollywood's fast lane. Late one night, after an all-day writing session, we met Danny's new girlfriend, Fawn Hall, at the old Café Figaro on Melrose Avenue in Hollywood. While we tossed back several whiskies, Danny told a welter of wild stories about his days with the Doors; Fawn shared with us stories about her old boss, Oliver North, and gave us the inside scoop on the Iran-Contra hearings; and I regaled them about my days with Joe Campbell, highlighting his stories about playing saxophone in a Greenwich Village jazz band and surfing with Duke Kahanamoku.

Finally, Danny leaned forward, and growled, "Fawn, do you know how *heavy* this is? What Jim Morrison was for me, and Oliver North was for you, Joseph Campbell was for Phil—a mentor!"

"That's true, Danny, that's true," she marveled.

There was a moment of awkward silence at the table as we dwelled on the unexpected turns of fate in our lives; then I asked Danny whether Jim had any mentors.

"No, that's the problem," Danny told me, ruefully. "First, Morrison started to tell the world that his parents were dead when they weren't, then he ended up hanging out only with people who told him what he wanted to hear. He was all alone at the end."

I was only too familiar with the story. For more than five years I had worked with John Densmore, the drummer for the Doors, on *Riders on the Storm*, his book about his life with the band. There was something in Danny's voice that made me think of a poignant vignette I had cajoled out of John during our close collaboration. John shared his memory with me the afternoon that he and I decided to tackle the story of the recording of the song, "People Are Strange," in 1968. I had the old LPs, the press clippings, and the record reviews, all organized around us, and read a few of them out loud to help transport John back into the surreal world of 1968; then I asked him what he recalled about the song. He sat at the computer and was suddenly so troubled he couldn't write. So I took the detachable keyboard from him and asked him just to tell the story, free associate, and I would type as fast as he could talk.

His eyes flashed and he recalled the afternoon that Jim came knocking on his door in Laurel Canyon "looking like the loneliest guy in the world." John said he was thunderstruck because by that time Morrison was one of the most famous young men in America. Yet there he was, all alone on a Saturday afternoon, lonely and vulnerable. As he spoke, I typed furiously fast, about how Jim just putzed around John's house for a little while, then disappeared for a few hours for a walk up the mountain, where he sat on the edge of the cliff and looked out over the vast expanse of Los Angeles. When Jim came back down the hill to the house he had written down the lyrics for the song on a crumpled sheet of paper: "People are strange, when you're a stranger...."

For many reasons that vignette has often come back to me over the years, because it reminds us how searing isolation can plague the famous, the infamous, the ordinary, and the extraordinary. The whole world is strange and threatening. "Faces look ugly," as Jim sang, unforgettably, "when you're alone."

These aren't merely the angry words of paranoid youth; they are the Expressionist-like observations of a young man who has amputated one intimate connection after another, with family, friends, lovers.

Thirty years after Morrison's tragic overdose in Paris, fifty-five after Dean's fatal car crash on a lonely highway in California, they are both enshrined in the mythic pantheon of young male heroes who symbolize the virtue and the tragedy of going it alone.

After drinks that night in Hollywood, we returned to Danny's home high in the Hollywood hills. I slept on a pullout couch in his office surrounded by gold records and photographs of the Doors, Iggy Pop, and other music legends. No doubt inspired by the talk that night about mentors, I had a peculiar dream that featured my Uncle Cy, who was trying to help me open a café in the abandoned saltmine tunnels underneath Detroit. When in the dream I balked that I didn't have enough money or time or energy, he handed me a shovel and told me to keep digging. I shrugged and started to dig in one of the tunnels, and soon it opened out into the back of one of his closets in his home back in Livonia. A treasure trove of books awaited me there, including the entire twenty-six volume series, *Man, Myth, and Magic*. I pored through them as my Aunt Barb looked over my shoulder, and one by one I passed them backward to my brother, my nephew, and several of my writing students.

My Uncle Cy McCann, photographed during World War II in front of the fighter plane he was later shot down in over Italy, circa 1943.

My Uncle Mentor

When I think of my own mentors, those men who somehow kept me from going it completely alone, even when my combustible young soul longed to, I think first of my Uncle Cy. He was my father's alter ego, giving me what my father couldn't, which is exactly the function of the mentor. My father devoted thirty-three years to the public relations department at Ford Motor Company's world headquarters, and always appeared to me to be in a kind of existential pain.

He would've hated the phrase.

My father fanned the flames of my interest in literature, art, travel, but I didn't see him a heck of a lot while I was growing up, which was very 1950s. He gave what he could, mostly his love of books, which over the years has often reminded me of the naturalist Loren Eisley's description of his own father's philosophy: "In the limitations of that day and time he had always defended my rights to read books. He had lived just long enough to think the books would lead me to someplace unknown."

There were only so many things he could give me, which is why fathers cannot be mentors. Fathers can only be fathers. The transmission of their knowledge and wisdom is direct and personal, which is why the relationship is often volatile. The mentor's relationship, as an aunt or uncle, close family friend, coach, or teacher, is by definition a few degrees off center, neutral, and indirect, which is important to a teenager for whom intimacy is usually a source of discomfort.

So there was a void, as there always is. That's where my uncle rushed in. As the Irish say, memory is a merciful editor, so I remember his presence nearly as much as my own father's. Cyril McCann was an adventurer. He boasted of serving in four different military forces: the French Foreign Legion, the Royal Canadian Mounted Police, the U.S. Army, and the U.S. Air Force. I was taken by him because he was an amazing storyteller, a twinkling Irishman with a magical touch when it came to introducing me to the mysteries of the outside world beyond the streets of Detroit.

His stories unfailingly gave me an adventurous picture of a world far beyond the one I grew up in. One of the tales that fired my imagination was about the time he parachuted into Italy as part of the squadron that was hell-bent on capturing Mussolini. They roared into the village where "El Duce" had last been seen, only to see him and his wife hanging upside down in the town square, having just been executed for their betrayal of their own people. My uncle told me that he watched in horror as the villagers cut open the bellies of the disgraced leader and his wife in search of the jewels they were rumored to have swallowed to pay for their life in exile after the war.

Then there were his stories about some local gangsters, the Purple

Gang, that he knew at Carl's Chop House, an old speakeasy in downtown Detroit. Once, when he took my family there for dinner, he pointed out their purple corsages to us, then quietly revealed to me one of their stranger customs. Whenever someone seriously crossed them, they would send a ritual warning. They did this by paying a local flower shop to cut off the heads of a dozen red roses and dye them black. Then the stems would be strapped down inside a box and the heads stuffed in on top of them, and the box delivered as a symbolic death threat. At that point in the story, I turned to my mother, who was a local florist at the time. I started to ask her if she had ever heard of such a thing—but her ashen face told me she had been one of those florists and she didn't want to talk about it.

My uncle's streetwise ways exposed me to a caliber of wisdom I wouldn't get at home or in books. He had been in two wars, then in business, sailed boats, drove all over the United States in his candy apple-red 1963 Lincoln Continental (the original Hot Rod Lincoln), hard-drinking, hard-driving ladies' man who looked like Cary Grant and sounded like Johnny Carson. And he did it all in constant pain.

One day after helping my uncle clean his pool, I noticed him wince; he made some offhand comment about his leg. He pulled his pant leg up and I noticed a ribbon of scars up and down his shinbone, which, he told me matter-of-factly, he had "earned" when he was shot down over Palermo in the war. It took several scotches to get him to talk about it, and even then he wasn't fond of the story. When I asked him why he had never mentioned to me before (I had just taken my first college psychology class), he looked at me like I had three heads.

"There are some things you just have to get over," he said. "That's what I did. That's what you'll have to do someday."

I turned crimson, resenting that he was aware of something in me that I had missed or ignored but was too proud to ask about. But I suspected it had to do with wounds.

His influence on me is profound. I suspect that beneath the bluster and bravado was the tacit knowledge that he was taking the war out of me as he was exposing me to the grim ways of the world. His war stories, often during the bodybag counts on the six o'clock news, did more to inure me to the romance of battle that many of my high school friends had already succumbed to than any number of talks on pacifism in my philosophy classes.

Then, in the middle of my parents' divorce proceedings, my uncle saved me by sending me straight to hell. After learning from my mother that we were suddenly cut off without any means of supporting ourselves, he got me a job at a factory owned by his best friend, Max Quarles, a place called Industrial and Automotive Fasteners.

I didn't realize it at the time, but it was just the initiation I needed.

Talk Like a Man

During my college years I had to work in an automotive parts factory to support my mother, brother, and sister. That's where I met another man who helped shape my future, which is another way to describe the influence of mentors.

Bob Schnekenburger was one of the original Green Berets back in 1964. He had been stationed in the Dominican Republic when his regiment got their orders to board a cargo plane in the middle of the night. The next thing they knew they were donning their parachutes and making a "night drop" into unknown enemy territory. They were going on a mission into hostile territory. That's all they were told about being the first troops in Vietnam.

I met "Schick" in the factory where I worked for nearly four years. As the hours of factory work increased, my spirits disintegrated. My vision of getting my college degree and traveling the world began to fade as the trials with my family worsened. I began to lose hope of ever getting out of Detroit, ever going on with my life. But steadily, by his sheer presence and the evidence of his own survival, Schick convinced me I had to survive the hellhounds of the factory, then get on with my life. He did it without preaching or lecturing; he did it by telling stories. While we worked together repairing forklifts or metal stamping machines, he would describe with a naturalist's attention to detail how to skin a deer in five minutes or how to take an engine apart and piece it back together again in less than a day. He also regaled me with exotic tales about the black market of Saigon, the cafés of Paris, the guerilla groups of the Philippines. One time, when we had to pull an all-nighter in order to fill a rush order of lock nuts for the Cadillac plant downtown, he broke down and told me how his best friend died in his arms in a godforsaken swamp, and how he had taken a round in his own leg and back. Eventually I realized there was a thread running through the stories: We have to keep going, no matter what.

The one who has no stories is dead, say the Somalis. Stories, and stories, and stories. This is what is meant by stories saving your life. Schick's stories, as well as the street tales of my fellow workers, of murder and gang warfare, were my introduction to the power of the night world and the wisdom of the well-chosen fight. At least once a week I found myself in a fistfight with somebody, usually over nothing, stupid territorial disputes, workload issues, or the release of terrific tensions.

One of the defining moments of my life in the factory came the night after my college philosophy exam; I was swaggering a bit because I had done well. It was the middle of winter and I was working in the shipping department with another Vietnam vet. The doors were open, and icy winds blew in, freezing our hot coffee in a number of seconds, and our hands if we didn't wear gloves. Suddenly, halfway through my rap on Schopenhauer, in which I was no doubt full of myself and secretly counting the days until my escape from factory life, the vet cut me off with a rigid, "Talk like a *man,* white boy." Later, I asked Schick what the guy meant and he said, "Careful who you tell your story to, Couzy, baby. Save it for the right man at the right moment. Don't throw your story away. We learned that in 'Nam. Stick with us, Couzy baby, you're going to get out. We're going to get you through this."

Together he and some of the other "factory rats," as they called themselves, did just that. Over the last two years, when the workload was sixty hours a week and I was taking eighteen or twenty credit hours at school, I was in utter sleep deprivation, averaging three to four hours a night. I was a menace to myself and to the heavy machinery supposedly under my control. As if we were all in the trenches together, they watched over my machines for a few minutes here and there so I could catch Thomas Edison-like catnaps, or even switch a shift with me so I could attend an important night lecture. Mostly it was solidarity through storytelling, standing with me shoulder to shoulder through the dark, cold nights, the oldest mentorship of all.

Making Men Out of Boys

Another early mentor of mine believed in healing your own scars. He was my high school track coach, Leonard Natkowski—Mr. Nat. After three decades, his voice still booms in my memory. "Let's go, gimp," he used to shout at me because of all my running injuries. "Let's go. Two mile warm-up, then eight 440s under seventy. Then after you chuck your cookies, we'll do a half-dozen 220s. Then I want to see you hit the high hurdles, then the long jump pit. C'mon, baby, don't fail me now."

Two fellow runners on our high school track team, Les Homan (left) and Bob Moore, flank our coach, Mr. Natkowski, as they present him with a plaque expressing our gratitude for his four years of mentoring and coaching, 1970.

The memory of Nat's voice brings back a mixture of love and dread. His workouts were tortuous, but I endured them for four years, and I couldn't figure why for a long time afterward.

Mr. Nat was a huge man in many ways, an ex-tackle from a small college somewhere in Iowa who had made Little All-America. That automatically earned him our respect, but we were also impressed that he taught different classes in two, sometimes three different schools in the area, plus coached football and sometimes basketball. To a lot of us he represented someone who had news about the world beyond our horizon. As great as he was in coaching technique, he embodied much more because somewhere along the line he learned how to talk directly to the heart and soul of young athletes.

Every season Mr. Nat began with an inspirational speech about the coming year, culminating in an admonition. "I can make you guys fast runners," he would say, his voice trembling with emotion. "I can help you run faster and jump higher, but that's not really why I'm here." Then he would pause, and we would all shift uncomfortably, our spikes raking nervously across the metal bleacher seats. "I'm here to help you become *men*."

What is astonishing is that we believed him. After practice he would ask about our classes, our girlfriends, our family lives, and our plans for college. He made it abundantly clear that to become men would take more than becoming fine athletes, and that it would take acts of will similar to what he was teaching us at every practice.

"I'm here to help you become men."

No one I've known since has pronounced the word *men* with such rigor and with such a sense of destiny. At a time when John Wayne and Archie Bunker represented the two ends of the spectrum of the American man, Mr. Nat gave us another ideal.

That's why we came to love a man who tortured us with run-till-you-throw-up practices, as comedian Bill Cosby cracked in a routine we had all memorized. We would have jumped through hoops of fire for him because we felt he saw something in us that we weren't getting from our fathers, qualities that had nothing to do with talent or raw ability. It had more to do with his belief that his role was to build self-confidence in us. While most coaches are on your butt about your times or distances, Mr. Nat sat us down at the opening of every track season and gave us a sheet of poetry, an anonymous poem about how to be fleet-footed on the road of life, and told us inspiring stories about great athletes, great performances. The poem was called "It's All in a State of Mind" and until recently I had forgotten that I had saved it all these years. The last stanza reads:

Life's battles don't always go
To the stronger or faster man,
But sooner or later, the man who wins
is the fellow who thinks he can.

As corny as it may read today, what I recall is the reverence with which it was handed to me. I've had the pleasure of hearing many of the great poets of our time read in public, but have rarely felt the same rigor and passion. If all poetry was handed over with a similar conviction that its lines and cadences and ideas were something you could live by, as Mr. Nat did, crowds would be lining the streets to get into the poetry sections of our great independent bookstores.

Recently, I asked and old friend and member of that track team, Doug Vega, what his recollections were of our coach.

I spent a good part of three high school years within the sphere of Mr. Nat's influence. His affect on me was to set me on a course whose affect is still being felt. At the time the ties with my own father were as tentative as my need to please him. How fortuitous it was for me to have Mr. Nat arrive on the scene at the time in my life when I was facing the impossible transition from boy to man. His influence was remarkable and simple. He spent time with us. He paid attention to us. He asked us to perform. And perhaps most important he told us what he expected us to do and how to do it: "Give me eight 440s under seventy-five seconds," he would shout. Then he stood by the track with his stopwatch in hand and would say, "Get set ... *go!*" He knew just how to prod us on as we gasped, rubber-legged, to our last quarter-mile. Always, there was the knowing smile as we whined our protests. How can we ever know the difference we make in someone's life? I only know that he did—and does.

I recall riding with Mr. Nat in his 1968 Ford Fairlane to track meets and basketball games while he would talk to us about the future, constantly encouraging us. His approval was the thing we most wanted in those years because we knew he was trying to show us the right way to win, and because he showed us we had destinies.

Later, during my college years, I'd occasionally stop by Nat's house to see him and just talk. He was always interested in how his ex-athletes were doing in the race of life. "Still looking for yourself, Cousineau?" he would chide me in reference to my tendency to brashly philosophize about this and that. "Found yourself yet?" I used to think he was still teasing me about my slow times. "Still looking, coach," I'd say, or "I find myself every day, coach."

Years later, at a Bogart revival at a beautiful movie palace in Berkeley, I heard Sydney Greenstreet tell Bogie, "That's wonderful, sir, wonderful. Yes, I do like a man who tells you right out that he's looking for himself. Don't we all? I don't trust a man who says he's not."

That moment was an epiphany for me. It was then I realized Mr. Nat had been encouraging me in his own goading way, in the age-old manner of the deliberately gruff mentor who nudges you along with contrary words, daring you to run your best because a cinder track is a powerful metaphor for the road of life.

Years later, my friend Joan Marler confessed to me that her mentor, Marija Gimbutas, the Lithuanian archaeologist, most noted for her seminal work on the culture of the goddess, was a kind of Baba Yaga, the impossible taskmaster, forcing her into the role of the callow Vassilisa. "She had no patience with fuzzy thinking or lack of preparation, and there were times I was cut to the bone, sinking in quicksand, grateful that I had brought my own mother's blessing. But Marija embodied an enormous depth and breadth of scholarship and heightened perception that continues to illuminate my path."

A reunion in 1995 with my high school track coach, Mr. Leonard Natkowski, at his summer cottage, at Houghton Lake, Michigan. After twenty-five years, he could still remember my running times in the high hurdles, 440-yard dash, and mile relay, as well as the times of many of my teammates.

Could it be that it is the mentor's role to set forth the task that we can't see for ourselves, in the darkness between thresholds, that throws forth the light that illuminates the rest of our lives? Where does that light come from? How does the mentor know what to ask of callow uninitiated youth?

Waking Up!

Every day Ruiyan would call to himself, "Master!"
And he would answer himself, "Yes?"
Then he would say, "Be awake, be alert!"
"Yes."
"From now on, don't be fooled by anyone!"
"Yes, yes."

"What is it that needs awakening?" ask the koans used in Zen spiritual training. The uncanniness of myths, their often strange imagery, is evocative of the mind-bender questions in Zen, whose focus is not on cleverness or competitiveness, but on what the scholar Thomas Cleary calls "the living application of insight." He cites the classical master Wumen's interpretation of the koan, "And if you imitate another, everything is wild foxy explanation," meaning we are all in danger of believing that our superficial personality is our real self.

"Right now, can you call and get an answer?" asks for profound spontaneity of the kind that mentors and masters attempt to help their students realize.

✳

When interviewed about the sometimes troublesome decision about choosing a teacher, the modern Zen teacher Robert Aitken said that the authority itself often frightens students in the West. "Everywhere I have gone here people have asked me how to choose a teacher. One of my own teachers first identified his teacher by a warm feeling *here* [putting his hand on his stomach]. But the questions you should ask yourself are 'Does this person have a sense of humor? Are they willing to be challenged? Can they admit to their own foibles?' And then, once you've decided to work with someone, it becomes *your* task to *make them* a good teacher."

Aitken's visceral description of the warm feeling in the pit of your stomach reminds me of the American Indian tradition of *orenda,* which is the flame that burns within. While we in Western culture generally talk about individual gifts or talent, individual gold, *orenda* is the group flame. When you are working on the self you're also working on enflaming the village, the tribe, the clan. This is accomplished by "walking the red road," the spiritual path you walk down with your relatives, in harsh contrast to "walking the black road," which they regard as the path of selfishness.

While we were working together on a documentary film about religious freedom for Native Americans, I asked James Botsford of the Indian Law Office what his relationship with the spiritual leader Reuben Snake meant to him.

Reuben Snake (center) leads an informal prayer meeting with Johnny White Cloud (left) and James Botsford (right) at his home, January 1992.

When I first got out of law school at age thirty-five and got my first lawyering job I had this green feeling like I hadn't had since I first sat in Buddhist meditation half my life ago. Armed with three college degrees I went to meet my first client, a "reservation Indian," with no college degrees. His name was Reuben Alvis Snake, Jr., and he was Chairman of the Tribal Council of the Winnebago Tribe of Nebraska. He was wearing blue jeans and so was I. He said he'd been waiting for me. Since I'd never heard of him before that week I wasn't sure what he meant. He took me under his wing (no small thing for a snake!) and before long he was introducing me to senators, governors, and medicine men. He wanted some legislation passed in Nebraska to protect the rights of Indians. With his guidance it got done. He wanted the Congress to essentially overturn a bad decision of the U.S. Supreme Court in order to protect and respect his beloved Native American Church. With his guidance it got done. Reuben put victories in my résumé and gray hairs in my mustache. He started as my client, became my friend, adopted me as his brother, and became Uncle Reuben to my kids. Through it all he was my mentor. He taught me, no, he showed me respect for absolutely everything, the value of relationships, the power of love in the rough-and-tumble world and how with humility, grace, and a healthy dose of humor, one can change the course of history. Reuben died in 1993, and since then I've only seen him in my dreams. He came a couple of times shortly after passing into the spirit world, bringing compassion and some last advice.

I was lucky. I was blessed. My mentor was my best friend. Not everyone has it that way. I'm over fifty now. People think I know what I'm doing. But when I have a tough challenge or decision in front of me, in the quiet of my mind I'm thinking, "What would Reuben do?" Then I'm guided by his presence, his voice, his spirit, or my inner sense associated with him. I can't tell the difference anymore. Man, what a mentor.

Michael Meade has recently revived a word from Africa called *litima*. This sacred word in tribal traditions refers to the inner heat, the inner flame. It helps to think about it in terms of inner heat or the gold of the alchemists. But that inner heat can be either positive or negative. It can be creative or destructive. The inner heat is what inspires, it's what draws people to each other, but if the heat isn't tempered it can burst out in violence, tremendous violence.

The Zulu *sangoma* or shaman, Credo Mutwa, describes how his grandfather taught him the secret art of breathing correctly, of melding his mind to that of the gods in the invisible realm, and how to sit very still so that he might summon "the hidden powers of my soul." The great healer goes on to explain a curious ritual of "the black people of South Africa...to banish certain fears from their children." Shortly

In this sixteenth-century miniature, the Sufi mystic and poet Mevlana Rumi (1207–1273) engages in one of his famous ecstatic conversations with a group of devout followers. The original caption reads, "The candle Mevlana lights is smaller, but keeps burning long after the others have melted away."

after the birth of a child he or she goes through a naming ritual during which each of the two grandparents sit on either side of the fire and throw the little baby so it passes over the flames. "This is intended to make the young child to grow up not afraid of fire."

Mythically speaking, the function of a well-balanced society is to recognize this heat or this flame inside ourselves and inside the young people in our community and not be afraid of it. Instead, the hope of the community is that its young learn to recognize and work with the heat, and as we grow older to recognize the flame in each other. The recognition of this quality of fire in a young person is the function of the elder and the mentor.

With passion and commitment, Meade describes many traditions around the world that teach that the flame must be tempered and occasionally cooled. It is no accident that the hippest word of praise since the late '40s, the war years, is *cool,* as if the genius of the culture is reminding us of something we can't afford to forget. "Chill out," "Cool down," "Lighten up," "Easy does it." These words and phrases mark a critical transition in the relationship to the light or the flame that we are describing.

The mentor or master, the guide, the soul guide, is the one who is observing just these worlds behind worlds, not just seeing surfaces, but glimpsing and authenticating a young person's inner world, recognizing the hidden beauty, the hidden soul, the hidden gold. Hidden out of self-protection and developing a relationship to draw that out, bring it out.

The mentor, as opposed to the guru, is the one who is there to help you make up your own mind, light your own fire, unfold your own myth. True mentorship draws out your mind, draws out your hidden qualities, puts the bellows to the soul, fans the flame, develops the gold that the mentor is trying to draw out. The mentor is the power of wisdom *outside of the family* because parents in this kind of mythological speaking cannot be mentors. Mothers and fathers initiate young people into the first round of power, so to speak: the mysteries of walking, talking, thinking, relating to immediate family.

The Ecstasy of Mentorship

In Roger Lipsey's pioneering work on the spiritual aspects of twentieth-century art, *An Art of One's Own,* he offers a vivid description of the three stages of creative initiation into the world of art and craft, and by inference into any tradition that requires long years of devotion and attention: apprentice, journeyman, master. Anyone aspiring to excellence in any creative arena, Lipsey reminds us, must first be accepted as a student. To become a master, one must apprentice to one. The training transpires "under the eyes of the mentor," he writes, whose every move, word, gesture, and suggestion is rife with meaning. Moreover, the authority that is wielded is not abstract; instead, "it is a personal influence intimately received." A guiding influence, by definition, is change, and change comes from overcoming ordeal, such as "menial service... long vigils over white-hot kilns in the middle of the night, the hours spent redrafting a design that fell short—are nothing in comparison with the opportunities for learning."

If the apprentice is devoted and inspired he or she becomes a journeyman. During this stage the apprentice works alongside the master, deepening not only her skill with tricks of the trade but with knowledge and reverence for the lore of the craft. Inevitably, as Lipsey points out, there is a "dark time" in which the creative fire of the apprentice interferes with the fire of the master. Awe and admiration often turn to disappointment and petulance as the flaws of the mentor are revealed. This period calls for "a subtle change of heart," if the journeyman is to transform into a master. Then a masterwork must be produced. It must be an original creation. It cannot be a copy. It must come from the soul and speak to the soul of others.

The Ideal Studio

For a few years in the early twentieth century, the French painter Henri Matisse played the role of *le maître*—the master—in his own art studio in Paris. In 1925, while recollecting those years of teaching what he loved most, Matisse cited an image that he used with his students to inspire in them the idea of steady progress in their art. In his book, *Ecrits*, he wrote,

I had the habit of telling my students...: the ideal thing would be to have a studio with three floors. On the ground floor, we would do a first study after the model. From the second, we would go downstairs rarely. On the third, we would have learned to do without the model.

There is a popular anecdote about Matisse that echoes the spirit of his belief that everyone has their own genius, which he believed they should strive to bring out of themselves. Two young American women who were hoping to study with him in Paris told him, "We want your color." The unflappable master replied, "If you haven't brought your own color, you will never get mine."

Matisse's image of the three stages of development in the career of an artist uncannily reflects the three stages of learning in the crafts, as well as the three acts in traditional drama (conflict, crisis, resolution), and the three stages of the rite of passage (separation, initiation, return). What all three models have in common is that they are images of change, theories of transformation, notions about growth from one stage of life to the next.

What is distinctive about mentorship, in contrast to all other forms of teaching and guidance, is the concern for the spiritual life. To draw out the soul is the mythic vision for education at every imaginable level. The distinction between the ordinary teacher, the ordinary foreman, the ordinary coach, and the true mentor is the focus on helping students to forge their own minds, light the fire in their own souls.

The Other Side of the Myth

If we don't own our own stories, our souls are in danger, whether we are young or old. Unfortunately, it may be difficult to see the problem unless we turn the mentor situation inside out. The gold is being hoarded, talent is being wasted, but it's only the wisdom of the well-lived, authentic life that is respected by the young.

The psychologist Eric Fromm writes that if people who are moving on to their twilight years don't use their power as elders, their mentoring capacities, they will feel betrayed by life and may not even know why. Should they buy instead into the very powerful myth that the ironically named "golden years" are meant to be lived in seclusion, in a world cut off from the young, they will be cheating themselves. The result of this tragic myth is that whole neighborhoods and cities of young kids are not being mentored. The unquestioned wisdom of retirement communities is creating generations of elders with no one around to mentor.

Throughout human history other cultures have been interested in those elders who have survived the fires of death, struggle, depression. Instead, our elders are banished into rest homes or retreat from the cult of youth into retirement communities. Such elders have figured out what keeps them alive—staying out of the way of youth. But it is a self-defeating strategy. The only thing that will help is for them to get involved with stoking the fires in the youth of the day. But how can they if they move away, leaving little behind?

The responsibility to pass the gift of hard-earned wisdom back to the community is epitomized in the work of Elie Wiesel, winner of the Nobel Peace Prize. Following is a passage from a commencement speech he delivered at Harvard in the early 1990s.

> One of my principles is that I must pass on what I receive to others.... I owe it to those who came before...and feel the need to pay back. Call it gratitude.... There is divine beauty in learning, just as there is human beauty in tolerance. To learn means to accept the postulate that life did not begin at my birth. Others have been here before me, and I walk in their footsteps. The books I have read were composed by generations of fathers and sons, mothers and daughters, teachers and their disciples. I am the sum total of their experiences, their quests. And so are you.... I also pray: Do not make someone else pay the price for your pain.... Only a fanatic does that—you have to learn to reject fanaticism. You know that fanaticism leads to hatred, and hatred is both destructive and *self*-destructive.... True education negates fanaticism.... I insist: All collective judgments are wrong.

This is the spirit of the genius mentor at work. Wiesel reveals here the true meaning of *education,* which means "to draw out," and by that he means both the inevitable pain of life as well as our God-given talents. The great teacher draws out the genius, the talent, the gold from the student, all the while ennobling his or her own wisdom years. Mentors are those along the road saying, You're on the right path. Keep going, keep going, keep going.

To accomplish this demands supreme trust in the one who is passing on the wisdom. "When I work with people in recovery," said Squeak Herman, a Navajo woman in the Indian Recovery Movement in Albuquerque, New Mexico, "I tell them who I am and what my story is. . . . Where my crippling is is where I go and do for them. [I'm not here] to rescue them and say you owe me. [I'm here] allowing them to grow and be. . . . I had a real tough time figuring out where I'm crippling *them* by doing [too much] for them. I finally figured I can share the wisdom and give them information, then let them go and do it for themselves. Then they're going to learn."

This compassion and selflessness marks an important transition, one that Ram Dass, the '60s renegade philosopher, now promotes as joyfully as he once encouraged his brand of "Live for Today" existentialism.

From Aging to Saging

In February 1997, Ram Dass, Ph.D. in psychology from Stanford University, ex-Harvard professor, pioneer on the spiritual frontier, soul friend to the dying, psychologist, and bridge between ancient and modern worlds, East and West, was felled by a massive stroke. Grievous as it was, leaving him with severe motor and speech disabilities and in a wheelchair, he has shown as much courage and resourcefulness in his recovery as he ever did with his intellectual work. In a sense he has played Parsifal to his own Grail King, asking of his own soul what was needed to be asked in order for the healing to begin.

For many, the name Ram Dass is synonymous with the "Be Here Now" counterculture of the 1960s, understandable since he coined the phrase. At Harvard University, he was "saved," as he describes it, from a life of behavioral psychology by a serendipitous encounter with Timothy Leary and Ralph Metzner. The triumvirate soon became cultural icons for creative and spiritual rebellion. For Ram Dass, spirituality needs to come out of personal experience and is nothing without "truly transformative practices." As Roger Walsh has written of his friend, few have lived with the combination of "pioneering experimentation and searing truthfulness" as Ram Dass, nor embodied the Buddha's *Kalamas Sutra* ("Do not put faith in traditions, even though they have been accepted for long generations and in many countries. Do not believe a thing because many repeat it"), as thoroughly as Ram Dass. His main message: *Take up a practice....*

✸

The latest chapter in Ram Dass' life is his work with the terminally ill. In this he has been emphasizing the possibility of "awakening the potential of change" in the elderly and bringing dignity to the aging process. In effect, moving an entire culture—ours—from aging to sage-ing, from a negative to positive attitude toward the natural movement of simply growing older.

During an interview I did with him in the spring of 1998, Ram Dass, now in his mid-sixties, recalled the night of the stroke. "Boy, this is a tricky thing," he said. His fingers drummed on the armrest of his wheelchair. His mica blue eyes shone brilliantly. "There was something I had to attend to. I prepared to become an old man. So I undertook what you might call an ancient ritual by going into a deep, deep meditation, living out a deep fantasy on another plane of consciousness."

For hours after the stroke, Ram Dass lay in bed playing out his game of active imagination, attempting his move from middle age into elderhood. Finally his assistant Jai called him in the middle of the night from New Mexico and could tell even over the telephone that something was direly wrong. Ram Dass assumed that the call—as well as the subsequent visit from two of his assistants, Marlene and Joanne, who live nearby—was part of his reverie. Quickly the assistants came over to his house and found him lying on the floor, half-paralyzed.

At the hospital, Ram Dass awoke to the sound of the word *stroke* being murmured by the hovering nurses and doctors. He recalls little else except for arguments with doctors, who, he feels, saw him as only as his "brain," and refused to know that "I wasn't just material." The doctors had no interest in how his inner life had been affected. They saw him only as a stroke victim.

Despite feeling devastated that he was being dismissed by the very "cultural pathology" about illness and aging he had long vilified, Ram Dass endured, using meditation and prayer. One person on staff, however, did perceive something different transpiring in Ram Dass' room. A doctor confessed to him, "In this hospital I cannot get any peace. Your room is the only room where I can."

"So when people say to me, 'What did the experience of the stroke mean to you?' I don't know, because I wasn't there. I was really on two different planes of consciousness."

The confluence of these realizations—the need for ritual during illness as well as wellness, ritual transition into elderhood—has strengthened his resolve.

"Our minds use what we live through as lessons for the soul," he concluded rather wistfully. When asked what kind of lessons, he just smiled, showing how painful change can still be spiritual grist for the mill of the soul.

❁

During the past several years there has been another focus, this business of moving from aging to eldering. In the early 1990s, at the Omega Institute in upstate New York, Ram Dass organized a conference called "A Council of Elders," bringing together highly respected spiritual leaders from different traditions. At first he got resistance about using the word *elder*. Some prominent people thought it had negative connotations, but he defended it as a word that has garnered respect throughout history. The fact that it doesn't elicit enough respect in our time, he said, is a reflection of the very problem the conference was confronting—that we don't honor the truth about aging.

In fact, Ram Dass wanted to stress that "aging consciously" can and must be part of the spiritual path. "Until I became sixty," he freely admitted at the conference, " I treated age as rather uninteresting. . . . I was busy being spiritual, and spiritual people don't focus on the age of the body."

He went on to say that in the West people are paying a high price for living in a materialistic society. An externalized way of life "measures people in terms of products and achievements," which he said invariably denies the need for a deeper understanding of aging and death. Trying to eliminate aging spots or lines on our face or banishing the elderly to retirement homes only adds to our suffering, because we make it harder to embrace what should be the crowning hour of our lives—the transition to what he deems "elderhood." His challenge to baby boomers is to embrace death, accept change, and find a way to age gracefully and courageously.

"We must recognize the stages of life and honor them," Ram Dass emphasized. "The art of being able to look directly at death and directly at suffering is a function of your ability to find in yourself that which is not changing, which is not separate, which is not vulnerable to time and space. That's the spiritual work. That's the journey of aging."

I asked him to say more about the price we are paying for living out "the myth of rugged individualism."

"The traditionally respectable journey from aging to eldering is complicated in our culture by our attachment to the strictly personal. The identity of individualism is opposite to the identity for community," he said recently. "The aged man or aged woman being a useful thing in society—*that's* community. The John Wayne myth is ego, because that kind of hero is not ready to go back into community. Community is being able to say, 'I am part of God,' or 'I am part of the community of things.'"

An ego-driven culture is also a youth-obsessed culture, one constantly implying that aging itself is the problem. Ram Dass' suggestion is to "see how you can use aging as a vehicle to help you in your spiritual work rather than being something that's an obstacle."

Still, the question remains, How? How do we learn to use our advancing years to our advantage? Ram Dass recommended learning how to recognize and honor the natural demarcations of life.

Traditional societies, he pointed out, like the Tibetan, Indian, and Japanese, were clear about marking the time and the way of making transitions from one age to the next, such as late-life pilgrimage and accelerated spiritual studies.

In our time, he noted, "There is no clear rite of passage when you are old." The transition tends to be sheerly economic—retirement or the start of Medicare—when you're no longer part of the workforce.

If aging isn't the problem, what is? According to Ram Dass, it is *change*. Change is the perennial fear—and fascination. At the Omega Conference, he compared the retirees sitting on park benches in St. Petersburg, Florida, who constantly complain about changes in their bodies, with people who were a still a force in their cultures at the same age—Einstein, Rubenstein, Picasso, Rembrandt, Shaw, Graham, Monet, Chagall, Bob Hope, Grandma Moses.

"You can't imagine them sitting around doing that same thing, can you?" he said to the laughing crowd. "So it's clearly not age, is it? It's where the mind grabs hold, and which changes it focuses on, right?"

In a filmed interview with Frances Vaughn in 1996, Ram Dass said that aging people have to create their own scenario: "The process of aging is itself a creative act. You are your own creation."

But he also issued a caveat: "Stop feeding the drama of aging. Realize that who you are has no age. Who you are is in a body that has a personality that is aging and changing, but you yourself aren't."

When I asked him what he thought about an American Indian description of an elder as "someone who carries knowledge of tradition and has wisdom of the heart, someone who walks in truth and dignity and humility," Ram Dass nodded warmly. Then he slowly ran the fingers of his right hand along the armrest of his wheelchair, and stopped at the edge.

"An elder is someone who has moved from doing—to being," he said.

To illustrate his point, Ram Dass described a recent event in San Rafael, California, when he participated in a march with Ron Kovic, author of *Born on the Fourth of July.* "There was a phalanx of wheelchairs behind us, homeless people, nice feelings and speeches. But when I attempted to speak from the microphone there was only static. I was blah-blah-blah. They couldn't hear me. But it didn't matter. I was impressed that they were [so] warm to me—because I was a symbol to them, not because of what I said." As it was for Gandhi, Ram Dass' message is his life, and he asks of us what message we are. He asks us to stop trying to hold back the clock, and instead to find and practice rituals that work at life's troubling transition points, to know that significant changes take place not in real time but in soul time, to accept with grace "the terrible beauty of nature's wisdom." We get old, he reminds us, but we have to *become* wise. Deepen into that mystery. And recall Martin Buber's advice, "To be old is a glorious thing when one has not un-learned what it means to begin."

One unexpected thing that eldering allows us to do, Ram Dass said at Omega, is to let go of trying to please everyone else and to become more eccentric, more and more ourselves. When I playfully reminded him that eccentric originally meant "out of the center" or "an odd, whimsical orbit," Ram Dass grinned and said, "Yes, well, it all depends on whether you're in the orbit—or are the orbit."

When I asked him to summarize what it means to be an elder, Ram Dass closed his eyes and folded his hands. For several minutes he pondered the question, then said softly, as though from miles away, "Being an elder is all about presence," he said, smiling radiantly. "The elder is moving toward God and the soul."

The Soul of Mentorship

In the summer of 1985, less than six months after my first meeting with Joseph Campbell, I was in his apartment on Waikiki Beach in Honolulu, Hawaii, with a full film crew to interview him about his life and work. While setting up for an interview with his wife, the legendary dancer and choreographer Jean Erdman, I stood with Campbell in the recessed kitchen. I happened to notice the long row of leather-bound books about Heinrich Zimmer he had masterfully edited, including *The King and the Corpse, The Art of India,* and many others. So I asked him if he had good memories of the long years of apprenticeship he had spent with the Zimmer material.

Campbell smiled and then tenderly ran his large, athletic hands over the tops of the books, back and forth, as if he were running his fingers through the hair of a child, and he said, "I spent one, two, three, four... eleven, twelve long years with this material, and it was a privilege. What I used to do was this. I would lay down a blank piece of paper in front of me, Heinrich's class notes to the left of me, and lectures and my own notes to the right. Then I would lay my left hand on Zimmer's notes and close my eyes and wait until I could hear his voice in my head.

"Then I would begin to write."

This anecdote illustrates to me that the greatest power of mentorship lies not in the obsequious following of a great teacher, the bowed worship before tradition, nor the romantic kowtowing before the Great Man (or Woman) theory of the world, but in what poet Donald Hall calls "absorbedness." This is the ability to absorb teaching, and then for the rest of your life to be able to draw on it at will and make it your own.

Campbell's constant exhortation to question what you read, what experts and authorities tell you, what priests and gurus demand of you, helps bring us full circle in our discussion about the mythology of mentorship.

It is also about learning to remythologize your life, retell your story or the story of your times when necessary. To this effect, I recall an afternoon with Marion Zimmer Bradley at her home in Berkeley, California, in the spring of 1985. We were meeting to discuss a literary tour of England, based on her world-wide bestseller, *Mists of Avalon,* that we were going to lead together. As we went over the itinerary, which included Glastonbury, Tintagel, Stonehenge, and Avebury, Marion's eyes suddenly beamed with gratitude and she confessed how the book came about. She told me that up until a few years before she was strictly a science fiction writer, but one night the sorceress Morgana LeFay

Standing at the foot of the Tor, Glastonbury, England, English scholar Geoffrey Ashe (left) discusses the legends of King Arthur, "the once and future king," with tour leader, Phil Cousineau (middle), and the author of the *Mists of Avalon*, Marion Zimmer Bradley (right).

from the Arthurian legends came to her in a dream and told her that the great round of stories needed to be retold. They needed to be reimagined from the woman's point of view so that the present generation of women would know how powerful women teachers were in the past. Marion told me she wrote for two years in an absolute trance and remembered virtually nothing about the process.

A few months later, together we climbed the Tor, the mythic hill that rises outside the medieval town of Glastonbury, the Avalon of yore, with fellow scholar Geoffrey Ashe. I asked Marian what it was like to be back at the heart of Arthurian England.

"I've never been here before," she said quietly, as we reached top of the hill and gazed out at the dramatic panorama of Somersetshire before us. Her hair blew wildly in the afternoon wind as she confessed, "I only saw it in my dreams. But it's just as I imagined it would be."

In this way she was able to revive an ancient myth, and as Camus recommended, breathe new life into it. Ever since then, her heroine, Morgana, has been an inspiration to millions of women around the world as a model of wisdom and mentorship.

I see Marion's experience with the Arthurian material as a creative response to the frequent question, "Where do myths come from? Where are the new myths?"

Myths come from the same place that dreams and art come from. They bubble up from the depths of the soul. They can't be forced or constructed, they can only be dreamed, or as Nikos Kazantzakis might have said, danced.

New Year's Eve with Zorba

Recently, I was bicycling past a Greek restaurant near Fisherman's Wharf in San Francisco, and I heard a snippet from the soundtrack to the Greek movie *Never on Sunday*. In the time-leapfrogging ways of musical cues I was thrown back thirty-five years to New Year's Eve, circa 1965. My father is feeling his oats, as he used to say, the effects of a rollicking good night with his best friend, Jack Daniels. He is wobbling over to our old oak stereo cabinet and turning the PLAY switch so that we can all hear the sprightly bouzouki music one more time. Surprisingly, he grabs my mother and they begin to dance, the only night of the year, besides their anniversary, when they do dance. These are the only times I can recall them being so affectionate. There is undiluted joy in my father's eyes as he dances, as he mimicked the earthy steps of Anthony Quinn in his other favorite Greek movie of the 1960s, *Zorba the Greek*.

I hit the brakes of the bicycle, pull off the Embarcadero, and walk the bike up to the chain-link fence outside, thinking of the dozen or so times I've seen *Zorba* since then, reeling with joy each time the final scene unfolds with the flamboyant Quinn teaching the cerebral English teacher, played by Alan Bates, to dance.

The narrator of the story is a youngish Englishman, theoretically a mentor figure to his students back in England, but demonstrably head-smart and soul-dead. When he arrives for a holiday on the island of Crete he encounters the saintly rascal Zorba, a local fisherman, who slowly brings him back to life. Zorba is headstrong, but soul-wise; his motto is "Live life and enjoy it." This is news to the teacher and Dante addict, who has an aversion to "pleasures of the flesh" but is soon introduced to the Whole Zocratic World (as Zorba himself refers to it) of food, wine, sensuality, beauty, old love songs, and dance. Slowly, Zorba helps the teacher to "make up his mind," not with another book, not with philosophical debates, but with lusty life and shoulder-to-shoulder friendship.

Through the course of the story he has seen through Zorba's vanity, his illusions, his selfishness, and he loves him anyway. Near the end of the movie, in the famous beach scene, the teacher has an epiphany and asks a favor of his wild friend:

"Come on, Zorba, teach me to dance!"
Zorba leaped to his feet, his face sparkling.
"To dance, boss? To dance? Fine! Come on!"
"'Off we go, then, Zorba! My life has changed! Let's have it!"

Zorba the Greek is a passionate and bawdy story brimming with wonder and awe at the mythic mystery of life, and serves us well as a feisty model of mentorship, one that is concerned with a soulful defiance and *playful* attitude toward life.

"For Zorba's dance was full of obstinacy and defiance," says the awed Englishman as he watches him leap into the air like a goat and seem to sprout wings like an eagle. It is a sagacious remark that helps set Zorba's rebellion against conformity a world apart from the cult of angry defiance we have seen in the recent outbreaks of teen violence.

"They hated everybody," said one of the classmates of the so-called Trench Coat Mafia in Littleton, Colorado. A deeply disturbing comment, but one that revives our question of where those boys learned to hate. Dr. Stuart Brown, in his essay, "Evolution and Play," writes,

What is shared by mass murderers, felony drunk drivers, starving children, head-banging laboratory animals, some anxious students, most upwardly mobile executives and all reptiles? They don't *play*. What do MacArthur "genius" grantees, historically renowned creative artists, successful multicareer seniors, and animals of superior intelligence have in common? They are full of play throughout their lives. There is something profound about play.

What do all these mentors with a thousand masks—writers, artists, teachers, coaches, and Cretan fishermen—share in common? I believe they resemble what the ancient Irish called *anam cara*, "soul friends." They are trusted because the young people in their charge know they have their best interests in mind. These mentors are committed to sustaining the relationship, often for years at a time, as symbolized by Mentor's twenty-year counseling of Telemachus. These soul-guides display an ability to share their gifts of wisdom, but in a literally playful manner; they *play* with ideas, virtue, insight, wisdom, compassion, even rebellion and defiance, because their deepest concern is for the souls of the young people around them, who secretly long to hear from someone who cares, someone who knows when to let go and say, with a firm but velvet touch, *"Now is the time for you to become yourself."*

FOUR

The Myth of Travel

From Easter Island to the Moon

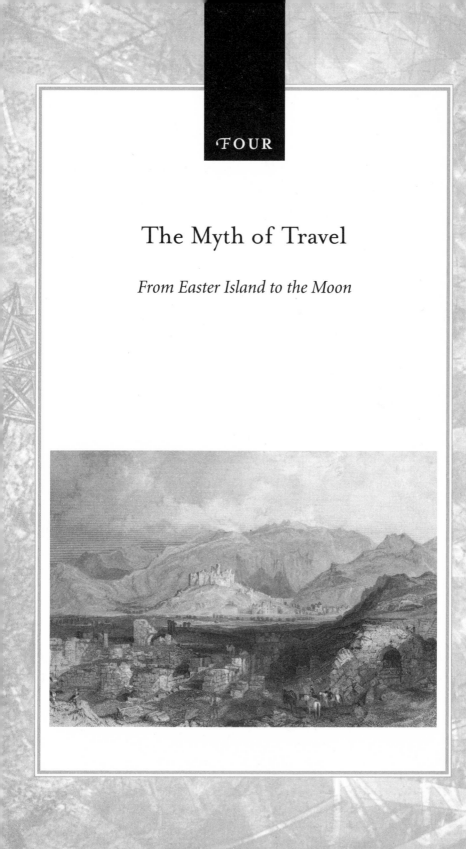

"What planet would you advise me to
visit now?" he asked.
"The planet Earth," replied the geographer.
"It has a good reputation."

—ANTOINE DE SAINT-EXUPÉRY, *The Little Prince*

or five hours and fifteen hundred miles there is nothing
but black sky and dark sea. I peer out the window of the
airplane to search for the island; it's as difficult to spot as
a speck of pepper on black crepe paper. Finally, two rows of runway
lights, shining like diamonds in the night, appear alongside the hulk-
ing shape of a volcano. They end when the island does, at the cliff's
edge a few hundred yards away. The drop-off darkness sends a shiver
of anxiety through me, a feeling of apprehension mixed with anticipa-
tion, at the utter remoteness of where we're landing.

When I step off the plane and onto the tarmac runway of Mataveri
Airport on Rapa Nui, better known as Easter Island, I am instantly
enchanted. The night air is sweetly fragrant as passengers are greeted
with garlands of white hibiscus. Two young kids riding bareback on the
same spavined horse along the perimeter fence shout gleefully to
returning friends. The owners of several local hotels rush the door of
the old wooden airport, calmly asking us if we'd like a room for the

One of the "living faces" of Easter Island in Polynesia, a mighty
moai or ancestral stone statue casts its haunting gaze across time
and space. The unplumbed myths and mysteries of the island
continue to beckon travelers from all over the world.

night. Chris Zelov and Henrique Kopke, the other members of the
small film team I'm traveling with, shuffle inside to collect our luggage
and equipment, but I pull back for a moment, seized by a strange sight
in the small garden just outside the customs office.

My heart pounds with excitement as I step into the giant shadow cast by the darkly silhouetted statue. I have to give it the old once-over-twice because I hadn't expected to see one of the legendary stone giants so soon. I wrongly assumed we would have to travel halfway around the island for our first encounter. But the adventure begins now. Looming before me is a ten-foot statue ruddily carved from volcanic stone. Its thousand-yard stare moves right through me and high into the night sky, as if communing with distant ancestors. Its brooding face exudes an otherworldly confidence, challenging me to read the meaning of its long silence.

Our drive through the small town of Hongo Roa seems oddly subdued for travelers who've come so far. We all look bewildered as the van makes its way through starkly empty streets to the Hotel Hangaroa overlooking the Pacific. After checking in, I toss my bags down on the wooden walkway near the office and shamble away from the lights to gaze at the Southern Hemisphere stars, which are wildly bright in the pure air of the island. The stars seem to have gone through a cosmic tumbler and emerged completely scrambled. I recognize nothing except for the Southern Cross. I'm completely disoriented, but love the confusion.

Wandering the grounds of the hotel, I discover another sleeping giant looking out across the night and back to the red dawn of time. I run my hands over the rough-hewn stone. The sheer good fortune of our unexpected side trip here still has me brimming with gratitude at my good fortune. While speaking with Juan Purcell, a visionary architect at Ritoque, a utopian community outside Valparaiso, Chile, for our documentary film on the future of cities, the interview took an unexpected turn. With avidity, he told us how his community had been influenced by the principles of sacred architecture, but that the influence had come from neither Europe nor North America. Their inspiration came from their own continent and from Easter Island, fifteen hundred miles to the west. Purcell told us he had taken some of his own students on field trips to the mysterious island to appreciate better the cultural links. If we really wanted to understand the origins of sacred architecture and communal living, he said, we had to visit the *moai* and ceremonial complexes of the ancient Rapa Nui people.

Seventy-two hours later, standing in the powerful presence of the *moai,* I feel like I've been beamed to the surface of a distant planet. I'm convinced there must be even deeper reasons we all agreed to come so far, besides the great trust and generosity of Chris, our producer. We could have found stock footage; we could have used still shots to cover this aspect of architectural history. But after much discussion it became obvious that all three of us had been hypnotized sometime in our lives by the mythic images of the island's giant statues that are found in books, movies, ads, and travel posters.

Gazing into the eyes of the statue, I feel a cold wind rush through me. Its tremendous *presence* is undeniable. Suddenly it occurs to me that we may be here for reasons similar to those that inspired the islanders who quarried the lava rock from the flanks of the Rano Raraku volcano and carved statues that have haunted the world ever since. In the words of one of the early anthropologists who excavated nearby, we're here for a "strong dose of *mana,*" that mysterious spiritual force granted by the gods or the ancestors and that moves all things. The English poet William Wordsworth experienced this once while hiking in the countryside:

And I have felt...a sense sublime

Of something far more deeply interfused,

Whose dwelling is the light of setting suns,

And the round of ocean and the living air,

And the blue sky, and in the mind of man;

A motion and a spirit, that impels

All thinking things, all objects of all thought,

And rolls through all things.

In the shadow of this beauty, I feel a page turning in my life, one that will reveal nearly every aspect of myth I've ever imagined. In that held-breath moment, I decide that I want to do more than "penetrate beyond the myths" of the island, as some other observers have recently boasted. I want to delve deeper into them.

Clearly, along with the Giza pyramids, the ruins of Macchu Picchu, and the Parthenon, the giant statues of Easter Island have come to symbolize to us everything that is exotic, remote, and mystical. Despite more than a century of fieldwork and explication, the statues continue to defy explanation, and I suspect there is something in that which our overdefined age enjoys. Here is a mystery that defies science, reason, and logic. Here is one of the last truly mythic worlds.

As I wait impatiently for Chris and Henrique to unpack and join me for the taxi ride into the small harbor town, I'm struck by something else unexpected: the *déjà vu* of the moment. Once again the fates have conspired to help me make a journey back to the beginning, to sacred origins. I shake my head in wonder at the odd sensation that, once again, there are invisible hands helping me along a path I need to follow. To live fully for me means to discover my personal and collective origins, which is partly behind my fascination with myths. As Mircea Eliade has presciently written, "To know the myths is to learn the secret origins of things."

So I've thrilled to front-page stories in the *New York Times* about the recent discovery of the origin of the alphabet along the Nile, thrusting the dates back to 1900 B.C.E. I am dazzled by reports of the discovery of the "recipe for subatomic soup" that might shed light on the birth of the universe, the first moment of all creation. Each origin story, from *coquilles Saint-Jacques* to coffee, seems to wipe the scales from my eyes and revivify my life.

Recently I came across the travel writer Bruce Chatwin's personal origin story, which was intended to at least approximate how his peripatetic life began. In 1966, at the age of twenty-six, Chatwin left a lucrative life at Sotheby's Auction House in London to travel to South America. Here is why:

One morning I woke up blind.

During the course of the day, the sight returned to the left eye, but the right one stayed sluggish and clouded. The eye specialist who examined me said there was nothing wrong organically, and diagnosed the nature of the trouble.

"You've been looking too closely at pictures," he said. "Why don't you swap them for some long horizons?"

Without ever formally declaring it my life's passion or compulsion, again and again I have found myself swapping my near-horizons for long ones, making pilgrimages back to the beginning of things that matter to me: from the origins of baseball at Cooperstown, New York, to the origins of cities at Catal Huyuk in Turkey.

For the first time in years I find myself thinking about the afternoon in 1991 I spent wandering around the excavations of the seven-thousand-year-old settlement in central Turkey, widely considered the oldest in the world. The day I arrived the wind was rustling through the ancient poplar trees. The air was pungent with the smell of woodsmoke that was pluming in far-off fields. I was ushered around the excavation site by the gentle caretaker, Suleiman. "Suleiman the

"Suleiman the Magnificent," the custodian of one of the ruins of Catal Huyuk, in central Anatolia, that dates from the end of the eighth millennium B.C.E. Its excavation by James Mallart in the 1960s revolutionized theories about the prehistory of the Old World.

Magnificent," he joked to me, echoing the legendary Turkish ruler. He told me in English as broken as the shards of ancient pottery that were still wedged into the old trenches that he had been there for twenty-five years and hoped his sons would take over after he died. He said he wished more tourists would brave the long dirt road drive from Konya, confided that he was impossibly lonely, and apologized for having nothing more to say in English.

As we gazed over the ancient grounds, he said, "But maybe you enjoy silence, too? It is best way to hear what old ones have to say."

"What did the old ones say?" I asked Suleiman. He looked surprised that I didn't know.

"Be silent and practice the art of silence. That's what Rumi said."

I'll never forget his gold-capped front teeth gleaming as he smiled. He was absolutely right. As much as my passion for history or my unabashed love of adventure, what I have come to love about ancient sites is their silence—and the unfailing way they move my heart and renew my soul.

The Polynesian Sphinx

After breakfast the next morning we load up our rental Jeep in a slashing rain. Ordinarily, as filmmakers, we would wait out the storm, but we have only three days to shoot on the island and it will be difficult to return. We drive tentatively a few miles north of town down muddy washboard roads to the ancient site of Ahu Vinapu. Through the steamed-up windows of the Jeep we can see the thrilling sight of a long row of *moai*, the mighty ancestral statues, poised on the *ahu*, a ceremonial platform constructed out of volcanic stones on the edge of the sea.

Stepping out into a tremendous storm, I huddle deep into my rain gear and trudge out over the wet grass. My first impression is one of surprise. After visiting monumental sites all over the world, I've learned to brace myself for crowds. But the only sign of tourism here is a small gray shack where a local villager quietly sells her hand-sized replicas of the statues.

The storm's blue fist pounds down on the island. Cold winds from Antarctica bluster in with huge foaming waves that crash against the rain-slick rocks of the coast. In every direction there are fifteen hundred miles of churning ocean. The isolation is spooky. An ancient melancholy hovers over the rocky landscape. But I love it in all its strange glory.

Despite my protection, the rain soaks through my clothes as I help Chris and Henrique set up the movie camera. After we get our "hero shots," as they're called in the business—the ones we believe will capture the mystery of the place—I wander alone in a cool reverie from statue to statue, taking photographs, making notes in a journal that becomes asterisked with ink stains oozing from fallen raindrops.

The statues have a strong presence, but they are not necessarily beautiful in the classical sense. There is no Michelangelo's *David* here, not even Matisse's rough-hewn *Large Seated Nude*. No doubt to some the *moai* even appear coarse and nearly identical. But I can't look away from them. They possess an ineffable quality that reminds me of the anonymous Italian journalist's infamous description of Sophia Loren as a woman whose mouth is too large, her nose too long, her chin and lips too broad—but somehow the combination of her qualities is beautiful. Before her days as a recognized icon of beauty, Loren struggled with the efforts of several producers to alter her looks. Finally, director George Cukor reminded her of something she already suspected: "If you are confident, you are beautiful."

No, there aren't any Sophia Loren lookalikes among the *moai*, only a mournful beauty that comes from their distant stares. What seems to bother scores of visitors is exactly what appeals to me. I see a beauty forged out of stone-cold confidence regarding the *mana* inside them, and see something else, a kind of visual echo of the faces of the ancestors that is barely detectable in their features.

I'm mystified by the sadness in the air, the hint of tragic history, but reinforced in my wonder about the effort that human beings have made throughout history to make "mute stones speak." The combination of wet stone and strange dislocation prompts me to remember an encounter years before with an Irish farmer who calmly asked me in a

The time-worn stones of the fifteen-hundred-year-old pilgrim road to the monastic settlement of Clonmacnoise, Ireland, one of thousands of pilgrimage sites that grace the countryside.

raging downpour, "Are you going to the stones?" How did he know, I wondered then, about my fascination with the old stone sites? The old County Clare man was referring to the megalithic sites erected by the ancient Celts six thousand years ago, one of which shimmered in the rain not a hundred yards away. His query was almost ritualistic, as evidenced by hundreds of centuries of farmers encountering pilgrims on the old stone-lined roads leading to the mystery sites.

Are you going to the stones?

The old farmer could just as well have been referring to the primordial urge to travel great distances to be in the presence of powerful stoneworks, whether dolmens, cathedrals, or sculptures. Why have people throughout the ages fallen under the spell of massive standing stones and sculptures? For what possible reasons? Healing? Fertility? Memory? Honoring of the ancestors?

They have faith in the nature of unseen things. And what is myth if it isn't the sacred story that dares to describe the invisible power behind the visible world?

Prowling for the Ineffable

Here on Easter Island I feel the archaic tug of travel like no other place I've ever been. There are few realistic reasons to visit here, unless you want to break up a long flight to Tahiti. Instead, the decision to make the journey often seems to be inspired by the desire to scour a land of pure myth, like the artist Piranesi who prowled the ruins of the Roman forum, or the painter J. W. Turner who brooded among the ruins of Stonehenge, or the indefatigable traveler Rose Macaulay who delighted in "the pleasure of ruins" as she roved over the ruinous islands of the Mediterranean and could practice "swimming down the hurrying river of time."

I understand these romantic compulsions. The world is increasingly noisy and busy. There are fewer and fewer places where we can literally brood, which means to sit on an idea like a hen on an egg, heating it, giving it time and love until it is time for it to hatch. There are fewer places to *moodle,* as an old writing teacher of mine used to say, a brilliant combination of *mood* and *doodle,* suggesting that the soul needs as much time to wander as our feet.

But what is it that we are prowling around for, what are we brooding over, why do we need to swim in the river of time?

❊

For an hour I hover around the colossal statues, snapping photo-graphs, helping my partners set up the movie camera so we can get some panoramas. I lean against the stones of one of the king's dwellings and watch the most rapidly changing cloud show of my life. Thunderclouds swirl away, followed by meringue-shaped cirrus. Soon after an armada of cumuli rise out of the west, thin tubes of wispy clouds flit overhead as if they were the telescopes of the gods searching for the secrets of the stones below.

While changing film in my camera it occurs to me that these sites are evidence of more than an innate wish to "understand or respond to the unseen," the common reductionism of anthropology. Something must have *happened* when these statues were raised and the islanders gathered in front of them, built fires, danced, and prayed, or the kings would never have kept ordering their creation. But what? What com-pelled these utterly isolated islanders to raise these enigmatic stone carvings?

As we pack up the equipment and make our way slowly down the washboard roads of the island, I recall how the Oregon poet William Stafford once suggested that the reason people worship, pray, believe in talismans, and teach their children to trust their dreams is that:

The world speaks.

❊

Stafford's words echo inside me while I rejoin Chris and Henrique at the local villager's wooden souvenir shack in the parking lot. They're pricing replicas of the statues when the owner's neighbor approaches. The owner tells Henrique, who is doubling as our interpreter, that she carved the small *moai*. Her profile reminds me of those in the paintings in my guidebook made by the artist on James Cook's ship that arrived here in the 1770s, and I'm impressed by her fierce pride.

I ask her what it's like to live near the old statues.

"Oh, the *moai* look out for us now," she says. "They take care of us. They bring tourists here. They help us more than the government does." Her eyes widen; her eyebrows arch. She smiles and adds, "The *moai* are still very powerful."

Her description wasn't limited to the past tense. The mighty statues were not relegated to the misty past, but were awarded a strong presence in her everyday life.

"Why are they still so powerful?" I ask her.

She grimaces slightly at my naïveté and gazes out over the wide lawn to the row of statues, and murmurs, as if to a child, "They remind me every day of our ancestors."

The Enigma

For a thousand years the ancient people of Rapa Nui lived on an island they originally called *Te Pito o Te Henua*, "The Navel of the World," or *Pito o te Henua*, "Land's End," dramatically isolated from the rest of the world.

On this island world measuring a mere sixty-four square miles, halfway between Tahiti and Chile in the South Pacific, around 1000 C.E. master sculptors began to shape the first of more than 1,000 sixty-ton statues out of the stone flanks of the Rano Raraku volcano. They cut colossal blocks out of soft volcanic tuff and with simple basalt hammerstones and chisels shaped them into images of their ancestors. This much the scholars generally agree upon. How the *moai* were then transported and raised is a matter of fierce contention. The current theory is that the statues were pushed and pulled over palm tree trunks for miles across the island, much as the great sailors of the island had transported their long canoes out to sea.

Arriving at the sanctuary, the statues were raised onto *ahus*, where they were polished, incised with symbols, raised, and revered through ritual prayer and ceremonies.

There they stood, then, their backs to the sea and eyes to the stars, unknown to the rest of the world until eighteenth-century European explorers encountered the island on their way to discover the "mythical" lost continent in the South. Their accounts are full of wonder and confusion.

"These stone images at first caused us to be struck with astonishment," wrote the Dutch navigator Jacob Roggeveen, who landed here on Easter Sunday 1724, "because we could not comprehend how it was possible that these people, who are devoid of heavy thick timber for making any machines...had been able to erect such images...."

"In the middle of the Great Ocean," wrote the French traveler Pierre Loti in 1872, "in a region where no one ever passes, there is a mysterious and isolated island; there is no land in the vicinity and, for more than eight hundred leagues in all directions, empty and moving vastness surrounds it. It is planted with tall, monstrous statues, the work of some now-vanished race, and its past remains an enigma."

The drawings and descriptions of the maritime explorers stunned the world, and slowly over the next two centuries the stone idols of Easter Island came to rank alongside the pyramids of Egypt, Stonehenge, the Parthenon, and the ziggurats of Babylon as one of the wonders of the world. Though some scholars continue to scoff at the seemingly useless activities of platform building and statue carving, travelers continue to venture here to brood over a mystery that eludes easy explanation.

The Lair of the Gods

Later in the day we venture down the rain-rutted coast roads to Ahu Tongariki, the site of ten resurrected giant statues. All along the way we see evidence of why Easter Island was once called "The Island of Broken Heads." Amid the heather and wild horses, volcanic rock and majestic loneliness, are hundreds of toppled statues. Some of the pummeled statues are evidence of the warfare that devastated the island at the end of the eighteenth century, others of the tidal waves that occasionally roar in from the sea, crushing everything in their path. After shooting a few rolls of slide film in the stunningly polarized blue light, I put my camera away and sit down among the decapitated stone heads and the rubble of long-lost *ahus* and ponder the unmistakable melancholy of old stones.

When the English explorer James Cook arrived here in 1774, he didn't report any damage to the *moai*, but subsequent visitors did. By the end of the 1800s all visitors reported that the statues were badly damaged. The implication is that during the intervening years war broke out between competing clans on the island, and one result was the toppling of the enemy's ancestral statues. By the nineteenth century, travel writer Paul Theroux writes in his book *The Happy Isles of Oceania*, "the island had flourished by being cut off, and then it became a victim of its remoteness."

After shooting some video footage, we drive over the washboard road to the majestic Rano Raraku volcano. It is a breathtaking sight. The grassy slope is riddled with more than three hundred half-carved statues, some still immured in the side of the mountain, others half-buried on the flanks. I climb by way of the ancient path of the stonecutters and joy fills my heart. This is an astonishment, but no longer a mystery. Recently, a group of anthropologists, the "wedge and lever" school, have demonstrated how the giant heads were probably transported across the island to their resting places on the platforms, which doubled as burial mounds for the ancestors.

The real mystery for me is their resemblance either to stone corpses in their final resting places, or even stranger, to the abandoned *kouris* that I found on the Greek island of Naxos. Those Cycladic sculptures are known for their size and their "archaic smiles," which signals for many scholars the dawn of consciousness or inchoate personality. A close look reveals the emerging mind in the expression carved into the faces. The parallels between the two forms, both lean, unfinished, in their primordial state, their stone souls not quite yet emerged, come to mind as I clamber up the trench running alongside and find a perch to gaze from down the hillside to the sea. A few feet below me is the colossal face of the *moai*, its own gaze frozen forever in what might be called the "archaic stare" down the mountain, across the valley, and over the ages. The strange gaze raises the hair on my arms, which is what usually happens when I get the chance to pursue what the Romantic poets used to call "ruin-gazing."

Underneath a Maxfield Parrish sky of teal blue and fleecy clouds, I recall how a century of archaeology has helped us answer many of the *how* questions, which is the typical province of science. But the *why* questions are the ones that have most taunted visitors to Rapa Nui, Easter Island—why and *when*. The answer is buried as deeply as the abandoned, half-carved statues that were left in these grassy slopes.

To paraphrase Winston Churchill, the island is a riddle wrapped in a mystery inside an enigma.

The Mania for *Mana*

In the beginning was a primordial egg. The egg gave birth to all living things. In the time before time began there was a god who named himself Makemake and created himself in the primordial form of a man with the head of a bird. In this time that wasn't yet time, before sky, earth, sea, moon, sun, and stars, he lived in utter darkness, his shell spinning wildly in space for millions of years. Eventually the goggle-eyed god pecked his way out of the shell, shed his feathers, and fell to Earth, thereby creating life through his very presence.

Down through the ages Makemake was worshiped on the island through a bewildering set of rituals designed to gain the force of his favor. Inevitably a priesthood arose. The members claimed to have direct access to the god. All across the Polynesian archipelago it was believed that kings inherited a spark of the divine power of the gods, that spiritual force known as *mana*. At some point on this wind-battered island the king had a dream, or a priest whispered in his ear, that the raising of silent stone figures might raise the *mana*, the magic power, the spiritual force that brings life, and a new religion was born: the birdman cult.

The sleepstrange story reveals one of the prime functions of myth, which is to "explain the inexplicable," as John Sharkey writes in *The Celtic Mysteries*. To know the myths, the scholar says, is to know the secret origins; but the reverse is also true. To know the secret origins is to know the myths. But what if the secret is lost? Are the myths lost as well? Perhaps the most compelling secrets of the remote world of the Rapa Nui died with the last of their priests who were captured by slavers and expired in the cruel guano mines of Peru, or expired with the tribal elders who were exiled to the leper colonies in the north of the island.

To comprehend the immensity of this kind of loss, it helps to recall the old African saying that each time an elder dies it's as if a library burns. If this is true, how do we gain access to the primary truths at the heart of the old way of seeing?

We learn to see again, as I learned from the blind poet on the slopes of Telegraph Hill. We do whatever is necessary to wake up and see anew, which is one element in our fascination with travel. Travel is flight, from and toward, but always movement, and it is movement that graces us with the new perspective we need.

Flights of Imagination

At breakfast the next morning we bump into the cameraman for another film crew that has arrived on the island. He is with David Attenborough's team from the BBC in London. They're here to shoot an episode for a program on "The Future of Life on Earth." Attenborough arrives while the camera operator tells us that his boss believes that the ancient Rapa Nui worshiped birds, and so they have constructed a special "robot camera." They plan to use it for aerial shots of the ceremonial village of Orongo, which is perched on a spectacular wedge of land between the Rano Kau volcano and cliffs that drop vertiginously to the wild ocean below.

As the operator assembles the robo-cam, I watch Attenborough in animated conversation with his producers, drinking his morning tea, and mention to the cameraman my thoughts about the uncanny parallels between the Easter Island "birdman" and *Birdy,* Alan Parker's movie about the Vietnam veteran who becomes obsessed with birds and his own fantasy to fly. Coincidentally, the cameraman worked on the film, even designing the special "bird's-eye view" camera that allowed the viewer to see through the eyes of Birdy as he flew.

Traveling through the dark before dawn, we head through a eucalyptus forest and upon a winding dirt road to Orongo. The sun stuns the horizon as we arrive in the parking lot and race to the summit with our equipment. There are dozens of drystone corbelled lodgings perched along the cliff's edge. They remind me of the beehive hermit huts on the remote islands off the coast of Ireland. The ceremonial dwellings here have doorways so low a visitor to the king would have had to crawl in on hands and knees.

From the summit the caldera of the volcano is glowing like a hot iron with the reflection of sunrise. On the other side of the promontory is a narrow pathway between boulders incised with carvings of strange birdgods that lead down the sheer cliff to the rocky beach below. The wind buffets us as if we're prayer flags. It's dizzying to stand here, as if on the bow of a stone ship, but I step closer to the crumbling edge anyway. My jacket fills with the swirling winds, and I lean over the edge, lifting my camera for a wide-angle shot of the birdman petroglyphs.

Adrenaline rushes through me like water through a fire hose, as if I were about to take flight, and I'm thinking exultantly, *Yes, this is why we came*—when suddenly Chris shouts out, "Careful, Phil, remember, you're a family man now!"

I back away, smiling.

When warfare over dwindling food supplies erupted on the island, construction of the statues came to a halt, and with it the religion based on ancestor worship began to fade away. Soon after, no one is sure when, the islanders developed a fertility cult based on their creator god Makemake, as if the mythology based on the dead needed to be transformed into a mythology based on life. At the heart of the new religion was a strange "egg race" that is rich in its mythic implications, since it was a mix of competition for divine grace and a Polynesian Ironman competition.

Each September the goal was to find for the coming year a new birdman, the living embodiment of the birdgod Makemake. The candidates were local warlords who chose their fittest servants or the finest athletes among the young men of the island to represent them. The fierce contest began with participants racing down the treacherous switchback path of the thousand-foot-high cliffs, followed by a two-mile swim on rush rafts through shark-infested waters to the tiny islet. There the warriors waited for the arrival of the terns and the first brown-speckled eggs of the season. The first to bring an egg back intact (many broke on the difficult return) in his headband would present it to his master, who was declared *tangata manu*, the man-god, the bird-man of Rapa Nui.

The proof of the new prestige bestowed on the winning contestant can be seen in the nearly five hundred petroglyphs around the island, which some scholars now suggest are portraits of the winners. As for the sacred birdman, his yearlong reign ended the *mana;* the magic power was believed to seep out of the egg. Tradition demanded it be hurled out to sea or hidden in the rocks at Rano Raraku and later buried in a sacred place when the birdman died.

Sitting on the edge of the Orongo ritual complex, I try to unravel the complex imagery of the ritual. I know that the islanders worshiped birds, especially the terns and the frigate birds, who were such strong flyers they were never seen to land. But why did birds and eggs hold such mythic power? In Polynesian mythology, as in many others, birds are messengers of the gods, but certainly there must be more to it.

I gaze out over the small islands offshore and for several minutes watch birds hovering and landing, hovering and landing. Then it occurs to me: Of course, birds come and go. An island without trees means an island without canoes. The Rapa Nui were essentially marooned, landlocked, and probably longing for escape. They were also caught in a catastrophic, downward spiral of internecine warfare, which meant the population was dwindling.

The birdman cult was the last-gasp ritual of an isolated people who longed for escape and life. As our innocent Easter eggs are symbols of the new life of the new year, so the egg was the symbol of renewal of life, the divine favor of the god.

Overhead, several wide-winged birds rise high in the thermals created over the cliffs, spin and dive for the tiny islands again. I think of the *hopu,* the old competitors in the egg race who were revered for their courage and strength and embodiment of the god, for having trained and accomplished a difficult task.

Now we are awed by the gods of technology that merely *simulate* the flight and ecstasy of the birdman with robots, cameras, and blue screens. It is a perfect reflection of our increasingly vicarious world, and a reflection of the emerging myth of the entertainment industry, which blurs the line between the real and the virtual in its attempts to transport people without their ever leaving home.

Flights of Fancy

Flight is one of the most ancient paths to the unknown. The shaman, the mystic, the witch, the creator of fantasy, and the mythmaker have much in common, as David Leeming has pointed out in *Flight,* his marvelous anthology on myth and fantasy.

"Each attempts to escape the illusion of the purely, temporal, physical life," he writes, "which to each of them is, at least in some sense, false. . . . Each moves toward what might be called a vision of God in the person of the universal, unmasked Self."

All around us this cold morning the stones are murmorous. The ghosts of countless generations of the Rapa Nui seem to hover over the restored dwellings. While Chris and Henrique battle the terrific winds so they can shoot some footage of the sunrise, I gingerly rub my hands over one of the birdman carvings on the rocks that act as a kind of threshold for the stone staircase that leads down to the sea. My fingertips linger on the wind-rubbed wings of the ancient birdman and I think of Icarus, as imagined by Matisse in his bright cutouts and by Breughel in his tumultuous painting of the young dreamer's flight from the labyrinth of Crete. Then I rub the "goggle-eye" of the birdman and recall the account of Charles Lindbergh of his flight to Paris: "My skull is one great eye, seeing everywhere at once."

Flight. It is the perfect metaphor for the longing of the spirit for independence from the body, the land, even time itself. The great texts of world religions are full of such descriptions.

An eighteenth-century engraving that was the frontispiece for a book
gracefully entitled "The Discovery of Dawn by flying Man or the French
Daedalus," after Greek inventor who gave wings to his son Icarus.

"Am I now more man or spirit?" wrote Lindbergh. "Will I fly my airplane on to Europe and live in flesh as I have before, feeling hunger, pain, and cold, or am I about to join these ghostly forms, become a consciousness in space, all-seeing, all-knowing, unhampered by materialistic fetters of the world?"

His descriptions could be that of an Easter Island *hopu,* or the medicine woman I encountered during a week of peyote prayer meetings in the remote mountains of Mexico, who described the sickness of one of the participants as a flight of the soul, and that it was her task to "cry for a vision" and bring the soul back.

The Other Sides of Myth

There are as many layers to the mythic reality of Easter Island as there are layers of rock in the deep craters of the island's four volcanoes. I'm thinking about these unexpected levels the next day while we drive the length of the barren windswept island to an unexpectedly lovely palm-fringed beach. Thirty wild horses gallop through the sand dunes. A bare-assed, long-haired swimmer cavorts in the soft waves of the only peaceful bay on the island. When he emerges from the scalloped waves I'm momentarily astonished to recognize him as one of the dancer-drummers from the traditional performance we saw the night before in the island's gymnasium. Then his face had been painted with the black and white spirals of the Polynesian warrior, and when he danced it was as if he were about to spin out of control, off the ground, off the island. Looking at him now pushes time out of joint and my mind wanders back to the founding story of the island.

❋

According to local legend, the great navigator Hotu Matua landed on this very beach some dim day around the fifth century. Recent voyages from Micronesia to Hawaii by replicas of the early long canoes have proven that there was some truth to the myths, and that the early Polynesians were the greatest sailors in history. Their voyages covered ten thousand square miles in the Pacific Ocean, using only the stars in the sky and the swells of the sea to guide them.

When asked why the revival was taking place, Mau Piailug, the revered elder among the traditional Micronesian navigators, said, "You know where you are going by knowing where you came from."

Many scholars still regard the account of the first settler's landing on Easter Island as purely mythological, in the derogatory sense, but now allow that there is a "good chance that it contains a sound framework of truth."

I saunter over to the restored row of six magnificent *moai* and listen in on a tour guide's description of another layer of mythmaking, the shadow side, that of the locally unpopular adventurer and self-mythologizer, Thor Heyerdahl. She knocks the head off each one of his theories, as readily as the warring clans here toppled the statues themselves. "Heyerdahl says that the Rapa Nui walked the statues with ropes and lines," she scoffs, "but all evidence shows that they were moved on sledges, using palm trunks." She throws her hands in the air, then points out to the sea. "Worse, he claims that Easter Island was settled by American Indians from the Pacific coast of South America, dismissing the Rapa Nui's belief that they are of Polynesian descent."

One well-read member of her group asks about the totora reeds in Rano Kau crater lake that Heyerdahl says come from South America.

"What he fails to mention," she hotly replies, "is the pollen study that proves the reeds have been growing in the crater for at least thirty thousand years."

Her passionate defense of Polynesian accomplishment reminds me of Paul Theroux's chapter on Easter Island in *Oceania*, which spares no vitriol in its description of Heyerdahl's position as "a display of deep bias, bordering on contempt, against Polynesians." In Theroux's words, Heyerdahl derides every island group he encounters as "too lazy, too uncreative, too stupid," yet he clings "to his discredited east-to-west migration theory, [and] is no more scientific than the Mormons, who believe that one of the Lost Tribes of Israel sailed from South America to populate Polynesia."

I spend the next half-hour climbing the promontory overlooking the bay, the legendary landing site of the heroic Hotu Matua, and an Olympian perspective on the statues on the *ahu*. Every inch of it as much mythscape as landscape. The wind, which began somewhere out around the Solomon Islands, buffets me around, nearly knocking me down. I think of how metaphorical this beleaguered culture is for the entire mythology of travel. The colossal statues on the *ahu* far below, framed by recently planted palm trees, staring out over the land, are an example of the iconic power of modern tourism, which attracts and repels, enchants and disturbs, simultaneously, as sacred images always have.

The swaying palm trees that fringe the bay like the tonsure of a monk were only recently planted by the Forest Department of Chile. Walking underneath them I ponder the commonly accepted theory of the relationship between the monomania that created larger and larger statues and the decimation of the island's trees, which were used as rollers for the transportation of the *moai*. One by one, the trees disappeared across the island. Soon none were left either for the statues or for canoe building, and then the Rapa Nui were incarcerated on their own island.

In the chilling words of the historians Bahn and Flenley: "The person who felled the last tree could see that it was the last tree. But he (or she) still felled it."

By the nineteenth century all the statues had been toppled and broken during the tragic tribal warfare. The trees were gone. The food supply was treacherously low. The dream had been broken. On this speck of island is evidence for the Janus-faced nature of mythic reality: one side faces the sublime, the other the demonic.

The *moai* are evidence for both the glories of mythmaking, the godlike power that can infuse a human being inspired by tradition and belief in the divine capacity within human beings. But there is also evidence for the madness of myth. On an island only slightly larger than my hometown of San Francisco, in a world of only a few thousand people cut off for a thousand years from the rest of the world, the psychodrama of the rise and fall of many cultures was acted out.

Sitting at the feet of dozens of the famed "living faces" of Rapa Nui, I'm convinced that with an as yet undescribed level of understanding, visitors come here from all around the world to do just this, to read the troubling mystery for themselves. In these dark, sad, brooding stone heads many seem to believe they can come face to face with the larger mystery of what endures and why and then, as an early explorer described his reaction, "marvel greatly."

The idea intrigues me. In my travels I've met many people who long to be surprised by wonder, moved by awe, but are genuinely disappointed by the "theme park-ing" of the world. The power of travel images slapped onto travel agency windows the world over appears to be in direct proportion to the lack of awe and wonder people experience in their own backyards. The disparity is comparable to the general thrust of advertising psychology: Make people feel they cannot possibly be happy until they have purchased your product. The myth of travel speaks to the part of us that needs to move, needs to tap into the living force that streams throughout the Earth. So we take journeys in hope that a great sea-change will take place inside our souls, hoping for the healing touch of art and history, or the spiritual forces of a sacred place to heal us.

As the sun sets over the only sandy bay on the island, a great bafflement falls over me, and a strange surge of energy flows inside me.

When the Thing Swooped Down

In the late nineteenth century the fledgling anthropologist Kathleen Routledge wrote that on Easter Island "the shadows of the departed builders still possess the land.... The whole air vibrates with a vast purpose and energy which has been and is no more. What was it? Why was it?"

There is a clue to this twisting question in the ancient tale that the twentieth-century anthropologist and mystic Teilhard de Chardin was fond of telling: that of Elias and the whirlwind in *The Book of Kings*. In an essay about the presence of spiritual power in matter that is remarkably evocative of *mana*, the God-haunted Jesuit wrote how "the man was walking in the desert, followed by his companion, when the Thing swooped down on him."

De Chardin was intrigued by the challenge of illuminating the occasional glimpse human beings have of the unseen power that lurks behind all things.

"From afar," he continued in the essay,

> it had appeared to him, quite small, gliding over the sand, no bigger than the palm of a child's hand—as a pale, fleeting, shadow like a wavering flight of quail over the blue sea before sunrise or a cloud of gnats dancing in the sun at evening or a whirlwind of dust at midday sweeping over the plain.
>
> The Thing seemed to take no heed of the two travelers, and was roaming capriciously through the wilderness. Then, suddenly, it assumed a set course and with the speed of an arrow came straight at them.

I see that spinning, whirling force as an echo of Makemake and many other vertiginous gods and goddesses who churn the world into existence, nevertheless the spinning of elements in the atom, the dance of the dervish, the drop of the curveball, the odd rhythms of poetry, and this: the way the sun just now slowly dips behind a curtain of clouds, turning the statues into silhouettes.

Now I will tell you a peculiar thing about the *moai*. In that odd flicker of tropical light I notice for the first time the exquisitely carved fingers sloping down across the belly of one of the statues. They are tentatively touching, even pointing for the rest of us to notice something about the belly. Could it be the Polynesian equivalent of the *chi*, the Chinese concept of the soul-like force in the belly? Is it a reference to fertility? Is it a suggestion by the priests, the master sculptors, the god himself, of the tremendous energy that lies waiting inside each and every one of us?

Some scholars believe that the gesture symbolizes the god's protection of ritual knowledge and oral traditions, but whatever the original intent the gesture is hauntingly beautiful. I believe it symbolizes contact with what the religious historian Huston Smith calls the "deeply real," evidence of encounters with the sacred dimension that lies behind the visible one. All cultures have attempted to reveal this numinous dimension, even here on the most remote inhabited island in the world.

Rumi writes of the movement of grace inside us that we occasionally see twisting in the world like unseen rain in a storm, in Coleman Barks' translation:

A secret turning in us

makes the universe turn.

Head unaware of feet,

and feet head. Neither cares.

They keep turning.

This is how I came to think of the enigma of Rapa Nui. These fantastic statues were sculpted to reveal the divine presence in the world, but not out of passive admiration like much art. Instead, they were erected so the people could tap into the power of their own ancestors. They were sculpted, transported, and revered, because something happened in the hearts and souls of the natives of Rapa Nui during their ceremonies of ancestor worship, which is one form of response to mythic reality. No doubt the islanders intensely believed that their gods and their statues could guide them through life, if they received their blessing, their *mana.*

This is how myths are born and then sustained, by way of sleeping and waking dream alike, through the sense of wonder at the power of faith, the faith in a power still invisible, out here on the sacred border between the known and the unknown worlds. Why do I marvel at their long-distance voyaging and their colossal sculpture? That they may have been able to tap *mana,* the sources of spiritual power. Perhaps myth itself is *mana,* the spiritual force in the form of a narrative, a story made sacred about how it all began *and we may begin again* every time we tell the story. The urge to sculpt these statues came from a place outside of time, and it touches a place in me that feels timeless, which is perhaps what all sacred sites are meant to do—offer a tantalizing taste of the infinite.

Contemplating the statues enables us, as the Chinese philosopher Lao Tzu expressed the goal of the spiritual life, "to practice eternity." Reflecting on them allows time to collapse for us, which is the beginning of all philosophical thought, the pondering of the ultimate meaning of our lives. I take Lao Tzu's advice to mean it is vital to the spiritual life to learn how to live in the lapidary moment, the multilayered image of time as past, present, and future. To do so we have to learn certain tricks of the eye and imagination in order to see the double nature of things, to witness for ourselves the beauty of the world, and the way it all began, here, there, and everywhere. We cannot take anyone else's word for matters of the heart, concerns of the soul. These things we must experience for ourselves.

And one of the strongest mythic metaphors we have had for this way of life is the road, the road of life, travel that takes us to sites that become sacred in the human memory because they allow us what the great traveler, Lady Montagu, called "an access to truth." Beyond the road of habit and routine, of dulled senses and drifting purpose, is the land of meaning, where time stops and we can hear the heartbeat of creation. It is there where we put the soles of our feet to the soul of the world.

Once and Future Gods

On our last night on Rapa Nui we dine on fresh grilled tuna, salad, sweet potatoes, and plenty of the good island hootch called *pisco,* and at Chris' prodding talk for awhile about the modern equivalents of *mana.*

"Where is it for us? Where do we go for *mana?*"

It surprises me how avidly he is asking us. He really wants to know. Our eyes keep going back to the lone *moai* a few hundred yards down perhaps the most cosmically named avenue in the world: The Center of the Universe Street. Whenever our gazes settle on the lone sentinel guarding the harbor and the mysteries of the island, the talk goes quiet again.

Being in the electronic and entertainment business, Henrique predictably votes for technology. "If you think of *mana* as a kind of life energy I think people go for it in live entertainment, music concerts. That's where I see it, anyhow."

My vote is for the world of the arts and literature and architecture, saying, "I think of it as the spiritual force, which can be amplified by telling stories or building great edifices on sacred sites."

Chris challenges me by asking what modern images have half the power of the statues on the island, and without thinking, I blurt out, "The monolith in *2001: A Space Odyssey*." Immediately, I feel like I'm on to something so I add, "And that reminds me of a story. Did I ever tell you about the Campbell-Kubrick connection?"

My mind moves slantwise back to the winter of 1968 and a curious moment in the life of my old friend, Joseph Campbell, who had not seen a movie in forty years. When he left for Europe in the late '20s silent films still ruled; when he returned to the States the "talkies" had arrived, and so had the "naturalism" and "literalism" he abhorred in any work of art.

"One blustery New York night," I began, "when his wife, the dancer Jean Erdman, was not feeling well he wanted to cheer her up. So he grabbed their coats and hats, took her by the arm, and said, 'Jeannie, let's go to a movie.'

"She was stunned, but delighted, as they hadn't attended one together for decades. They scurried around the corner of their Greenwich Village apartment, and ducked into the first movie house they could find, the Waverly, not even looking up at the marquee to see what was playing.

"Inside, the house lights dimmed, the cone of light from the projector beamed across the dark theater, and the opening strains of music came up, and the credits scrolled for *2001: A Space Odyssey*. The scholar watched intently as the story opened up in prehistory, on the plains of Africa, then segued to the dark caves of a clan of shivering Australopithecines. In the middle of the night, one of the protohuman apes squinted as a strange light shown into the cave. His head lifted; the hair stood up on the back of his neck, his eyes dilated as he watched the moon rise through the opening of the cave.

At that moment it all clicked in for Campbell and he elbowed his wife, and said, 'They've been reading my books.'"

✳

Several years later, Campbell spoke with the film's director, Stanley Kubrick, and the filmmaker confirmed Campbell's suspicion of his influence. After reading the Arthur C. Clark short story, "The Sentinel," it took years for Kubrick to figure out how to turn it into a movie. The breakthrough came, he told Campbell, when he discovered Campbell's book, *The Masks of God: Primitive Mythology,* and discovered the mythic images he had long been searching for. In that book Campbell isolated what he thought to be the primordial moment of the origins of human consciousness, the one that separated us from the apes: the awakening through awe and wonder of the human heart. Campbell was thrilled he had unwittingly helped an artist give voice to what he thought was the emerging myth of modern times: the image of Earth-rise made possible by space travel. Campbell was so moved by the movie and his subsequent collaborations with the astronaut Rusty Schweikart that he wrote a book-long essay partly inspired by their encounters called *The Inner Reaches of Outer Space.*

✳

The day after Stanley Kubrick passed away, I was driving through the Presidio Park in San Francisco listening to a tribute program in his honor on National Public Radio. One of his recent biographers commented that one time he asked Kubrick about the possible meaning of the black monolith in *2001.*

"Well," Kubrick replied, "the stone is God, of course."

Later that day I read in his obituary a description of him as "the foremost man of mystery in modern cinema.... The myth of Stanley Kubrick is now intact, unlikely to be broken." In another eulogy, an excerpt from an interview with *Playboy* magazine helped explain the effusion of the first. It said in part that Kubrick had attempted to "create a visual experience, one that bypasses verbalized pigeon-holing and directly penetrates the subconscious with an emotional and philosophic content...just as music does.... You're free to speculate as you wish about the philosophical and allegorical meaning." In *The New Yorker* magazine Kubrick was quoted as going even further: "On the deepest psychological level, the film's plot summary is about the search for God, and it finally postulates what is little less than a scientific definition of God."

For some this reimagination of an ancient vision was a modern epiphany; for others an antiseptic and sterile view of the past and future.

One man's myth is another man's menace.

❋

Nine years later, in 1977, another Campbell-inspired film, *Star Wars*, premiered and introduced another icon that continues to define the times. In the first movie George Lucas revealed his warp-speed notion of *mana*. "The Force," as his mystical Jedi Knights describe it, is the energy field that sustains life. It is never explained, only summoned in times of crisis, which is in keeping with other forms of spiritual power that can appear anywhere—in dreams, one's inner voice, the Holy Spirit, or the inspired sculpture of sacred stones.

❋

Eight thousand miles from "this tiny mote of land lost in the endless empty seas of the southeast Pacific," and seventy years ago, Robert Frost wrote,

> We sit in a circle and suppose,
> While the secret sits in the middle
> And knows.

Long ago the ancestors of Rapa Nui sat in circles around their secret-bearing statues and longed to tap the force locked inside these stones. Where there was once *mana,* there is now our own practice of mythic mimicry in churches, movie theaters, art museums, science exhibitions, any modern sacred sites that spark an infusion of soulful insight into our perplexing existence, which is why we speak of our heroes and heroines in those worlds as gods and goddesses.

I like to imagine that we travel to sites like this because they renew us. Our pilgrimages to old ruins, crowded museums, cold cathedrals, and now, for the cosmically inclined, into outer space, restore us in ways we can only barely comprehend. But in our attempt to understand the mythic power these places have on us we breathe life into our own souls. When we recite the first stories, we recreate the world and ourselves, which is our secret longing. Yet these journeys do even more than entertain and renew us. They mythologize our lives; they provide the chapters for the sagas of our lives.

✳

Later that night we attend another traditional dance performance, then walk back along the seashore to the hotel and retreat to our rooms to pack and catch a few hours sleep before our early flight. But I can't sleep, and I wander back outside and sit in a lounge chair for one last contemplation of the shadowy stone giant a few yards away from me.

Chris' question from dinner continues to taunt me. He came as a skeptic about the iconic power of this place, but he is leaving a believer, even if he can't quite put his finger on the source of the power here. Starlight pours down from the Milky Way and across the face of the *moai* in the hotel courtyard. For a few seconds its eye sockets seem to glow with life and in those fleeting moments I try to imagine why so much effort went into the creation of these ancestral statues. Inexorably, I am drawn back to the source of the strange mystery.

The Eyes Have It

In the darkness around the ancient one, I sit pondering the presence of the past. I can hear the crashing of the breakers that have rolled in for thousands of miles, and see the silhouette of a wild horse in the mist along the perimeter road. The air is pungent with salt and frangipani; I don't think I've ever smelled air so pure. Above me the Southern Cross rotates across the heavens. Below me the sea surges. Around me four volcanoes sleep. I'm held in thrall by all the shimmering elements. The night fills me with affection for all creation. I lean against the seemingly self-luminous statue, and the island hints at a thousand more secrets.

My mind goes back to a poem by Guillevic that I read amid the ruins of Carnac, France, many years before:

> From the midst of the menhirs
> It seems that the world
>
> Was born right here
> And here returns

In the silence between crashes of surf I hear something moving in the night. Is it the horse? A hawk? A fellow sleepless traveler? The spirit in the stone stretching for another thousand years?

Something tectonically deep within the island wants to cry out, but I cannot tell yet whether it is a cry of joy or anguish. It's as mournfully ambiguous as the truth behind Quasimodo's crying out to the gargoyles on the towers of Notre Dame, "O, why was I not made of *stone* like this?"

Dawn is approaching, but still I don't want to sleep. It's harder to ward off the temptation to think about returning home tomorrow and the life I left behind than it is to ward off the desire to sleep. Rumi's words keep returning to me like an exhortation toward alertness: "Stay here, quivering with each moment, like a drop of mercury."

We travel great distances at great expense to be in the presence of stone and glass and paint and ink that will raise our spirits out of the doldrums of our desperate everyday lives, feel the mystery, as the preachers used to sing, from out of the darkness for a few fugitive moments so that we might feel the presence of our own hearts pounding as if we were falling in love again for the first time.

A colorful retinue of Japanese pilgrims, priests, entertainers, commoners, and soldiers traverse the Nihonbashi Bridge, one of 53 stations on the 312-mile long Tokaido road between Edo and Kyoto.

I believe we travel to these primordial places, back to the origins, to the beginnings of great things, to "activate the *mana*," like the old Easter Islanders. We expend tremendous effort "to see with new eyes," as the statues did when the islanders "opened their eyes" by inserting the white coral and red scoria into their eye sockets—and do to this day, but only for certain rare ceremonies. The Rapa Nui apparently believed eyes to be the animating force behind the statues, a belief that must have arisen out of deep observation.

No mere coincidence, this. In our own tradition eyes are the proverbial windows of the soul; a glint from eye of one we love reveals one of the few sources we have for any sense of continuity. While the flesh changes the eyes alone seem unchanging from youth to old age. Yet knowing this, how often do we "put in our true eyes" compared with how often we walk with hollowed-out eyes, seeing nothing? Looked, but did not see, or saw, but did not learn? Didn't the sage say, in the *Panchatantra,* "Knowledge is the true organ of sight, not the eyes"?

I am no different. I dread the thought that the reason I travel so much is that scales form over my eyes at home and I have to leave again and again to learn see once more. In this way I am living out one of the myths of my times, that the road will save me, infuse my life with more meaning. Many times it has, but only when I meet it halfway, on a spiritually challenging journey.

That belief and model is of one of our most enduring myths, one of our most sacred stories, which is rooted in the hope that the world will change us if only we go far enough, long enough, feel the presence of mysteries that baffle the experts. If we can trust the transportive power of reverie activated in these sites, and our own deep urge to go back once in a while, so we might go forward. Our souls are revitalized with the images we find there. Which reminds me of a story.

In the sweltering jungles of Papua New Guinea during the early 1930s a British explorer by the name of James Taylor ambled down a dirt runway toward his airplane. An eerie sight awaited him. Tied with vines to the fuselage of Taylor's plane was one of the villagers from a mountain tribe he had been the first outsider to ever contact. The man said his good-byes to his family as Taylor approached, telling them that no matter what happened to him, he had to find out where the plane had come from. And so it is with us.

The Once and Future Riddle

What unfolds forever, but never moves? challenges the old English riddle.

The road, answers the sphinx of paradox.

Far above me and the hundreds of *aringa ora,* the "living faces" of the island, a satellite blinks its way across the night sky. Watching the red eye of the night sky, the birdman cult doesn't seem quite so far-fetched when seen in context of our own far-flung metal dreams, our own living myths of flight and escape and discovery. On the plane ride here from Santiago, Chile, I read in a magazine about hundreds of crazed calls to NASA in hopes of signing up for space shuttle flights to the moon. How will our descendents three centuries from now—the length of time between us and the rediscovery of Rapa Nui—think of our rocket-fueled attempts to take flight from "This Island Earth," as the old science fiction film called our orbiting planet? Will they think of us as primitive and superstitious, as so many people still regard the Polynesians? Or will they give us the benefit of a doubt that our own stumbling exploration is but an expression of our irrepressible urge to surpass ourselves?

The Wings of Myth

At the Wright Brothers Museum in Kitty Hawk, North Carolina, there is a small photograph of the first airplane flight across the sand dunes at 10:30 in the morning of December 17, 1903. *American Heritage* magazine recently called it one of the few photographs that have captured "the thunderclap of an event that changed everything."

The iconic image shows the dark-suited Orville splayed out on his stomach clutching the controls of the rickety aircraft. Wilbur runs beside the plane, his fingertips inches away from the wing, ready to balance it should the plane falter.

A mere forty-foot run then—flight—twelve seconds in the air—a hundred and twenty feet—the long marvel of airborne flight come true, across what Wilbur later called "The Infinite Highway of the Air."

So many visitors have rubbed the laminated surface of the museum's photograph, as if they were medieval pilgrims touching a sacred relic, that it has to be replaced every few years by the curators. Perhaps the visitors are startled that an image exists at all. Maybe they hope that the magic will rub off on them. Whatever the motivation, the gesture

One of the truly mythic images of the twentieth century is the photograph
that captured the moment of origin of human-powered flight. On December
17, 1903, on the dunes of Kitty Hawk, North Carolina, Orville Wright took
flight while his brother Wilbur steadied its gossamer wing, and a friend
snapped the shutter of their glass plate camera.

reminds us of how deeply the hard facts of history may touch us, and
how touching it is when history turns and deepens into myth and
legend.

⊛

At the Smithsonian Museum of Space and Technology in Washington,
D.C., there is an unusual display a few yards inside the entrance. The
exhibit is constructed of glossy steel columns, reminiscent of an
ancient shrine. Above it hangs the Wright Brothers' plane, suspended
by steel wires. Next to it is John Glenn's heat-scarred space capsule.
Inside the high-tech shrine a new kind of relic is lying across a steel
plate. It is wedge-shaped, no more than a few inches long. It practically
begs to be touched, rubbed, which is exactly what everyone does when
they realize they are staring at an actual moonrock.

When I was there in early 1999 I watched a little girl in braids and green jump suit look at her parents for approval to touch NASA's postmodern relic. They nodded and she tentatively reached in and stroked the stone as if she were touching the soft fur of an animal, then she sighed and danced away, hand in hand with her parents.

After she strode away, I sidled up to the rock and rubbed my own fingers on it. As I did, a sudden image flashed in my mind of the famous photograph of Earthrise followed by a recollection in his book, *The Way of the Explorer,* about astronaut Edgar Mitchell's epiphany on Apollo 14 following his descent to the lunar surface in the coincidentally named *Kittyhawk* lunar lander. Mitchell described something I find classic understatement, that following a "job well done" on the moon he was left with only a minor assignment of monitoring the spacecraft systems, which left him "time to quietly contemplate the journey." He used the precious few moments to ponder their slow movement across the heavens through the module window, and in that serene state of mind he felt tranquility, a sense of wonder, and "tuned in to something much larger than myself." It was this rare chance for "contemplation and the process of resurrecting memories," he wrote, that led to the startling realization that the true state of the universe looming before him through the porthole was like nothing he had been taught. "There was an upwelling of fresh insight coupled with a feeling of ubiquitous harmony—a sense of interconnectedness with the celestial bodies surrounding our spacecraft." It was altogether, he described his experience as "an ecstasy of unity," but an essentially ineffable experience, one with mythic implications for all of us.

Later, he concluded, it is our destiny to explore the universe.

✳

Is it any wonder that Plato said, "He who understands has wings"?

In many cultures the mythic image for the soul is a bird in flight. This makes perfect sense when we think of the thrill the world felt watching the flights of Charles Lindbergh, Amelia Earhart, or John Glenn, but also when in the presence of skyward-spiraling stone, such as the sculpture of Brancusi, or even the flights of cartoon characters like Superman who continue to satisfy our secret longings to rise above ourselves and journey to sacred places that just might restore our faith, revive our energies, renew our souls. This is why after many millennia we too are held in thrall by mysteries that sweep us away on the wings of imagination to places and times of the public dream that is our mythic heritage.

As if on one of the thousand-mile-long swells that wash up on these rocky shores, mythology is the *movement* of stories and images across time and space, carrying souls like us along with it, like the long canoes of Polynesia searching for new worlds.

We live in the hush of time it takes to move in between those stories. Every age, to paraphrase the archaeologist, gets the Easter Island it desires and deserves.

The riddle of renewal endures.

FIVE

The Myth of the City

*From the Walls of Jerusalem
to the Cafés of Paris*

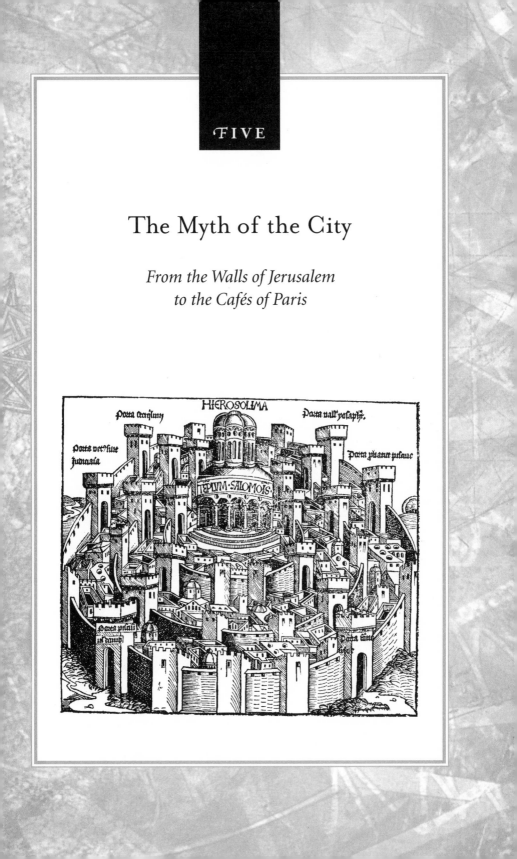

I dream'd in a dream I saw a city invincible to the
attacks of the whole of the rest of the earth,
I dream'd that was the new city of Friends.

—WALT WHITMAN, *Leaves of Grass*

One Sunday morning in the early 1990s a Paris radio program reported that the French philosopher Marc Sautet was meeting with colleagues at the Café des Phares in the Bastille *quartier* to discuss the recent phenomenon of "therapy with philosophers" that was springing up in nearby Holland and Germany.

"The Sunday after the radio program," Sautet later recalled to the *International Herald-Tribune*, "ten people showed up, asking, 'Is this where the philosophers meet?' It was a big surprise for us, very strange. We talked about death. The following Sunday there were ten more people. We talked about art. As the group got bigger and bigger, we needed a moderator. I agreed to do it and I kept going because it gave me pleasure and I was also very touched by the hunger to talk."

Steadily, the word spread around Paris about Sautet's effort to take philosophy out of the jealous grip of academics and bring it back to ordinary people. Suddenly, it seemed possible and desirable again to partake in the ancient art of exploring the world of ideas, especially in the louche atmosphere of a bohemian café.

"A New Passion for Philosophy," announced the daily newspaper *Liberation;* "Philosophy Everywhere?" asked the book review section of *Le Monde,* where the philosopher Roger-Pol Droit wrote, "Attention is turned toward the ancients, seekers of wisdom, rather than toward the moderns, builders of systems." The owner of the café told Jacqueline Swartz of the Toronto *Globe and Mail,* "I want to recreate the ambience of the old Deux Magots, where there were cultural encounters and people like Sartre were regulars."

Anne Marie Leblanc, from one of the ringside seats at the Café des Phares in 1996, told the *New York Times,* "It helps me to pause, and I find the promise of wisdom very exciting. Most of all it's the pleasure of being together, and while being together, question ourselves."

Marie, a young Parisian friend of mine who worked at one of the multimedia companies in the Bastille *quartier* told me recently, "You know, I get so tired talking business, business, business. At the 'café-philo' I can, how do you say, think out loud about things that used to matter to me when I was a student. This is why I came to Paris from my home in Clermont-Ferrand. I wanted to sit in cafés like Sartre and de Beauvoir and just *philosophize* about ideas that make my heart move." She pronounced the noble verb like the name of a long-lost lover.

At a typical gathering the *animateur* (not "amateur" but "ani-mater") steers the careening discussion for the crowd of people who have gathered over *café crèmes* and Gitanes cigarettes to explore questions such as: "What is the right way to act in order to do good?" "What is passion?" "Do I have a body, or am I a body?" "What is our fate after death?" "Is there a beginning to the universe?" "Religion: transcendence or obscurantism?" "Why is there something—rather than nothing?"

To paraphrase the French philosopher Pascal, the philosopher cafés caught on for reasons that reason does not know. By the end of the 1990s there were more than twenty of them around Paris, plus two hundred more around France, and many others scattered like so many coffee grounds around Belgium, England, Greece, Argentina, Uruguay, Switzerland, Japan, Canada, and the United States. Their discussions have been reported in books and magazine articles all over the world. Some have charged it is nothing more than the latest version of French navel-gazing. Others have claimed that the search for meaningful conversation and community is the logical result of an essential nihilism at the heart of existentialism that duped a gullible public into believing that we are ultimately alone in the universe.

"Popularity of debates called sign of widespread angst," bruited a headline in the *San Francisco Chronicle* in 1997. The article reported that "many French people are reverting to philosophy to assuage their anxieties." A Sorbonne philosophy professor, André Comte-Sponville, told the *Chronicle*, "If people are turning to philosophy today, it's because of the decline of ready-made answers given by politics or religion." The phenomenon of the revival of interest in philosophy itself, according to the *Economist* in early 1997, reflects a "recurrent feeling that the world is in a mess, that Western civilization may be on the verge of dramatic change, that one should reflect on man's place in the universe."

Sautet so strongly disagrees with the trend of many philosophers to dismiss the nettlesome questions about the meaning of life that he initiated the first private philosophy practice in France. In *Un Café Pour Socrates*, his book about philosophy-therapy, he recounts the emblematic story of his first client, a middle-aged businessman who was suffering from terminal ennui and was threatening suicide, but changed his mind after reading and debating the ideas of Socrates with Sautet. The relevance of Socrates' work, in Sautet's view, is that he reveals the classical ideal of someone who "cares about his or her own soul and also about the body politic."

Apparently, this is relevant enough for the waiters at the Café des Phares who advertise Sautet's book on the back of their shirts, but not relevant enough for traditional psychotherapists, many of whom dismiss his "philosophy-therapy" as a substitute for their work. Sautet demurs, saying that they have things backward. People seek him, he says, because of their anxiety about diminishing community life.

"Accordingly," wrote Jacqueline Swartz in the Toronto *Globe and Mail* in 1997, "the new popular philosophy is big on the notion of the 'city' as intellectual and moral community, the only antidote to the injustice, narcissism, and 'Internalization' of society.'"

The Japanese painter Foujita greets a few bohemian friends at an artist's café in Paris in the late 1920s.

So much for the much-vaunted death of French intellectual exchange and the dread of dwindling café life due to—*quelle horreur!*—the invasion of television and fast food restaurants. So much for the stereotype that the French are too proud ever to change their mind in a discussion.

"You will never hear a guest say, all right you have convinced me," Michel Polac, the "provocateur" host of the television show *Droit de Reponse ("The Right to Reply")* told Mary Blume of the *International Herald-Tribune.* The droll implication is that the French love to talk but not necessarily listen.

If so, what are we to make of the iconic café images in Atget's photographs of old friends in intimate conversation over Gitanes and espresso, Degas' paintings of dancers drinking with prostitutes and politicians in lonely bistros, or Edith Piaf's and Serge Gainsboroughs' ballads of tortured lovers mourning lost love? Are they simply reflecting *fumisteri,* smoke-in-the-head self-indulgence—or is there a connection between coffee, conversation, and civilization?

That delicious old proverb, "Squeeze a church, you get wine," could have been updated with the opening of the first coffeehouses in Paris near the end of the seventeenth century to, "Squeeze a café, you get coffee—and conversation."

From the beginning, the two went hand in hand, or at least cup in hand. The famous Le Procope, founded in 1686, on the Rue de l'Ancienne Comedie, became the favorite haunt of Napolean, Danton, Rousseau, Georges Sand. The café and its habitues helped launch the coffee craze that became all the rage, and then more. Within the hothouse of Paris intellectual life, coffee itself became mythologized as the ambrosial drink for thinkers and philosophers. Coffee was what you drank to think more clearly, rationally, and soberly, especially if you wished to hold your own in rigorous public debates. As Arab drummers drummed to *mihbaj,* the rhythm of coffee grinding, so too did French intellectuals talk and think to the rhythm of café life. Soon the prodigious outpouring of work by writers such as Balzac and Voltaire was attributed as much to their legendary coffee consumption—up to fifty cups a day—as much as to their genius.

However, not all were instantly converted. As the coffee madness spread, devout Catholics pronounced coffee to be the drink of infidels and the sinful. Eventually, Pope Clement asked for a cup before he declared the Church's position but must have gotten quite a caffeine buzz, because he decided to publicly *baptize* the brew and thereby lend it official Christian status.

By the eighteenth century, coffee became *the* drink for the aristocrats and the rising bourgeoisie, upstaging wine and beer, in the belief that it stimulated clear thinking and hard work. Thus the drink that aided the rise of bohemianism was transformed into the drink that accelerated the rise of capitalism.

The confluence between coffee, cafés, and capacious conversation helped create the myth of Paris as the most intellectual and cultured city in the world. As is often the case, the origins of the word *conversation* itself uncover the roots of its mythical significance. Its Latin root is *conversus,* meaning to "turn around," as in the act of walking with a good friend, perhaps through a bosky wood, around the garden, or down to a favorite café, before returning home. Conversing is what friends do when they walk side by side. Not only does this essential human act solidify friendships, it also forges community.

"He that converses not, knows nothing," goes the old proverb. "Sweet discourse makes short days and nights," says another. "In many words, the truth goes by," advises a third. "Think with the wise, but talk with the vulgar [common people]," recommends a fourth. The Lithuanians say, "Strange smoke initiates the eyes," an oblique reference to the wispy atmosphere of old cafés and taverns rasping with revolutionary talk. "While all was doing," writes Ovid in his splendid retelling of the Greek myth of Baucis and Philemon, "they beguiled the time with conversation." To enjoy one good conversation, the American philosopher Ralph Waldo Emerson once remarked he would walk a hundred miles through a snowstorm.

Conversation, friendship, ideas, passion, and philosophy are notions one doesn't often associate with modern urban life. But in certain communities, the forces of design and culture invite its denizens to contemplate the things that matter most in life. In Paris, contemplation is a public pursuit, and architects are encouraged to plan for it. In 1998 an architectural board was formed to create more *lieu de contemplation* in the city, more public places that consider the needs of the soul.

The exhilarating exchanges in the philosopher cafés are a paradox. The city of Paris epitomizes the sound of passionate conversation—enveloped by the silence of urban loneliness. It is at once the most fraternal and most solitudinous of places. While being as real as stone and steel, Paris is also a metaphor for the kind of city that reconciles these apparent opposites, a sensuous symbol for the connection between private passion and public idealism.

As all things mythic are metaphorical, the city, since Hammurabai's Babylon and Solomon's Jerusalem, looms large in the imagination as the place where the gap between the dream of community and the reality of isolation may be bridged. This has long been one of the great tasks of urban life, as attested to by the Roman adage, *Magna civitas, magna solitudo*" ("A great city, a great loneliness").

The greatest of cities have been places that have embraced a mythic vision, a way of living that allows and encourages both community and privacy. But it is exceedingly difficult to see just how this happens, because the real beauty often eludes the eye. The French war hero and author Antoine Saint-Exupéry echoed this idea in his masterpiece, *Le Petit Prince*, where he wrote, "What is essential to the human heart is invisible not visible." So too Italo Calvino, in his surrealistic novel, *Invisible City:* "Cities also believe they are the work of the mind or of chance, but neither the one nor the other suffices to hold up their walls. You take delight not in a city's seven or seventy wonders, but in the answer it gives to a question of yours."

To discover the source of this plangent power is a mythic quest, one that reveals the inner meaning, the poetic truth, what the ancients used to call the soul of the city. To discover what the soul is, we must seek the origins, the center, the *story.*

The Paris of the Midwest

In these questions, discussions, and debates at the philosopher cafés, I hear echoes of what the philosophers of old called "the long conversation." The very phrase suggests to me a pulsing chain of ideas across the centuries that is revived every time we ask what my tough Jesuit philosophy professor in college called the "Irrecusables," the fundamental questions of life that shouldn't be rejected for lack of time in your schedule or frustration with the opacity of so much postmodern thinking.

My own twenty-five-year love affair with Paris has been a constant challenge. Over the course of more than a dozen visits, life there for me has been an alternating search for culture and solitude, community and anonymity. The mythic brew turns out to be just what my soul needs.

In *The Timeless Myths*, scholar Alexander Eliot reminds us, "Myths keep spinning back into the mainstream of time, into history and personal experience...thanks to religious ritual, folktale, fairytale, literature, painting, sculpture, architecture, music, dance...and sacred legend. But the power of myth also appears to us in the sky, at sacred sites, and special landscapes." While many of our deepest beliefs can be illuminated by a look at myths of the natural world, much of our modern behavior can be amplified by contemplation of the myths we tell about the great cities of history.

I have been driven to understand city life since leaving my hometown of Detroit in my early twenties. When I left home I was embittered by memories of deadly riots, muggings, homicides, factory life, university days behind barbed wire, omnipresent fear, and the corrosive cynicism of most people I encountered around town. For years I wandered, from London to Jerusalem, Paris to Lisbon, Dublin to Manila, before finally settling in San Francisco, in hopes of finding a city that was as alive to me as Detroit was dead.

Senator Bill Bradley has written in *The Vision Thing,* "Myths help to explain why things are the way they are by placing them in a context of the way they've always been." In this sense I have discovered that the myths of the modern cities that I've visited and lived in can best be explained by considering them in the context of ancient myths of the "noble cities," "cities of destiny," the hieratic city states, even Utopia, Paradise, and the Promised Land. These mythic images are tenacious in the way they influence our decisions about our travel destinations, as well as form—or limit—our ideals for where we might spend our lives. Uncannily, these images also parallel, in ways that continue to astound me, the search for the mythical lost continent of the place we once called home.

The French philosopher Voltaire once defined history as *une fable convenue,* an agreed-upon fable. To read the history of American cities, or even to glance at their Chamber of Commerce pamphlets, is to realize that the mythic imagination is working as hard on outer space, the places where we actually live, as it does on inner space, the places where we dream.

The America I grew up in has its own twentieth-century myths about cities. The recent Ric Burns PBS documentary series about New York City reveals a world already enshrined in mythic memory, by way of being rhapsodized by Walt Whitman, scored by Duke Ellington, novelized by E. L. Doctorow, and filmed by Woody Allen and Martin Scorcese. Meanwhile, Chicago is not only a crossroad of commerce and skyscrapers but the city of demonic gangsters, godlike ballplayers, and all-powerful politicians. New Orleans is more than a port town; it is the birthplace of the blues and the new Rome, the center of the modern Saturnalia, Mardi Gras, and now a pilgrimage destination for fans of Anne Rice's vampire lore. More than the grim surface of endless concrete highways and a thousand suburbs in search of a city, Los Angeles has churned out its myth of the city of angels where the touch of a celestial being's wing might turn you into a star. San Francisco is the phoenix of cities, rising repeatedly from the ashes, but originally spawned from a motley mix of rapscallions, fortune seekers, railroad tycoons, gamblers, and prostitutes. J. B. Holliday recounts the old ditty, "The miners came in '49 / The whores in '51 / And when they got together / They produced the native son." The tale of the Gold Rush is a splendid example of the once and future myth at work, as evident in the "rush for riches" in Silicon Valley today.

Finally, one of the more unlikely examples of mythic cities is Detroit. While I was growing up in Wayne, twenty miles away but within its undeniable gravitational force, cynicism and fear about the benighted city itself ran corrosive and deep. But my father was fiercely proud of its history and made sure his kids were aware of it. By dint of voracious reading he trained himself to be an amateur folklorist of Detroit history, World's Fairs, and his own employer, the Ford Motor Company. The Stanley H. Cousineau Collection at the Henry Ford Museum in Dearborn is testimony to his tenacious mythologizing of our little corner of the globe.

So besides homeschooling us in the classics, my father taught us about the local Indians, Chippewas and Hurons, who had lived along the river before the French arrived; lectured us about Antoine Laumet de la Mothe Cadillac, the French adventurer who planted the seed of a dream of a great city along the river; and tried in vain to convince us that his hero, Henry Ford, was, as he put it, "the modern Daedalus," the American da Vinci. My father regarded Ford as a boy genius, a divinely inspired inventor, the man who single-handedly

The Ford Rotunda, constructed as a pavilion for the 1934–1935 Chicago World's Fair, then reassembled in Dearborn, Michigan, for use as an International Visitor's Center. It burned in 1962.

invented the horseless carriage and that harbinger of the future, the assembly line.

More pertinent to our family mythology was the curiously touching way in which my father convinced himself that he was destined to spend his life working in public relations at Ford's because it was Ford himself who brought my grandfather to Detroit from Canada.

One day, the story goes, in 1923, a Model T arrived in Sudbury, Ontario, the nearest town to the family farm. The driver handed out leaflets to the burly young men of the town, one of whom happened to be my Grandfather Horace. The flyers advertised the now-famous five-dollar day "on the line" at the River Rouge Plant down in Detroit. That was twice what my grandfather was earning as a farmhand, and it was just a train ride away.

Thus I grew up with the chorus of voices proclaiming a proud heritage for the very city the rest of the world was mercilessly maligning.

But my father had no truck with the nay-sayers, so to speak, and wouldn't allow us the slightest bit of criticism about Detroit. To his dying day he refused to accept my own angry charges that it was "The Big Three" in Detroit who conspired to destroy the trolley companies across the country, leaving us at the mercy of cars and freeways. To him, the city was synonymous with cars, which in turn were stream-lined symbols of freedom, glamour, and efficiency. To him, the mighty factories were as historically important as European cathedrals and castles. In fact, my father sometimes reminded me of a medieval raconteur regaling his family with legends of a noble world. His task was to reveal the heart and soul of this world to me, as he knew it, in the wonderful local museums, theaters, parks, and the last remnants of its Indian and French history.

In this way he slowly mythologized my world. His affection for Detroit was as genuine and unswerving as any Frenchman's for Paris, which is perhaps why he never made it there. Perhaps he thought it would have been redundant, knowing as he did that Detroit was known as the "Paris of the Midwest" during the 1930s, or maybe it would have been too painful for him to admit the world of difference between the two cities. I often asked him; he always changed the subject.

Still, his influence must have gotten to me, as reflected my devotion to the local sports teams, my passion for Motown music, my allegiance to Mustangs, Falcons, and Thunderbirds, and the way that the city, to this day, haunts my dreams.

Slowly but surely the city seeped into my soul.

The Demythologizing of our Cities

While my father mythologized Detroit, our actual hometown of Wayne was being demythologized.

In the mid-'60s, when I was in junior high school, the city fathers ripped out the heart of the Civil War-era town "in the name of progress." I've been suspicious of the phrase ever since I first heard it uttered by the mayor when he was trying to sway the opinion of the editor of the *Wayne Dispatch,* the town paper where I worked while in high school. The mayor would have been more precise if he had said, "the myth of progress."

The potency of this myth is in its steamrolling message that all change is inevitable and good, and just trust those that promise it. In our case, the venerable Hudson's department store (of Thanksgiving Day Parade fame), twenty miles down Michigan Avenue in Detroit, had promised to build its long-awaited second store in our suburb if there was enough space in the center of town. Seduced by the myth, the bulldozers came in and the bricks came down.

Lured by the prospects of fame and money, Wayne turned its back on the beauty of its humble pre–Civil War beginnings. In fact, it was founded in 1824, and local legend has it that the town was one of the stops for the "underground railroad" on the old Indian trail between Chicago and Detroit. During the '50s, *Life* magazine named it as one of the 100 Best Small Towns in America. Then the wrecking ball pulverized our past. The soul of the town was detonated and down came Gladstone's Shoestore, Lazar's Clothing Store, Chum's Donuts, Workman's Feedstore, Leo's Jewelry Store. Graders broke up the brick streets and new streets were laid in hopes of a new town. It is as if my hometown was ashamed of its own roots, and longed for the imprimatur of big-city sophistication.

I witnessed the architectural mugging from the second story window of my junior high school class at Wayne St. Mary's. While the Sisters of the Immaculate Conception droned on about the fallacy of evolution and the genius of Saint Augustine, I watched dump trucks haul away the beautiful old red bricks and hand-painted store signs. Over the next several years, one fiasco after another prevented the vaunted urban renewal. Hudson's withdrew, as did other big chains. A minor mall was built that resembled a hastily built airplane hangar. Parking garages were built for customers who never came. Where once were soulful nineteenth-century streets and buildings now rose soulless ruins.

Thirty-five years later, the town center still resembles a punch-drunk boxer's face. There are vast tracts of empty, weedy land between a few sorry modern replacements, as if the town's front teeth are missing. The travesty of the mall squats where the center of town used to be; a bruise on the cheekbones of history. After all the urban renewal, it looks more dilapidated than the hundred-year-old buildings that came tumbling down in the interest of a myth gone bad.

❋

Those are the outer facts; the inner meaning of this ignominious topic is best revealed by the telling of a recurrent dream of war I had as a boy. I was in a battalion with my boyhood friends. We fought bravely in a place that looked like the bombed-out fields of France against a faceless but repugnant enemy who had ignited Armageddon. Exploding shells, mustard gas, corpses caught on barbed wire—nothing could hold us back if we fought together. These were exhilarating dreams because they always featured a chance for me to do something heroic, throw myself on a grenade, vault over the wire into No Man's Land, rescue kids from an orphanage, sacrifice myself for my girlfriend. What was disturbing about the sulfurous images of the dream is that they took place on the streets of Wayne, my own hometown. Invariably, they rekindled my sense of lost friendship, the feeling my war-hero uncles described to me as the bonding in the trenches that they had never been able to recover. I suspect this peculiar association of friendship and warfare and the desire to save my home has its roots in a calamitous decision made by the town when I was still a boy.

❋

Every few years I return to Wayne, and while driving down Michigan Avenue into the city limits, again and again I've been haunted by the image of a children's book—*The Phantom Tollbooth,* written in the early 1960s by Norman Just—that was one of my favorites while growing up. The wistful story has its young hero, Milo, driving a magical little car toward a city that keeps fading away. The author uncannily captures the sinking feeling of millions of Americans who are losing their heritage to the steamroller of progress. The anxiety of losing our past intensifies the desire to find it elsewhere.

All this is to say, No wonder I had such an unabashed sense of wonder when I encountered those mythic destinations I had scribbled on the back of my factory locker door—London, Barcelona, Rome, Venice, Athens, Cairo, Oslo, Stockholm, Munich, Brussels, Amsterdam, Jerusalem—as incentive to get away from home. No wonder I was magnetized by my father's passion for Detroit and by the myth that cities matter that was propagated in the books and movies I loved. Sure, I loved the great outdoors. I was a camping fool when I was young; I loved hiking in the woods and fishing in the Great Lakes. But my destiny, like my father's and my grandfather's, was in the city.

The Myth of the City

But how did it all begin? echoes Roberto Calasso again and again. To him, this is the question that drops us into the mysterious underworld of myth.

Ten thousand years ago, ancient people began to settle together for the simple reason that it was easier to feed themselves that way. The first examples of cities have been found amid the ruins of Ur and Babylon, sites encrusted with as much legend as history. The rediscovery of these sites whose names evoke romance and mystery heralded the rise of archaeology and gave them profound metaphorical power.

Since then the chronicles of urban life are divided between the real and the fantastic, as men and women have dreamed of golden cities, hidden cities, invisible cities, ruined enchantments such as Pompeii, mystical realms like Shambhala, and labyrinthine worlds like Jorge Borges' Tlön, where "they seek neither truth nor likelihood; they seek astonishment." Elaborate urban mythologies are devoted to Shiva's vision of Benares; Athena's patronage of Athens; the royal reverie that founded Shanghai; Boswell and Johnson's conjuring of a London built of ale, books, and gossip; the Joycean feverdream of turn-of-the-century Dublin.

"Famous cities have exhibited a persistence that transcends their geographical location," writes René Dubos in *A God Within*, "the quality of their climate, or their natural resources. Like the hallowed sites, they have remained true to their character despite changes in religions, economic, and political philosophies." These often ineffable qualities can be discerned while reading centuries-old descriptions of Paris, London, Venice, or Marrakesh, and realizing that the *genius loci,* the spirit of a place, defies time and challenges us to perceive them in a different way.

"Cities are not only the structures we see," writes Eduardo Ruach in an essay for *Parabola* magazine in 1992, "their present life, that which the senses offer us of their being. Cities are layered: archaeologically, in the memory of themselves and in our memories, and between the living and the dead. There is also an unconscious city within us."

In his 1938 classic *The Culture of Cities,* Lewis Mumford described cities as "energy converted into culture." "It is in the city," he wrote, "the city as theater, that man's purposive activities are formulated and worked out." And, unexpectedly, but reassuringly: "A city should be an organization of love." In a similar vein, Anne Sofer wrote in the *London Times* in 1984, "Throughout history, from the vision of battlemented white towers on a distant hill as in Renaissance painting, to the glitter and raucous vulgarity of New York's Broadway in the 1930s—'the city' has been an idea to quicken the pulse and lift the heart; it is a quality of excitement which London on a warm spring evening still abundantly has...."

Character, energy, heart, love, and one other vital ingredient. Toynbee emphasizes it when he writes, "What is essential is that the inhabitants of the city should be a genuine community in fact." T. S. Eliot literally brings home the point when he asks, in his long poem, "The Rock," what kind of life is it that we have in modern cities if it is "dispersed on ribbon roads" instead of spent together?

> When the Stranger says: "What is the meaning of this City?"
> Do you huddle close together because you love each other?
> What will you answer? "We all dwell together
> To make money from each other?" or "This is community"?

Leave it to a discerning poet to illuminate the difference between a profane city and a sacred one. Cities are of course crossroads of commerce, but if that is all they do the spirit of the place will dry up like a well gone bad. How can a sense of community prevent that, especially if we only think of it as a synonym for walled-up suburbs?

Architect Paolo Soleri believes, "The good city is a sacred locus. It is the *Civitas Dei*. It is that complex machine of information which by the non-expedient ways of design also becomes knowledge in itself.... The emotional impact that a landscape or cityscape has upon a person is a combination of the exhilaration of understanding and at the same time the anguish of realizing the massiveness of the unknown that such an environment makes tangible."

If the city can indeed be a sacred crossroad, then certain things are required of it by the hopes and aspirations of those who live there or seek refuge there. In an increasingly pluralistic world this means an ongoing debate about what it means to transform the misery of urban failure into successful city life.

"The mythic vision has been set into place," writes Thomas Berry in *The Great Work: Our Way into the Future.* "The distorted dream of an industrial technological paradise is being replaced by the more viable dream of a mutually enhancing human presence within an ever-renewing organic-based Earth community. The dream drives the action. In the larger cultural context the dream becomes the myth that guides the action."

The Collective Dream

During a 1999 film interview for the Knossus Project at the Open City, the experimental community in the rolling sand dunes outside of Valparaiso, Chile, the local architect Juan Purcell told me, "There are two kinds of cities, the old European cities that last long, like Rome, and the Aztec cities that lasted only one generation. So every generation had its own cities. It's another point of view. So America says something different than Europe about that special theme." However, the working methods of the Open City actually combine the cultural heritage of South America with the leaping imaginative techniques of French Surrealist poets and reverence for the mystical spirit of the sand dunes

Created out of an abandoned quarry by the mayor-architect Jaime Lerner of Curitiba, Brazil, this complex of a lagoon, outdoor theater, and architectural offices is an inspiring example of sustainable design.

themselves. As Purcell's mentor Godofredo Iommi has written, "Eros must be present in one's capacity to fall in love with the work." The planners of the Open City infuse eros into their community by grounding every design in the reading of poems, the writing of plays, and long conversations in their public "agoras" about what it means to live with "intimate grandeur." In this way, Juan Purcell told us, the creation of every building is a "poetic act" and the molding of a community is an adventure.

Purcell's poetic vision for urban life reminded me of Jaime Lerner, the charismatic architect-mayor of Curitiba, Brazil, the most environmentally and socially conscious city in South America. When we interviewed Lerner in his office in 1993 for our film, *Ecological Design: Inventing the Future,* he harkened back to the notion of collective thinking in order to revive communities the world over.

> Cities, like a monument, should represent this shared cause. It's the only way that we can achieve a collective dream. There is no challenge more noble than to achieve a collective dream. When a city can improve its quality of life, when it respects the people that live in that city, when it respects the environment, when it prepares for the next generations, the people assume that kind of co-responsibility, and this is a shared cause—it's the only way to achieve that collective dream. How beautiful it is to achieve that collective dream of a city.

✸

The loamy roots of the word *community* lead us back to the philosopher café, the lost art of conversation. It derives from *commune,* which means "to converse intimately, exchange thoughts and feelings." The way the Spanish surrealist filmmaker Luis Buñuel described this in his book *The Last Sigh:* how he sought out his fellow countryman, the poet Unamuno, at the La Rotunde café in Montparnasse and "sometimes I'd walk Unamuno back to his apartment near the Étoile, a distance that gave us a good two hours of conversation." That desire is at the core of mystery of the city, not just the temporary loss of isolation, but the permanence of some new thing discovered, noted, delighted in.

When Eliot's stranger asks what is the meaning of this or that city, do we respond, "To move money from bank to bank, wallet to wallet?"

or "This is the place where I live with family and friends and have conversations about things that move my soul. Conversations I cannot live without."

I believe that this is what the noble cities throughout history have in common. They are places that are loved because of their intimacy, their continuity, their beauty. They ask us how can we possibly settle for the banal myth of consumerism when we are beckoned, as if by Aphrodite herself, by the soulful myth of beauty?

But the beauty of a city is not to be measured only in the way its buildings are designed. Aphrodite is also an elusive and fickle goddess, one who is difficult to pin down. She appears in the way ideas and feelings and images can move between real people. Cities are mythologized when they transcend the perfunctory demands of the day and stand for something larger by encouraging timeless pursuits, something sacred. The archetypal psychologist James Hillman writes in his book, *City and Soul,*

> Without images, we tend to lose the way.... The soul wants its images, and when it doesn't find them, it makes substitutes: billboards and graffiti, for instance.... How we see into each other, look at each others' faces, read each other—that is how soul contact takes place.... We also need body places. Places where bodies see each other, meet each other, are in touch with each other, like the people who leave their offices in Paris and swim in the Seine River.... This emphasizes the relationship of body to the daily life of the city, bringing one's physical body into the town. In other words, I am emphasizing the place of intimacy within a city, for intimacy is crucial to the soul.... A city that neglects the soul's welfare makes the soul search for its welfare in a degrading and concrete way, in the shadow of those same gleaming towers.... The soul that is uncared for turns into an angry child.

Marketplaces are often considered the soul of a city. This etching of the old market and arcade of Saint Peter's Port, Guernsey, in the Channel Islands, illustrates why in its depiction of people shopping, trading, and sharing stories, the stuff of everyday life.

The Symbolic Center

The mythic city is a soulful city. Its qualities are intimate, timeless, connective, in depth, and original, meaning both that vital things began there and that it is unique. A city is mythic when it symbolizes the sacred center of the world. Joseph Campbell wrote in *The Flight of the Wild Gander* that mythologically based cities mirror the divine order and become places where "art and custom shape the soul: art [is] lived—as ritual." The holy cities of the ancient world—such as Angkor, Babylon, Konya, Mecca, Benares, Peking, Chichen Itza, and Jerusalem—were associated with gods, heroes, prophets, divine kings, holy temples, or the dream of heaven on earth. They were cities not just of subsistence but of revelation. But often where visions are brightest, the longest shadows are cast.

Of all the cities in all the world, the most mythic is the city of Jerusalem. In the Land of the Book, Jerusalem is to cities what myths are to history: volatile and incomprehensible, mysterious and indispensable, revealers of our sacred origins.

My first encounter with the collision of competing myths occurred there. World atlases regard the great city as three thousand years old. Historians estimate that it has been conquered eleven times, and razed five others. Religious scholars regard it as containing more shrines than any other site on Earth. The "Holiest of Holy Cities" is the home of three mighty religions, Judaism, Islam, and Christianity, and all three have struggled to the death for the right to live and worship there, because each believes that access to heaven is easier there than on any other place on Earth. Jerusalem is the consummate example of the old adage among mythologists that when a myth is taken literally rather than symbolically or metaphorically there is only one way to prove it if it's disputed—violently.

It was 1975. I was twenty-three and working as a volunteer on the Ashdot Ya'Akov kibbutz, two miles south of the Sea of Galilee. I had ventured there after a year on the road where I heard innumerable recommendations from fellow travelers that a few months on an Israeli kibbutz was an adventurous way to learn a culture from the inside and get a glimpse at a fascinating utopian experiment. I worked in the date groves and harvested bananas, six grueling days a week under the hot sun with an eighty-year-old broad-backed kibbutznik by the name of Shimon. He was one of the founding members of the kibbutz. Back in 1909 he had planted the very trees we were now climbing, trimming, and harvesting. He treated them like his own flesh and blood. My conversations with him as we worked in the groves were worth the scorpion bites, the pre-dawn risings, and the fear of attack from terrorists just across the Jordan River. From him I got my first real humbling in history. One day I was high up in a date tree arguing with Mikkel, a regular guy from Brooklyn who came to Ashdot for two months every summer, about the virtues of American communes, Chinese collectives, and the Jewish kibbutz. Just as it was getting combative, Shimon ordered us down out of the tree, threw his gloves and his machete down on the ground, pulled up the powder blue sleeve of his work shirt and showed us a serial number tattooed on his wrist.

He could have easily and righteously said, "Neither one of you know what you are talking about." I wouldn't have blamed him. Instead, he simply, softly, said, "During the war I went back to Germany to help my family but we were all sent to Auschwitz. I lost seventy-one out of seventy-two members of my family. After the GIs liberated us I came back here to start life over. To begin again. To start a new family. Together with my own people. There is no other way now."

Shimon picked up his machete and donned his gloves. His skin was sunburned, his face was scarred from being tortured by the British Army for hiding guns during the 1948 war for independence.

"I don't know if what we are doing on this land is right," he said, "but it is all that some of us have left. But we must be careful not to do to others what has been done to us."

Silently, we went back to work. I noticed for the first time that Shimon said a small prayer each time he climbed one of the sixty-foot date trees and how he always took a moment to appreciate the miraculous beauty of his vast groves.

After several weeks had elapsed, a fellow volunteer from Pittsburgh named Marianne invited me to accompany her to Jerusalem for the weekend. The moment I saw the glorious walls of the Old City I was instantly transported back in time. Passing through the Mandelbaum gate we entered the dusty bazaar teeming with rug sellers, fruit vendors, spice merchants, camel and donkey drivers, butchers and cobblers, purveyors of silk, and fleecers of pilgrims. We treaded the maze of shops, visited the Church of the Holy Sepulchre where I filled an empty film canister with holy water for my mother, and walked around the Dome of the Rock, where we listened to the thrilling sound of the muezzin's call to prayer cascade over the city. Once, we passed an American hauling a cross down the Via Dolorosa, the mythic Road of Sorrow, blood streaking his naked back, reenacting Christ's last walk. Twice we were stopped by Israeli soldiers with Uzi machine guns who searched our bags and asked us if we had had any untoward conversations with strangers. Recalling only too vividly that our kibbutz had been shelled recently, we complied, wordlessly.

At the Western Wall, we watched hundreds of devout believers tuck prayers written on simple sheets of paper into the open cracks of Solomon's Temple wall. As Marianne explained to me, the Temple is the most sacred site in the world to Jews because it is believed to be the place where earthly and heavenly forces meet. She said that the Temple wasn't only beautiful but powerful due to its sacred geometry, its proportions being laid out like a musical composition, which were meant to reflect the original harmonies of creation. Every portion of the Temple was designed to symbolize an aspect of heaven or earth, all of which were echoed later in St. John's Revelations in the New Jerusalem. Listening to her, I recalled William Blake's tantalizing lines, which I had learned by heart as a child:

I give you the end of a golden string,

Only wind it into a ball,

It will lead you in at Heaven's gate

Built in Jerusalem's wall.

The great mystic poet's vision of a golden string is a marvelous mythic image for the strong pull that has tugged on the hearts and souls of Jews, Muslims, and Christians for centuries. Blake's image of heaven's gate is also a common theme to sacred sites everywhere, referring not to a theory but an experience of spiritual transport by hundreds of generations of worshipers.

Near twilight, as we made our way back through the bazaar, an elegant man sitting on a stool before his clothing and carpet stall invited us inside to look at his wares. We were taken by Ahmet's kindness and accepted his offer of a simple cup of tea, knowing full well the timeless choreography of bargaining. After an hour of graceful displays of his work, we bought a few shirts and bags between us. Then, to our utter surprise, Ahmet invited us to his home for dinner. Marianne quickly accepted, whispering that it was an extraordinary opportunity to experience the "other Jerusalem."

Upon our arrival at his simple two-storied home on the outskirts of the Old City he ordered his wife to prepare a feast for us. We sat down at the family dinner table and were soon surrounded by curious neighbors and relatives, who stared unblinkingly at us. Through the open window I could see swaying palm trees and a single, noble cypress tree in the courtyard, and the faces of neighborhood children. Minutes later, I was startled to hear the *thud* of an axe as a sheep was summarily slaughtered, for our benefit and honor, we were told.

"Welcome." Ahmet toasted us with a glass of Turkish coffee. "I am proud to have you in my home." For the rest of the afternoon Ahmet quizzed us about our views on the Yom Kippur War, which had taken place only three years before, the plight of the Palestinians in the refugee camps in nearby Jericho, the plague of tourist groups in the Old City. In turn, he described his life for us in the city of his birth, one that often made him feel as if he were only half a citizen. He feared he was a father giving his children a painfully uncertain future. But he would live nowhere else.

Finally, Ahmet's wife and daughter brought in our dinner, roasted sheep on a platter of rice and date palm leaves. They set it before me, the honored male guest, with the two eyes of the lamb staring at me from atop the heap of rice. The room was quiet as I stared right back at the glassy eyes, and everyone else's eyes focused on mine. I vaguely heard Ahmet explain that sheep's eyes were a delicacy, and would I honor him by sharing one with him?

For the sake of literature, I said to myself, or something to that rushed effect, and plopped one into my mouth, and immediately felt the need to gag. Before I could I reach for my glass of juice, Marianne had handed it to me and I quickly washed it down, then passed the platter down to my host, who smiled and followed suit.

After dinner, out in his courtyard, he took me aside and said something I'll never forget: "This is the glory and the hope of Jerusalem, the only city in the world where a Christian man and a Jewish woman can come together in peace into an Arab home. If only the politicians could see this. All my life, it is my dream that Christian, Jew, and Arab live in peace. Only the politicians separate us. Only ordinary people can make peace, like this, like this."

To this day I recall listening intently to our new friend and thinking of the mythical story of the Tower of Babel, from Genesis 11:1–9:

> And the whole earth was of one language and of one speech. And it came to pass, as they journeyed from the east, that they found a plain in the land of Shinar and they dwelt there. And they said to one another ... Go to, let us build us a city and a tower, whose top may reach unto heaven; and let us make us a name, lest we be scattered abroad upon the face of the whole earth. And the Lord came down to see the city and the tower, which the men builded ... and scattered them abroad from thence upon the face of all the earth: and left to build the city. Therefore is the name called Babel; because the Lord did confound the language of all the earth.

At one time, throughout the world, the story tells us, human beings first lived together in cities and shared the same language. They understood one another. But it was not to last. The dream of paradise is inseparable from the dream of common language. The Tower is no mere building project; it is an act that separates men from each other, an attempt to be godlike, and is punished the way acts of hubris always have been. This early version of the "technology run amok myth" tells us that God destroyed the tower and dispersed the people by casting a spell of confusion over the city. Suddenly they could not understand one another. The story says that the price we pay for trying to be gods is exile from the paradise of understanding one another.

But myths are always lapidary, containing layers of hidden meaning. This tale also tells in the vivid picture language of myth (think of Breughel's magnificent painting of the Tower) that the sudden "babel" is also the creation myth to explain how and why different languages came into being.

The biblical legend of the Tower of Babel is commonly regarded as a parable about the hubris of "storming heaven" or challenging the almighty power of God. But it is also a mythic image illustrative of the chaos that erupted when human beings made the transition from the village, where everyone spoke the same language, to the city, where, suddenly, many tongues struggled to be heard and understood.

During that splendid moment of reverie at the merchant's home, the city of Jerusalem epitomized to me the "confounding of language," the agony of miscommunication, resulting from three different cultures attempting to storm heaven simultaneously, amid a babel of incomprehensible voices.

It was only two years after the Yom Kippur War and twenty-some years before the Intifada. Still, the dream lives on in this sanctuary of spiritual aspiration. It lies as deep and is as difficult to reach as the original roads that the prophets, Jesus, and Mohammed walked, which are now, after some thirty-five centuries, sixty-five feet below the surface of the modern meandering lanes of the Old City.

Again and again I returned over the next few months, hitchhiking, getting lifts from the kibbutz trucks taking chickens to the slaughterhouse, or rides in the back of army Jeeps. Every chance I got I made the long ride through the Jordan Valley, past the ruins of Jericho, across the West Bank, and into the Old City. Once there I walked first to the Western Wall, where I prayed and was transfixed by the devotion before the Holy Temple. Then I set out for a café in the bazaar, where I went out of my way to engage in conversations with soldiers, spice merchants, bus drivers, missionaries, and travelers from all over the world. Often I felt something I'd never felt before, that I was in a place watched over by God, holy ground where He could hear my slightest whisper; always I wondered why a place so obviously blessed by the divine could have such a tragic destiny.

"No other city lingers quite so tremendously in the memory," writes the maven of travel writers, Jan Morris. "When once you have entered the gates of Jerusalem, you are never quite the same person again." Is this not the quintessential description of the mythic city, the place that feels as if it has always existed, the place you never leave and never leaves you, the site that symbolizes the origins of all we deem sacred?

The Singing Streets, the Talking Stones

But how did it all begin? asks the mythic imagination about that other sacred city in my life, Paris.

The English historian Arnold Toynbee wrote in *Cities of Destiny*, "No one conscious of being part of Western civilization has since the Middle Ages ever been able to enter Paris wholly as a stranger. He comes conscious of a fundamental debt, and confident of recapturing an ancient inspiration. Even as a man in age may revisit a lover of his youth, or an exile after long wandering return to a second home."

This image of the second home is striking and illuminates for me the mystery of why Paris evokes more nostalgia than perhaps any city other than Jerusalem in all the world. Curiously enough, *nostalgia* refers to "the returns," the various attempts of the surviving Greek soldiers to return home after the war against Troy. What the word, the old stories, the new myth are telling us is that there is something fathoms deep in the Western soul that is not at home in the world, or is always striving to find a second home.

In the beginning, according to conventional history, Paris was founded by the Parisii tribe of Gauls around 250–200 B.C.E. when they set up their huts on the islands in the Seine. Those are the facts, which the mind needs, but as Nietzsche observed, "There are no facts, only interpretations." There are facts of the mind and there are facts of the heart. Our inward life demands a story that touches the soul.

Accordingly, during medieval times Paris joined the ranks of "the noble cities." What made it unique was its range of influence, which was, as Toynbee points out, "royal, ecclesiastical, mercantile, and intellectual," at a time when the University of Paris came to symbolize to the rest of Europe the importance of an "awakened curiosity stimulated by the presence of great teachers filled with ardor, and from the enthusiasm of a multitudinous student body eager to learn."

The "long conversation" of culture and civilization has poured down the centuries from the classrooms and cafés of Paris like water flowing through a log flume in a gold mine. During the seventeenth and eighteenth centuries, it enticed young travelers on the Grand Tour who were following in the footsteps of Abelard, Aquinas, Dante, Rousseau, Madame de Stael, and Voltaire. Many of the grand travelers walked—so they could talk, in the salons, brothels, parks, cafés, or classrooms. In the early days of the university, classes were held outdoors, along the Rue des Fouares, near Saint Julien-le-Pauvre, the sixth-century abbey near the Seine.

Ever since, like pilgrims of old returning to the mysterious source, travelers and seekers of all stripes have gone to Paris in search of their own experience of that "awakened curiosity," on a quest for ideas and pleasure. Or was it pleasure and ideas? The pleasure of ideas? The ideas of pleasure?

Over the last century, Paris has been mythologized for a multitude of reasons, but largely because modern art has its origins there. This is the source of its secular sacredness, if by sacred we mean what is worthy of our reverence, which is exactly the view of the arts that has evolved over the last couple of centuries. The writers, painters, sculptors, and filmmakers who have become identified with Paris embody what the French adventurer, author, and minister of culture, André Malraux, meant when he described art as the modern religion.

The belief in the saving grace of the life of the mind and the creative imagination is as embedded in the soul of Paris as the dirt ground into the cobblestones of her oldest roads.

The Mythmaker's Paris

"I have no money, no resources, no hopes," wrote Henry Miller while living in Paris. "I am the happiest man alive.... I no longer have to think about [art].... I am." This is the Miller that the amorous Anaïs Nin fell in love with, the one she described as having "the brilliancy of a fate in motion."

I recognize in Miller's euphonious praise of his life in Paris the qualities that inspired my own fascination and love for the place. His essentially bohemian stance holds a key to the legendary status of Paris as the place you traveled if you wanted to live well on a shoestring budget, eat better than you could at home, fall in love, immerse yourself in culture, or simply slow down and walk—for days, weeks, even years, at a time.

There is a mythic sensibility to his description that lies behind the bountiful stories of *fin-de-siècle* Paris, *les années folles,* the Crazy Years of the 1920s, and the postwar years of the expatriates. Those years, first of Ernest Hemingway, Josephine Baker, F. Scott Fitzgerald, Gertrude Stein, then of Janet Flanner, James Baldwin, and many others. Those years intrigue me not only for the prodigious output of art and literature, but for the fact that mythic Paris exists alongside, as if in a parallel universe, to the "real" Paris of banks, sewers, schools, hospitals, crime, and municipal strikes. There is the Paris for Parisians, the Paris for tourists, and the Paris for the seekers of the Eternal City. They might be French, English, Algerian, Greek, Irish, Canadian, or American. Sometimes their paths cross with the others, but the latter share one thing in common: the hope that one's own dormant "genius" might awaken in Paris alongside the *genius loci,* the spirit of the place.

The folklore of artists, writers, travelers, even politicians is replete with stories and images of the mythic transformation of foreigners here: Turgenev, Chopin, Strindberg, Mozart, Picasso, Diaghilev, Emerson, Jefferson, Franklin, Rhys, Gershwin, Josephine Baker, as well as those who were graced by the gods to have been born in Paris. Their stories support the ancient notion that behind every myth is a truth dying to get out, a kernel of truth about the human condition that needs an image.

Of course, Miller's Paris doesn't exist anymore. It is far too expensive, and modern people are less inclined to romanticize urban life, even in Paris. But it lives on in the mythic imagination; deep within the chambers of the collective soul is the notion that ignites inspiration. That is one reason why the place is still so vitally important to tourists, lovers, philosophers, and artists alike. It the immortal Paris of café and street life and a pervading cultural atmosphere that encourages relishing *la bonne vie,* the good life, the mythic art of living.

"The streets sing, the stones talk," Miller said, "the houses drip history, glory, and romance." This Paris does live on, in song and poetry, movies and literature, as a compressed metaphor for one of the last places where people still live with capacious appetites for joy, beauty, ideas, politics, and sensual pleasure, in other words a life of soulful rather than materialistic pursuits.

Its importance as the absolute center of culture has diminished, as its many rivals are happy to point out. But underneath its sometimes cloying reputation as the "City of Lights," where poseur painters in berets work at their easels along the canals and feverbrowed anarchists loom underneath every other lamppost, it maintains a singular stature among world cities. David Applefield, the publisher of *FRANK* magazine writes, "The idea of pulling up stakes and pursuing the life of the writer or artist in Paris never seems to lose appeal."

Nearly 70 million people visit France every year, the most of any country in the world. As Applefield writes, many of them, mostly Anglo-Americans, stay on, at least for awhile, leaving around two hundred thousand expatriates walking the boulevards of Paris alone in pursuit of the ghosts of art, literature, and infamous history. The steady flow of visitors and media coverage, he adds, "reinforces the myth that being in Paris makes you happy and creative."

In many traditions the act of naming is the equivalent of ensouling. An intimate aspect of the city of Paris is the way in which names are bountifully visible on street signs, buildings, political or artistic movements, and even café menus, as in this classic one from La Coupole, the Montparnasse bistro.

This siren song to artists, lovers, and philosophers is hard to resist. The tune is relatively unchanged: There is something missing in life back home, and the solution is to be found in an idealized place loosely referred to as "somewhere called Paris," with its sundry charms of beauty, culture, fashion, sensuality, cheap wine, bountiful food, and freedom from Puritanical values. These qualities are inferred in the name of the most famous street in the city, les Champs-Élysées, the Elysian Fields, "the mythical paradise where the Golden Age lived on."

But as Alexander Eliot wittily reminds us, "Myth cannot be understood, let alone reimagined and reshaped, other than mythically." It requires a special form of seeing, like the early form of movie projector, the Zoetrope I saw years ago at the Musée du Cinema. If you peered through slots on the outside of its revolving drum you could view a band of photographs of old Paris that were mounted on the inside, thus creating the magic illusion of a "persistence of vision." What we see through the twirling "slots," are tears in the fabric of the merely visible world. We may catch a fleeting glimpse of doors that swing open to reveal hidden courtyards, the street names that tell the tales of the city, the faces of the old people in the parks that evoke the photographs of Cartier-Bresson or the paintings of Renoir, the rain on the cobblestones—all these impressions create what filmmaker Gordon Parks called "a carnival of imagery."

The Carnival of Imagery

"I dawdled over my work in Paris..." Somerset Maugham wrote. "I thought I should be a fool to allow work to interfere with a delight in the passing moment that I might never enjoy again so fully." Speaking of the sensual rhythms of the city, biographer Noel Riley-Fitch wrote in her guidebook to Paris café life, "Wasted time? Certainly not. Idle time. In part. There is time to sit and contemplate, to dream and observe life. Time to plan the next story or the word order of a poem." For the greatest diarist of the century, Anaïs Nin, "The hours I have spent in cafés are the only ones I call living, apart from writing...."

"It was the summer of a thousand parties and no work," lamented F. Scott Fitzgerald as he was leaving Paris in the late '20s. "Was it fun in Paris?" his wife Zelda asked him.

> Who did you see there and was the Madeleine pink at five o'clock and did the fountains fall with hollow delicacy into the framing of space in the Place de la Concorde, and did the blue creep out from behind the Colonnades in the rue de Rivoli through the grill of the Tuileries and was the Louvre gray and metallic in the sun and did the trees hang brooding over the cafés and were there lights at night and the click of saucers and the auto horns that play de Bussy...?

Their friend, the publisher Harry Stearns said, "It was a useless, silly life, after one particularly champagny season with the effervescent Fitzgeralds, and I've missed it every day since."

❋

Helen Keller lived for a short time in Paris. One day she received permission to have a private audience with the statues at Rodin's studio. She stood on a chair and caressed *The Thinker* with her hands. Later she wrote, it was "primal, tense, his chin resting on a toil-worn hand. In every limb I felt the throes of the emerging mind." Touching the bold forehead of Rodin's *Balzac,* still a work in progress, she said she felt the same strength she did when she first understood from her teacher the breakthrough word *water.*

❋

Shortly after Picasso met Gertrude Stein and her "charmed circle" at the 27 Rue de Fleurus he asked if he could paint her portrait. She readily agreed, again and again, some eighty sittings in all. For months he never showed her a thing. She describes him in *The Autobiography of Alice B. Toklas* as coming around to her Sunday salons, and even asking her for advice on his poetry, his eyes glaring like a bull's. When he finished the portrait, which revealed her as an imperious, aquiline Roman empress, she was deeply disappointed. "It doesn't look anything like me," she complained.

"It will," said the man who once quipped that art is the lie that tells the truth.

It did.

⊛

In the late '40s, novelist Herbert Gold went abroad to "study France and the meaning of life," and was nearly ensorcelled by Anaïs Nin (her word). Years later, he wrote of her, "So many myths, but so little paper in her notebook."

Of Paris herself, he wrote sagely, "The myth endures; the need is great."

Why the myth, why the need?

Why the city?

The Mythic Sensibility

Beauty, wine, coffee, cigarettes, creativity, dream, seduction, pleasure, authenticity, conversation, freedom, power, time, happiness, leisure, madness, loneliness, anxiety, meaning, imagination, revolt, gods, joy, love....

Of such words are myths born. The vocabulary of those on the quest for idealized beauty. The stuff of everyday life and the words and images chosen and repeated for decades combine to describe the "great need" to mythologize Paris. They suggest to me that even in our days of secular humanism, there is still a strong desire to reimagine our cities the way Paris has been by poets and travelers for the last eight centuries, and make them as sacred to us as the ancient holy cities were to their denizens.

The cacophony of the modern city, the noxious air, the foul smoke in the cafés, the thunderous bigotry from the far-right racist, the frequent disdain for foreigners are all undeniable problems, but not enough to prevent the beauty from catching our breath or the phantoms of times past from appearing, as if behind a scrim.

Herb Gold recently recounted to me in a North Beach café how he found himself telling stories to his grown-up children about nearly every street corner when they visited the city together a few years ago. After one too many "I remember whens," one of his sons rebuked him, "Dad, you're just seeing ghosts."

True enough. That's the mythic point. Father and sons seeing two different images in the same looking glass. That's why we return again and again to enchanted ruins and places with names that still pulse in our veins. In Paris the phantoms of Abelard and Heloise, Dante and Rousseau, Sartre and de Beauvoir, the rebels of '68, Truffaut and Gainsborough, are still part of the landscape, memorialized in the very street names—Rue Danton, Rue Monge, Rue Voltaire. The rude lights of the *bateau mouches* spewing diesel fuel into the Seine and noisy disco music into the quiet houseboats are not so bad that the message of Paris behind the images, however fragmented, like jagged pieces of ancient frescoes hanging in the Louvre, cannot be heard.

The Place to Loaf In and Invite Your Soul

As we have seen, all cities have a veneer of myth, but there are innumerable layers of storied varnish on Paris. The City of Lights is such an integral part of world culture that many people who have never been there feel they have already experienced it, in books, movies, music, and that a real visit would be redundant. The fan of Edith Piaf's torch songs, Matisse's paintings, Rimbaud's poetry, or Hemingway's novels has already felt the pang of romantic love in the city's garrets, seen the dance of light over the Seine, and tasted a cool Pernod at the Café Contrescarpe. Those who finally visit feel like they've already been there.

"For those who visit Paris," writes Noel Riley-Fitch, "the myth may become a reality." The fortunate visitor may fall in love, discover the glories of art, poetry, and literature, but it is just as likely that the noise, the pollution, the high prices, the language barrier may sour the experience.

"Nevertheless," Riley-Fitch insists, "the myth persists."

All this is to say that I too rode into town on the back of a myth, in fact, many myths. Not unlike the pilgrims to Jerusalem's Western Wall, I followed a golden thread in search of a hidden gate.

For me the spell cast by the myth of Paris began in childhood with family stories about the French family connection on both sides of my family, the Cousineaus and the LaChances. To this day, my mother is tickled pink to tell anyone within earshot that her father had to shorten his surname when he was a young man from "LaChance du Pepin de Paris" (The Luck of the Pepins of Paris) just to fit on his Canadian driver's license. My cousin Pierre claims to have traced the LaChances all the way back to Charlemagne himself. Be that as it may, from high school writing classes right through college and into my years of writing for hometown newspapers, far more than genealogy it was the Hemingway myth that reigned in me.

As I learned it, the twenty-one-year-old reporter out of Kansas City boasted to his friends the night in 1921 he left home for Paris that he would return seven years later as the most famous novelist in the world. Seven years later, he went home with a copy of *The Sun Also Rises* under his arm, and the rest is history, or myth. On the surface the story may be only the wild boasting of a callow author. But below the surface, in the myth is a metaphor for the transformative powers of the city of Paris. The Hemingway myth is emblematic of the mysterious power that the spirit of a place has over our own spirits. His books, letters, and legend depict the life of the *flâneur,* roaming the streets, haunting cafés and bistros, and seemingly in constant conversation with the greatest artists, writers, soldiers, and politicians of the age.

In a word, Hemingway personifies the myth of a young man transformed into an artist by a city. As he concluded in *A Movable Feast,* "It would be pretty to think so."

My first ten visits or so to the city tied me up in Gordian Knots, creatively speaking. Initially I was content to play tourist, seeing the stupendous sights. Eventually I learned the city well enough to lead, in 1987, a literary tour titled "Bohemian Paris." Afterward, I spent several months there, in the Writer's Room of Shakespeare and Company Bookstore, courtesy of its owner, George Whitman, and my friend

Sarita's apartment near the Rue Mouffetard. Several dissolute months disappeared down the rabbit hole of Parisian café life.

Years later, I would find an apt description of my life during that time in Herb Gold's book, *Bohemia,* where he wrote that the bohemian life was "a soulful image for goofing round." I was goofing around but wasn't so sure it was soulful. I only knew that somewhere along the road of life I had forgotten to enjoy the simple but sacred details of everyday life. In truth, my soul was leading me in the direction of everyday beauty, and whispering, "Later, later, later you will write. Right now pay attention to the treasure at your feet."

One late autumn night I decided to ride the Métro out to the twentieth *arrondissement* to attend a screening of Bernard Tavernier's film, *Round Midnight,* at the classic Rex Theater. Twenty minutes into the smokily atmospheric story was a scene that brought a wall-to-wall grin to my face, one that readily captured the elusive soul of the city in all its rainy, cobblestone splendor. The sulfurous saxophone player Dexter Gordon, playing a character based on the late Lester Young, is scolded by his landlady for being poor and miserable. "Yeah, but I'm poor and miserable *in Paris,*" he growled.

Around dawn the next morning, the smells from the bakery below woke me as gently as the nudging hand of a lover. But this time a sliver of dream hovered in my mind. I had a vague image of the actress Isabella Rossellini, and she was handing me something bizarre, a body cast buzz-sawed in half. Then a smile spread across my face. It was inspired by a strange tale I had heard the movie critic Roger Ebert tell the year before at a press party at the Cannes Film Festival. Apparently, when Rossellini was a teenage girl she had a serious illness and was bedridden in a full body cast for nearly a year. When she recovered she still felt oddly attached to the body cast and took to sleeping in it at night. Finally, her mother, Ingrid Bergman, threw the cast out and Rossellini became furious.

Rarely do I have an immediate take on a dream upon waking, but that morning I read the dream as a parable for my having brought with me from America a kind of body cast that was keeping me from moving or moving on with my life. It needed to be thrown out so I could walk again. I can't think of a more vivid image than this to express the myths we sometimes carry around with us even after they are worn out, outgrown, and need to be replaced. The dream prompted the recollection of the famous question from Carl Jung's autobiography, *Memories, Dreams, and Reflections,* in which he described a midlife breakdown, when he was forced to ask himself, "Am I living the myth, or is the myth living me?"

The strange dream told me that when the myth no longer fits, change it. Start over. Go home.

The Uncanny Influence

When I returned home to San Francisco in September 1987, I felt restless but enlivened. Though I came back with little to show for my time, in the usual sense, I was happy with the first drafts of my stories and the journals I had filled. More mysterious, I felt different, as if I had endured an ordeal.

However, there wasn't much time to dwell on the curious changes going on inside me. I was scheduled to fly back to Europe in early October to screen *The Hero's Journey,* the documentary film on Joseph Campbell I had co-written, at the Cork Film Festival. The day before I was scheduled to leave for Ireland I called Stuart Brown, the stalwart producer of the film, to iron out the final details of the screening. On a hunch, I asked him about the "psychological biography" on Campbell that he had been working on for more than two years. Glumly, he confessed the manuscript wasn't working out like he had planned. His disappointment was palpable, and as I began to sympathize something happened to me, something opened, as if the golden string I had been following for years had indeed led to Jerusalem's Wall—and the gates of heaven opened for me.

Time stood still. It was one of those rare moments in life when everything and anything is possible. The blink of an eye turned out to be a sly wink of fate. Until then I doubt if I would have had the confidence to leap at the opportunity I saw opening up before me, but something had changed.

Motivated about my writing in a way I had never felt before, I asked if I could help. I offered to take a look at what he had written, even take it with me to Ireland, if he could express mail it to me. To my eternal surprise and gratitude he managed to mail off the manuscript, which I toted with me in my satchel all the way to Cork, and which I read over the course of the film festival. From the first page to last I saw how the entire manuscript could be changed into what should have been obvious from the beginning, a companion book to the film.

Within a week of my return from Ireland, I had revamped Brown's proposal for Harper & Row Publishers (now HarperSanFrancisco), and to my utter amazement my bold suggestion of a complete change of direction was enthusiastically embraced by his editor. A week later I signed my first book contract as co-author for a book about my own mentor. Over the course of the next two years, as I transformed our seventy-odd hours of footage into a book, my heart was overwhelmed with a sense of gratitude for my time in Paris, which I was sure had readied me for the Campbell book project. I hadn't metamorphosed from a *boulavardier* into Marcel Proust overnight. I was simply nudged a little further along my own road. And that was enough of a miracle. *C'était formidable.*

The Storehouse of Marvels

And then suddenly I was back.

In the spring of 1989, I returned to Paris, and with the help of my friend Jeannette Hermann, reprised the "Bohemian Paris" tour. Afterward, I took up the generous invitation of my Corsican friend Jean-François Pasquilini to live with him in his family's sprawling Montparnasse apartment.

Ceremoniously, on my very first morning there I tacked a *Paris Plan* onto my bedroom wall and made my own plan for the next six months. Every morning, I vowed to myself, I would circle a neighborhood in one of the twenty *arrondissements* and walk there, no matter how far, with the idea of *finding a story there*. With the passing of only two years I felt the press of time like never before. The very next morning I purchased a 120-franc pass that gave me free access to more than a hundred museums around the city, four new journals, a sketch pad, and a box of sketching pencils. I borrowed a tape recorder and loaded my camera with film. For the next six months I walked ten to fifteen miles every day, reveling in the old bookstalls along the Seine, intrigued by the vitality of the outdoor market on the Boulevard Raspail, where the best chefs in the city secretly did their shopping.

My working principle was that each encounter with the city should inspire a new piece of writing. To paraphrase Annie Dillard, I was "teaching the cobblestones to talk," at least talk to me. In this way, an afternoon of brooding in the old Roman Arena, which had been covered with the city's refuse for fifteen centuries, inspired a story about "the enchantment of ruins" through history. An evening's drinking of Pernod in honor of Hemingway at the Closerie des Lilas café triggered memories of Michigan, which compelled me to write a story about a boy's coming of age while hunting for Indian arrowheads. A breakfast at La Palette, across from L'Hotel where Oscar Wilde died, with an irascible Irish television producer named Dave Gallagher, earned me a month's worth of work writing a short script about Wilde's phantasmagorical last hours. Often, the ritual reading from one of the volumes of poetry or books set in Paris that I carried with me in my leather satchel inspired my own poetry or a short story, as when I read Baudelaire in front of the Hotel Lauzun, where he had staged elaborate hashish parties, or Madame de Staël's redolent letters in front of the Musée de Paris.

My café rendezvous were planned to spice up my newfound regimen of long stretches of solitude with conversation, the news of the day, and whenever possible, the learning of new ways to see the city. At La Tartine on the Rue de Rivoli I often met up with Anne, a French literature student from Alsace who taught me the virtues of sitting still and listening to the rain on the red awning outside, slowly savoring a Beaujolais, and playing the venerable Parisian game of trying to imagine the life story of people passing by. Charlyn, a friend of hers, convinced me that a weekly outing to Au Gamin restaurant in the Marais district for their spectacular mousse au chocolat was not self-indulgent, but "*necessary* for the happy life," as she put it. One day she brought a friend of hers from Saltzberg, who was apprenticing at one of the most brilliant restaurants in the city. He proceeded to give a two-hour disquisition on why the presentation of French food resembles Impressionist painting. "*Ç'est logique. La raison être beau.*" Stewart, the South African border guard who was on the lam from the authorities, shamed my self-pity about my finances with hair-standing tales about political atrocities. Maurice, the Tunisian bass player whose claim to fame was playing with Charlie Parker and Dizzy Gillespie in the 1940s never tired of sharing stories with me about the "good old days" when jazz and blues musicians were ignored in the States and revered in France. To him, Rimbaud and Miles Davis alike were active mythic forces in the life of Paris.

Steadily, the city changed from a place that was outside of me to a place that was inside of me. I came to love my night walks in the rain when the fog turned the city into a moiré of gold and silver. I came to love the simple beauty of sitting on a wooden bench on one of the city's thirteen bridges every evening to quietly watch the sunset, along with enflamed young lovers and forlorn artists enduring that peculiar form of French melancholy called *le cafard,* the existential blues. A favorite observation point was the Île de la Cité, where, as the seventeenth-century writer Corneille wrote, "twilight turned its bushes into palaces." His transfiguring imagination is an example of the mythic vision that has brought so many millions of us to Paris.

When I thought I had exhausted café life and the inspiration of studios and museums, I turned back to conversation about books and the writing life with a few of the guest lecturers from my tour who often frequented George's bookstore. One day I had lunch with William Wiser, author of *Paris in the Twenties.* We spoke for hours about his favorite topic, *les années folles,* the crazy years of the '20s. His most charming story was about the afternoon he spent with the guards at Père Lachaise cemetery when they showed him Oscar Wilde's "balls"— the marble ones that local bluenoses had ignominiously hacked off the Lipschitz carving of the Sphinx on his tomb. Even more vivid than that symbolic castration was a conversation about his life in Paris during the late '50s and early '60s, when there was very little café life and little fraternizing among writers, yet he learned to write anyway. When I asked him how, he said, "It is the city that inspires me, not the so-called literary scene. There's something peculiar and lovely about the light and the way that the city is horizontal and not vertical, like New York or London, that makes me more human, even feminine. It's the city...."

And then his voice trailed off as if he were talking about an old lover.

✳

Often, I simply sat in the parks or museum gardens, such as Ossip Zadkine's *Sculpture Forest,* one of my favorite contemplative places in the city. For hours I would sketch the rough-hewn works that seemed to me to combine the corrosive beauty of Modigliani and the muscular melancholy of Bourdelle. I loved those moments in the garden, surrounded by chestnut trees, the smell of roasting coffee from the museum café, the clanging sounds of restorers in the shed, the exuberant yells of children from a nearby school. Another favorite was the Place de Furstemberg, the most tranquil spot in the heart of the city, according to Henry Miller, and often, to my joy, the place where saxophone players and flautists practiced.

Many nights, I ended up on the terrace of Le Select on the Boulevard Montparnasse, which opened in 1925 and became the favorite watering hole for the likes of Isadora Duncan, Hart Crane, photographer Robert Capa, and Hemingway. Part of its charm was watching people come and go across the street at La Coupole, where Josephine Baker used to walk her cougar, and Lenin, Trotsky, and Ho Chi Minh used to drink and plan revolutions. Once ensconced at the Select I would sit for hours. The lighting was bright enough to write and read by, and espresso was only nine francs.

✳

Slowly but surely, over the course of those months, the alchemy of the city, its alternating rhythms of conversation and silence, fraternity and solitude, highbrow culture and lowbrow street life, worked its magic on me. My one true life was lured out of me by the genies of time, beauty, solitude, and work itself. I grew to trust my passion for transforming my daily impressions into words on the page, not caring a whit, for the first time, about the great dragon doubt or the exigencies of the marketplace. I walked and looked and I wrote and that was enough.

One evening, as winter approached, the steel blue sky turned metallic, and the very clothing of the citizens darkened considerably until it seemed the whole city was dressed in black coats draped with red scarves. The café tables and chairs moved inside. The plane and acacia trees lost their leaves. Then, the old loneliness began to steal over me, and I huddled deeper into a story I was working on about an afternoon in Nottingham, England, spent with a distant aunt of mine, Floss Thornywork, who looked like my grandfather and sounded like Alfred Hitchcock. In the story I was trying in vain to describe the great psychic divide for a writer/photographer like myself, who is constantly torn between the desire to turn every encounter into words—and the equally powerful pull to freeze-frame them with photographs.

As I was rewriting the ending of the story for the fifth time, I overheard a stylish Frenchman flirting with an English woman by conveying his philosophy of life to her, an old lover's trick in Paris.

"When I started to live my life the way I wanted to," he began, determinedly, "it didn't even matter anymore if I was happy—happy is just a *bourgeois* word. What did it matter? *Ouf!* I was *creative.*" It worked. She swooned. He sighed.

I couldn't help but smile to beat the band. It was a strangely liberating comment for me. Laughing to myself, I resolved to stop counting the stories, poems, and essays that were stacking up in my room back on the Rue Regis.

Ouf! I was writing. That's all I had ever wanted. Just time and the sight of cobblestones in the rain, the sound of Debussy coming from the café, and the strange blue light of early winter in Paris. That's all.

The Fountains of Life

There is a wonderful moment in the movie *An American in Paris* when the horn player reaches deep down into his soul for the right notes to echo the aching love of the Stranger, played by Gene Kelly. That was the sound in my soul my last night in Paris that year. Buoyant with happiness, I packed my small bag, filled my leather satchel with my notebooks, and walked across town to Shakespeare and Company Bookstore to meet an old friend who never showed up. Not to worry, I thought, as I sat on George's green bench on the terrace with a bottle of new Beaujolais. There was a strong breeze that shifted fast-moving clouds across the city, casting shadow-puppet movements on the towers of Nôtre Dame just across the river. I thought of my father, who never made it to Paris. I planned the books I would write for the rest of my life and the journeys I would take. I wondered if I would ever be this happy again.

The water murmured out of the dark green Wallace Fountain in front of me, bringing back the story of its provenance that I had learned from an old bookseller. In the nineteenth century, Henry Wallace, an English explorer, got lost in the Arabian Desert. He was dying of thirst when a troop from the French Foreign Legion found him and slaked his thirst with fresh water from a cold canteen. Upon his return to Europe, Wallace left his fortune to the state of France with the provision that they construct water fountains to be placed all over Paris so that travelers would never go thirsty.

For those on a quest, everything is a metaphor. The longer I stayed in Paris the more I was able to read into it, interpret its stones and streets as metaphors and symbols, then slowly let even that go. An epigram by René Daumal became my mantra: "Live first, then philosophize, then live again." This was a philosophical moment. I pondered a simple beauty of the fountain and began to think of it as symbolizing the city as an ever-flowing fountain intended to slake the deep thirst of people for beauty, art, and culture.

The Man in the Gray Fedora

If you travel far enough, a wily old traveler once told me, one day you will recognize yourself coming down the road to meet you.

The last time I saw Paris was in the summer of 1997, eight years since my previous visit. I had returned with my partner Jo and Jack, our then one-year-old son, to co-lead yet another literary tour around the city, this time with architect Anthony Lawlor. The day after our farewell dinner for the tour I filmed a television pilot called "The Soul of Paris." One of the three people I interviewed on camera was George Whitman, owner of Shakespeare and Company, who gave me one of the best descriptions I've ever heard of the living mythology of his adopted home.

"I found out that in the 1600s this building was a monastery," George told us while on camera. "Now I've tried many things in my life, and failed many times, but at least I was able to take over the traditional function of the most eccentric monk of the monastery who used to be the lamplighter of Paris. I have been keeping the lamps lit in the world with my books for the last forty-five years. Paris is a city of imagination built by architects and poets and artists and storytellers and all kinds of magicians. So in Paris there is no exact boundary between earth and heaven. And in such a city you can hope to meet the angel in everybody."

The next day I saw one, or at least a ghost. Or was it all a dream?

I was strolling with Jo and Jack down the Rue Mouffetard on the last day of our month-long visit. It was the violet hour of late afternoon, what the French call *entre chien et loup*, the hour between the dog and the wolf. I thought I passed myself in the corner table of the Café Contrescarpe.

I thought I passed myself.

Stunned, I paused, my hands gripping the baby stroller. There I was, a ghostly lookalike of myself, ten years younger, poring over red-lined pages in a notebook, table stacked with books to be devoured, peeking occasionally at the pretty French girls passing by after school, gazing longingly at the green painted house where Hemingway lived with

Hadley and broke her heart, then across the plaza at the *boite de nuit* where Louis Armstrong and Josephine Baker sang and danced during *les années folles*, down the street to the gutter in front of the little house where Verlaine collapsed and died, and across to the little park in the center of the square that Beckett immortalized in *Waiting for Godot* as the place where his two existential hoboes wait and wait and wait. I saw him check his blue Clairefontaine notebooks, clutch his pen, smile with sublime satisfaction at the pages he had filled with stories.

Then I'm sure I saw him pull down his gray fedora over his forehead, swirl the last of his *café crème* around in the cup, as if trying to read his own fortune, and whisper a silent vow to himself that someday he would return to this same café as a published writer, maybe a father, a husband, possibly even happy. Then, like a plant turning toward the sun, he turned and cleared his throat, and began an uneasy conversation with two bashful young female students from the Sorbonne.

Watching him for a moment, as inconspicuously as possible, I thought of the café-philo we had visited that morning and of Sautet's recently published comments about his hero, Socrates, who had explained, in the immortalizing words of Plato, how we may be set free by philosophy, dialogue, drinking, and talking, beauty and love, all those ideal forms that lure us out of the "gloom of our cave of ignorance," not through mere information but through the beauty of dialogue, the flowing of words and ideas between people, that connects the self to what the Greek called the *daemon*, the divine presence within. There, I thought, is the myth of the city, unfolding right in front of me, three lonely people in a loud, chaotic modern city, brought together by the promise of soulful conversation.

Smiling, I pushed on, the wheels of the stroller clattering over the old cobblestones, a light Parisian rain falling silently over the city I had come to love, the place where I first began to take seriously *l'entente de la vie*, the art of living, which means for me writing until I can reach the roots of my life.

The Imaginary Homeland

After immersing myself in myths all my life, I have come to believe that their beauty and their strength derives from their capacity to transform us. The mythic tenacity of ancient stories, modern models of belief, and certain sacred places, from Jerusalem to Paris, work on us in ways it may take a lifetime to understand.

My own experience of mythic places is that they are absorbed in my imagination, becoming part of what Salman Rushdie calls "imaginary homelands," cities and countries of the mind, sometimes agonizingly disconnected from ordinary life at home, but often profoundly linked to the new worlds we must create for ourselves out of the fragments of our lives.

Perhaps the finest lesson I have learned from my time in far-flung places like Jerusalem, Dublin, Sintra, Manila, and Paris is a new commitment of attachment to my own home ground. This has been the challenge of all travelers on the road of life. It is the moral of Zgibert Herbert's retooled myth of Antaeus. In his book of marvels, *The King of the Ants,* the Polish writer retells the ancient tale of the hero whose strength derives from the connection of his feet to the earth. Antaeus is only defeated when Hercules lifts him off the ground and holds him in the air until he could no longer breathe. What is memorable about the retelling is Herbert's interpretation.

"The myth of Antaeus," Herbert writes, "is [about] attachment."

The first time I read that story, in the poetry room of City Lights Bookstore in San Francisco, I thought of the philosopher Nietzsche as having been only half-right about an artist having no home, save Paris. The beauty of the myth of great cities is that they teach us, like American Indians say, that every place is in the center of the world, including our own home. While mythic cities may inspire awe and devotion, the greatest of them all don't defeat us through spiritual or cultural intimidation but remind us to take that devotion and attention home with us.

There isn't a day that goes by in my life here in the old Italian neighborhood in San Francisco, where I live now with Jo and Jack, when I don't think of Paris. Occasionally, I miss it, usually when strolling around the pine trees in Pioneer Park, near Coit Tower, because it reminds me (as it did Simone de Beauvoir, who lived here in the 1930s) of Montmartre. I think of it when wandering by the French-Italian bakery down the hill and recall living over the bakery on Rue Broca. I am swarmed by nostalgia when walking down the narrow North Beach alleyways, which remind me of the Latin Quarter, or see crowds of old people in heated discussions on the benches of Washington Square Park. Recalling how often I have been helped by local people in my own travels, I have developed my own daily ritual of coming to the aid of a lost or baffled tourist every day. Pointing them toward Coit Tower or City Lights Bookstore, sharing some local lore, such as where Alan Ginsberg wrote *Howl* or Sam Brannan ran into the streets with a bag of gold dust shouting the news that would change the world: "Gold!" Each gesture renews the myth of the city for them and for me.

Mostly I am simply grateful for the time I had there when I was a younger man and the context it lent me for everywhere I've lived since. It embodied the myth that gave me the courage to take my life more seriously, more *creatively.* I've come to learn that I must find everywhere what the poet Paul Valery found in Paris: "Tell me. Have you not observed while walking in this town that among the buildings which people it, some are dumb, others speak, and yet others, that are the rarest, sing?"

Gratitude and love for the beauty I discovered there on an everyday basis, not only that found in the museums, galleries, and gardens, but in the way the light played off the cobblestones and glinted off the Seine, the way the bells of the churches ring out like crystal chimes, or the way flowers festoon the sidewalks. Gratitude and love for the splendid prism it has given me for my life in the equally mythic city of San Francisco.

Sunset over the Golden Gate Bridge, San Francisco.

Tonight, I am sitting in a rickety lounge chair on the roof of our little cottage on top of Telegraph Hill, musing over my life in Paris. I gaze out over the rooftops of North Beach, with their heavenly gardens and telescopes and lounge chairs for gazing out across the slithering fog to the Golden Gate Bridge. I try to imagine the tumultuous years of the Gold Rush, when hundreds of ships lay in the Bay bringing the hopeful from Boston, Valparaiso, Sicily, and even Paris, to California and the fever-dream of the gold fields where a few nuggets might set a poor man free for life.

Paris is a dream to me now, but it's not like I long to return to those days. Instead, the revamped dream is the most ancient one of all, that of the realization of an "enchanted ordinariness" in my life here and now. The real lesson I've brought home from Jerusalem and Paris, even Detroit, is reattachment to home.

When we hear Bogie remind Bergman in the ultimate escapist myth, *Casablanca,* "We'll always have Paris," a strange ache comes into our hearts, an ache, I believe, for the mythic home, paradise, the garden, the green land where we will find love, find ourselves, make the hard sacrifice, and, finally, do the right thing with our lives. This throw-away line in a wartime movie, expected to disappear soon after its release, has come to capture the ineffably romantic charm and promise of the timeless place called Paris, the city that transformed a cynical café owner into a self-sacrificing war hero.

"Naturally," wrote Gertrude Stein in the legendary 1920s, "one does not know how it happened until it's well over beginning happening."

Stein was writing about the mysterious moment of inspiration, but she was writing in that polyfabulous, that many-storied place called Paris, which is never over beginning happening in the mythic imagination.

SIX

The Myth of Sports

*From the Fields of Olympia to
the Field of Dreams*

It is not only a business for making money,
but for mythmaking, hero worship,
the elevation of gods.

—DONALD HALL

In the middle of September 1999, I returned to San Francisco
from a month of lectures and filming in Brazil and Chile, and
the first night back home I dreamed that I was back in my
boyhood bed, underneath the bedcovers, clutching my white plastic
crystal radio set. In the dream the time was on the far side of eleven
o'clock, long past my bedtime, but my hometown team, the Detroit
Tigers, were playing the Angels in faraway California, and I had to find
out who was winning. I rolled my thumb over the volume switch and
was thrilled to hear the crackling static of voices as if from a distant
planet. I adjusted the plastic earphone in my ear, wiggled the metal
clip on the windowsill for better reception, and heard through the
static that was sheer magic to me the soothing Southern voice of Tiger
announcer Ernie Harwell saying, "Kaline swings and it's a long belt to
left field. Wagner goes back, back, back. It's gone! Kaline hits one into
the boondocks. Home run number twenty for the veteran slugger Al
Kaline. The Tigers lead it, 5-4."

The dream then segued to a strange image of a baseball scorebook
with the phrase "Myth, Magic, and Mystery" embossed on the cover. I

leaned over it and with a baseball bat-shaped pen I entered the symbol "HR" next to Kaline's name and circled the word *Hometeam.* But instead of ink, what came out of the magical pen was powdered chalk, the kind used to line basepaths on a baseball diamond.

Then I woke up.

It was near dawn. The dream drifted away, like a boat leaving me on a pier. Utterly baffled, I got out of bed and walked into the kitchen, allowing the images to play in my imagination. "Seize the image!" I remember psychologist James Hillman exhorting us at a lecture years ago. "Don't analyze your dreams to death!"

I poured a glass of iced tea, and it occurred to me that this was my second baseball dream in the last month. Two weeks before, in a São Paulo hotel, I had dreamed of Kaline himself inviting me down to Tiger Stadium for batting practice, where he showed me how to swing naturally, how to take a carom off the right field wall gracefully, then turn and throw to home plate, all in one motion.

As I took instruction in the dream from my boyhood idol, there was a lucid moment in which I became slowly aware of how deeply he had influenced my youth. The Hall of Fame right fielder wasn't flamboyant like some athletes, smug like many movie stars, or even rugged like my father. His nickname was "The Line," because his every move on the field looked straight and smooth. Kaline had what all great athletes have: stillness in the heat of the action, even when in pain, as he was throughout his injury-wracked career. It was the same calm that reigns at the center of the torso-twisting statues of ancient Greek athletes, the composure that the philosopher Emerson noticed in the hero who is "immovably centered."

It was the stillness that impressed me, then and now.

Standing bleary-eyed in the kitchen, shivering in the coolness of the hours just before dawn, I found myself trying to shake off the jet-lag effects of a fifteen-hour flight from South America and the unnerving influence of a perturbing dream. Absentmindedly, I turned over a copy of the local paper on the kitchen table and flipped to the sports pages. In the baseball boxscores I saw the words "Tiger Stadium" and the phrase "last homegames ever at the old park," and my pulse began to race. There was the word *home* again, and it reverberated through me.

"Dreams are wiser than men," say the Omaha Indian elders. But where was the wisdom lurking in my strange sports dreams? I wondered. Were they reminding me about the promise I had made to myself a few years before, when it was announced after years of bitter political battles that the Tigers were building a new stadium downtown and would be shuttering the old stadium forever? Were they reminding me of my vow to see at least one more game? The magnetic pull from my boyhood "field of dreams" was stronger than I suspected, but if I longed to go back, why had I procrastinated?

In truth, it was too painful to think about. Sure, I had been boasting about taking my three-year-old son Jack back to Detroit so he could see the ballpark my father had taken me to when I was a boy, but some unconscious belief must have prevented me from confirming any plans, as if it would have meant admitting that the fight to save the stadium was over. I ached to see one last game, but was feeling a bit uneasy about being so vulnerable to the notorious nostalgia of baseball.

Sports still had a terrific grip on my soul. I still loved playing ball, attending games, and following my favorite teams. But a peculiar voice had hounded me about my passion as I grew older, whispering in my ear that maybe I should think about doing more constructive things with my time. But I held tight to my old fascination with baseball, partly because it connected me to one of my few fond memories of growing up in the Detroit area. No doubt, Tiger Stadium was one of the most mythic places of my youth, the ground where my heroes walked and my dreams flew. But Detroit isn't a place you go back to lightly. The name alone has become a loaded metaphor for American ingenuity, soul music, violence, and the riots of 1967. Under the circumstances, going back had all the promise of returning for a family funeral.

With only two weeks left in the season, it seemed impossible for me to get tickets. My heart dropped like one of former Tiger hurler Jack Morris' famous sinker balls when I thought of being shut out of the ritual farewell.

On the way back to our bedroom I passed our son Jack's room, where he was still sleeping. He was wearing an old baseball shirt. I read the moment like a base runner taking a sign from the third-base coach as he rounds the base: *Go, go, go. . . .* then, *No, no, no. You're broke, you're exhausted, you're beyond this nostalgia business.*

Out of the blue came the image of Jack's face when he saw the miniature Tiger Stadium that my sister Nicole had sent to me a few months before. He was instantly enchanted, even though he wasn't quite sure what it was. When I told him it was a model of a baseball park he nodded and ran his fingers along the basepaths, touched the stands, the dugout, and the tiny home plate. Squinching his face up till he looked like a little bulldog, he asked me if he could ever "go there." Of course, I had said, Yes, of course, buddy, dumbstruck to hear my father's voice in mine.

Looking at him asleep I had one of those "now or never" intuitions. At that moment I knew I had to take him back and show him where I grew up. It was my chance to begin what I hoped would be a lifelong conversation about heroes, competition, freedom, camaraderie, health, exercise, hope, courage, discipline, the joy of accomplishment, the story behind every game, and the beauty of play. It could begin ritually, by our being there together, shoulder to shoulder.

It was time to show my son how I learned to *play.*

It was time to remind myself.

For the next two days, a gemlike flame burned in me. I quickly got on the phone and called my frequent flier program and admitted being five thousand miles short for two award tickets. Being nearly broke, I pleaded for mercy, confiding to the airline rep that I needed to take my three-year-old son back to Detroit to see the last games ever at the old ballpark where I went when I was a boy.

The dead air was chilling. I was afraid that my plea sounded sentimental. "That's so sweet," the representative said, genuinely touched. "Of course, I can help you. I see on my computer you've been one of our premium customers for years, so I think there's a good chance you'll be good for the miles later on. Why don't we just give you credit? Listen, you don't even to mail away for the tickets. They'll be waiting for you at the airport."

I thanked her profusely and contacted my brother Paul, who was living in Louisville at the time, and he leaped at the idea of a rendezvous at the old ballpark, then called our boyhood friend, Jack McCaffrey, who volunteered to get tickets for two of the last three games at the old ballpark. "Hey, I just want to help," he said. "I think it's pretty cool that you want to bring your son home."

Twenty-five years had gone by, but to my old friends it was still my real home. Over the next few days of preparation for the journey, the way my childhood friend pronounced the word *home* got me thinking about the whole notion of home again. As I prepared for the trip, I thought about the mythic image of home as intertwined with my deep identification with sports. I recalled Salman Rushdie's description of "imaginary homelands," countries of the mind, memory, imagination, and faith, the composite homelands of the new world of accelerated immigration, what the English scholar of fairy tales, Marina Warner, has called "existential dislocation." In a restless world home is a moving target. The modern anxiety about homelessness and rootlessness intensifies the urge for creating home in the world of the imagination, sinking roots however we can, an impulse that is at the heart of myth-making. The Caribbean poet and playwright Derek Walcott, in his stage adaptation of the *Odyssey*, has Menelaus, King of Sparta, say, "We earn home, like everything else."

This profound push out of the soul to get home is at the heart of pure nostalgia, but what of what religious historian Mircea Eliade called "nostalgia for paradise," the deep yearning to return to the place that will renew us?

Surely, my journey back to Detroit was no return to paradise, considering what had happened to the place over the years—or was it? After all, *paradise* was simply the old Arab word for "walled garden," and wasn't that a poetic way to describe the green fields of a ballpark, especially a garden within the often war zone-like atmosphere of a city like Detroit? And mythically speaking, wasn't paradise just the sacred place you returned for renewal?

"In mythical geography," Eliade wrote in *Images and Symbols*, "sacred space is the essentially *real* space, for in the archaic world the myth alone is real." That is the secret power of myth, the search for the deeply real. That's what I wanted to feel again and pass on to my son, the raw and the real, what we used to call "down home."

That's my myth, and I'm sticking to it.

The Green Cathedral

Faster than you can say "Rocco Dominico Colavito" (another of my boyhood baseball heroes), my son and I were back in the land of urban legend. In my parent's time Detroit was known as the City of Champions, a robust city that prided itself for putting the world on wheels. By the time I was growing up, in the suburbs a few miles away, it had decayed physically, spiritually, and politically. By my third year at the University of Detroit, in the early 1970s, life had become so dangerous for students and teachers that a barbed-wire fence was erected along the perimeter of the campus. Every journey downtown for a class, a movie, an art show, or a ballgame was like a trip into a war zone. Many fled the Motor City in those years, but the siege mentality also fostered a fierce resolve in those who stayed and tried to revive the city. Loyalty was at the heart of the devotion to the local sports teams. I vividly remember that sense of pride, the solidarity with friends at school, the mailman, the grocer, aunts and uncles, sportswriters, and the players themselves. In a besieged world you sink roots any way you can. You hunker down together. You learn to care—or be corroded from within by the rust of cynicism.

Twenty-five years after leaving home to see the world, I was standing with my son and Ed Fallon, an old family friend, on the corner of Michigan and Trumbull, staring at the huge white fortress of a ballpark. The stadium, the oldest ballpark in the land, was built on the site of an old haymarket in 1896, the year when the young Henry Ford was tinkering with the combustion engine and gold was discovered in the Klondike. The original park was expanded, renamed Bennett Field, and officially opened on April 12, 1912, the week the Titanic went down. Later it became Navin Field, then Briggs Stadium in 1938, and finally Tiger Stadium in 1961, the year I first remember following the team on a day-to-day basis. I was nine, an age susceptible to hero worship and mythmaking, and I followed the Tigers by radio that year while they ran neck-and-neck with the Yankees of Maris and Mantle, until fading in September. From then on I was consumed by baseball, listening to every possible game on radio, reading two sports sections a day, memorizing all the statistics of all the players in both leagues, playing fantasy ball on a board and disc game, and most important, from the first thaw of winter to the last fallen leaf of autumn, playing sandlot ball dawn till dusk down the street at Forest Park, the site of our neighborhood baseball diamonds.

My passion for the team peaked in 1968, the year the team beat the Cardinals in the World Series, but the dramatic victory was significant in ways that transcended baseball. It was the year after the '67 riots, when tanks had rumbled through the streets of Detroit while it burned for five days, and forty-three people were killed. The city was under siege as the 1968 season opened. More guns were bought by distraught citizens than at any time in its history, turning the city into an armed camp.

But then mythic things began to unfold down at the old stadium. The team began to win in April and never stopped, creating a distraction from the social turmoil, but also providing a window of symbolism. The harmony of black and white teammates playing together escaped no one.

After Mickey Lolich beat Bob Gibson in the seventh game of the Series, the city was turned, as the *Detroit News* reported, "into a madhouse of joy," and "Detroit exploded in delirium. It was Christmas, the Fourth of July, Halloween, New Year's Eve, V-J Day, and the Mardi Gras rolled into one. Strangers kissed and cheered, horns blatted over and over and over." The day after the great victory the *Detroit Free Press* wrote, in an unsigned editorial:

> There was laughter in the streets and the canyons overflowed with a joy long overdue. Until then, it had been a difficult year. The snow stayed too long and the coming of spring brought not beginnings but the destruction of two magnificent lives [Martin Luther King, Jr., and Bobby Kennedy] whose loss made it painful to try to hope again.

Our sorrow was a shadow that clung to the months ahead and the days were gray in spite of their sunshine. In a game, we found solace and a happiness that could be made to last through a summer afternoon.... From a game, we learned that hope is worth having for the joy that it can bring. In the ecstasy of our afternoon, something of ourselves returned and told the truth about the kind of people we really are: capable of happiness and selflessness and commitment. With love and abandon, we celebrated into the night. This hope, at least, had come true. Their victory was ours and it felt full and fine.

It was a summer of mythic struggles, a season of rebirth, inspired by a game that healed a wounded city. My main memory is aural, the sound of the games coming not only through the little transistor radio that I carried with me everywhere that summer, but the sound coming from house after house, neighborhood after neighborhood, car after car, the sound of a game played by men who had not forgotten how to be boys, a game that rallied lost dreams. I have been trying to figure out why ever since.

I suspect it begins with the "green cathedral," the "church of baseball," as Susan Sarandon refers to the ballpark she visits religiously in the great baseball movie *Bull Durham*. In the spring of 1981, the batting coach for the San Francisco Giants told sportswriter Lowell Cohn, "When I think of a stadium, it's like a temple. It's religious." The first time he saw Yankee Stadium he almost cried. "It was very moving. My God, Ruth played there and Gehrig.... They left their spirits there. I know it. I hope I've made myself clear. I've never said those things before. I didn't know they were in me." The coach's self-surprising reflections lead us to the heart of the matter of the mythic dimension of life. The mythic reveals depths we have been ignoring—or never knew existed.

The Mythic Magic

As we walked across Michigan Avenue, Jack was overjoyed to point out the red bricks and trolley tracks still visible underneath the old street.

Knowing trains were the love of his young life, I told him my father used to ride the trolleys to the ballgame when he was a boy. His eyes widened and suddenly everything about the Tigers was twice as cool.

As we nudged our way through the well-burnished wooden turnstiles and into the cavernous concourse, I thought of my first visit with my father, back in 1963, as if only a day—or a ballgame—had passed. Ed and Jack and I made our way through the teeming crowd to one of the souvenir stands. All around us were crumbling concrete walls and rusty pipes, but I was fonder of it by far than the cookie-cutter stadiums that had cluttered up the landscape the last twenty years. I thought to myself, *God, I love this place.* It smelled the way a real ballpark is supposed to smell, of beer and sauerkraut hot dogs, and sounded like one, with the *thwack* of fungo bats resounding across the ballpark, the jibing of jostling fans carrying tattered leather baseball gloves, and everywhere the glorious Gothic D on the caps of players and fans alike.

Still, I had a strange feeling as I bought a scorebook for the game, ice cream for Jack, and beers for Ed and me, and led them to the ramp that would take us to our upper deck seats. The stadium appeared to be on the verge of becoming another one of Detroit's ruins, as some were referring to the vast number of abandoned monuments around the city, like the old train station and steel plants. Recently, I had stumbled across a Web site with a virtual tour of its latter-day ruins, whose images reminded me of the illicit after-hour tours of the catacombs below Paris. I flashed on the moonlit night in Rome years before when I hopped the guardrail with an old buddy and snuck inside the moonlit Coliseum, and descended into the maze of gladiator quarters that lay below the arena floor, reveling in the evidence that history was real as stone. The ruins of the Old World had helped preserve memory, a sense of continuity with the past. *What will happen to the New World,* I wondered, *if we keep destroying our links to the past?*

Suddenly my reverie was broken when Jack asked me, "Papa, where's the park? You promised to take me to a park today."

"I said *ballpark,* buddy. A ballpark is a place where they play ball. This is it!"

As we strode up the shadowy ramp leading to the third deck, I tried to explain to him where we were and why we were there.

"Jack, buddy, *this* is the ballpark, this is where they play baseball," I said softly, stroking his face with the side of my hand. "I used to come here with *my* papa, and he used to come here with *his* papa, and he used to come here with *his* papa." It was true. My Great-grandfather, Charlemagne Cousineau brought my Grandfather Horace here to see Ty Cobb tangle with his archrival Babe Ruth back in the 1920s. Later, Grandpa Horace brought my dad here in 1938 to see Hank Greenberg challenge Ruth's home run record. In the 1960s my dad brought me to watch Kaline chase down fly balls in deep right center field.

For me, this was the secret charm of baseball: its continuity, the passing of tradition, ritual, ceremony, the very soul of culture. Those of us who grew up in the Detroit area in the 1960s knew it was no accident that our town had given the world soulful athletes like the boxer Joe Louis, hockey star Gordie Howe, and basketball phenom Dave Bing, *plus* soul music geniuses like Smoky Robinson, the Supremes, and the Temptations.

With all this running through my mind, I was almost whispering as we made our way to our seats. It felt like we were entering a sacred temple, and my face turned crimson with embarrassment. But Jack was concentrating solely on his ice cream bar, which was dripping all over his sleeve.

Looking up, Jack asked me again, "Papa, where's the park you're taking me to? You *promised*." He looked more confused than ever and began to sniffle and whimper that he wanted me to take him to a *real* park, the kind with slides and swings. I had the shivery sensation of my heart melting while trying to control a burst of laughter.

Then we reached the upper deck and the glorious panorama of Tiger Stadium. Stretching out before us was to me one of the most beautiful sights in the world. The green grass of the outfield and the sea of blue seats seemed to shimmer under the lights like an American mandala. Gazing at it for even a few moments was calming and meditative, even as the infield was a blur of bright white baseballs and hustling ballplayers, razzing coaches and frenetic sportswriters.

"See, buddy, it's out there." My voice was cracking as we paused for a moment next to the guardrail. Jack gripped my hand and shouted, "Oh, look, Papa, I see it. There it is, there's the park!" Everything was suddenly, miraculously, okay with him.

"You're right, buddy. There's the park.... Beautiful, isn't it?" I said.

Uncannily, just as I was feeling bewildered by the beauty of the place, I overheard the fellow next to me, his face painted with orange and black Tiger stripes, confess to his girlfriend, "You're right, it wasn't the most rational thing in the world to do. But I don't care how much money it cost us to fly back from Europe. This is more than just a ballgame. This is *family*. It's like saying good-bye to my youth."

I clutched Jack's hand and felt another surge of befuddling emotion as we plunked down into our seats. "C'mon, let's get settled," I said, restlessly, and helped him with his ice cream, pennant, and peanuts, then gave him a hug.

"Papa, this is *great*," he said, as he looked around the ballpark and his eyes widened at the general carnival atmosphere. Thousands of flashbulbs were going off across the park as fans began documenting their own last games. It was some consolation that I wasn't the only one who was almost dizzy with sentimental attachment. It had a scuffed-up soul but still looked beautiful to me, as gorgeous as the day I first saw it, back in that summer of '63 when my dad brought my little brother and me to see the Tiger's Jim Bunning duel the Twin's Camilo Pascual, only to lose 12-1. If I squint, I swear I can still see Harmon Killebrew pole-axing two homers into the seats and Norm Cash crushing a solo homer into the upper deck in right. If I close my eyes, I can smell my dad's menthol aftershave and see him in his white Marlon Brando-style T-shirt as he studies his newspaper while his boys watch the drama of the unfolding game.

The exactitude of that memory is at the heart of the myth of sports. The way that afternoon stands out in bas-relief to hundreds of other experiences with my father underscores the game's symbolic importance, its elegiac quality, its transcendent possibilities.

Settling into my seat, I gazed out over the great green expanse of the outfield and sensed what W. P. Kinsella called "the thrill of the grass" in his cult classic, *Shoeless Joe.* Most of the pantheon of baseball heroes had played there: Ty Cobb, Babe Ruth, Tris Speaker, Mickey Mantle, Joe DiMaggio, Ted Williams, Willie Mays, Hank Aaron. I imagined their ghosts shagging flyballs one last time, like the old-time ballplayers in *Field of Dreams,* phantoms who came back—to a cornfield in Iowa—for one more chance to play ball, one last chance to redeem themselves. My kinescopic memories reminded me of something that the old Tiger slugger Darrell Evans said when asked back in the late '70s about losing Tiger Stadium, "It would be a real shame to lose that place.... Where would all the ghosts live if it were torn down?"

Ghosts, spirits, phantoms, presences. *Is that what makes the place mythic?* I wondered. Is that what connects this old ballpark with the other sacred sites of the world? A sense of presence and celebration?

The crowd was far more celebratory than any I'd seen in a long time. I had expected more anger about the abandonment of one of Detroit's greatest sources of pride and tradition. Apparently those battles had already been fought, and lost, when the city decided to build a new stadium a few miles away as part of another attempt to revive the moribund downtown area. Was it resignation about the corruption of local politics? Was it a loss of pride in the genuine past?

No, there was something else, rarified and wonderful in the air as we sat down in our seats. I looked around at the vast range of fans, ranging from factory workers to lawyers, grandparents to newlyweds, white, Latino, and black, and was struck by the solidarity, and one unexpected word came to mind: love. It's not too strong a word. It was love for the rusty old ballpark, love for the losingest team in the league, love for the besieged town, love for the mystery of the game, love of the play. Love for the *uniform,* as Jerry Seinfeld had once joked to David Letterman on *The Late Show* about the true source of his devotion to the Yankees.

But as the man said, "The play is the thing," and the man on the field is the umpire, whose hand shot up in the air, and who bellowed, "Play ball!" Fifty thousand strong roared with the hope that springs eternal, which is aroused at the beginning of every sporting event, the philosophical lesson that is learned there perhaps better than in any other human endeavor.

At that moment, I felt like I had come home.

Affectionately, I rubbed the top of Jack's baseball cap, as if to remind myself why I had dragged him clear across the country. Since he was a baby his mom and I had surrounded him with books and stories, things we deeply believe in, but there was this other part of life I wanted to share with him, the pageantry of sports. I wanted to show him how learning to "root, root, root for the home team," as the seventh-inning song goes, is one way to learn how to sink roots in your home.

I wanted to tell him how I had grown up with the notion that the well-rounded life included devotion to the mind and the body. In fact, it was drummed into me. We read books, but if my father caught us inside the house on a sunny day we were physically thrown outside and told to play, and often weren't let inside until the sun went down. Every day, sunny or stormy, we were shunted outside to play in the yard or down at the ballpark.

It wasn't only in great books and movies, but in stadiums that I saw men become heroes, and heroes become gods, and time stand still, and thousands of people find a little unity and pride about their life and times in the midst of an intensely fractured life. As I began to play, then compete, in baseball, basketball, track and field, I learned that sports could be as profound a source of spiritual awakening as art, literature, nature, or even love.

The beauty of it is elemental. It is play first, raised to an often magnificent level. According to Johan Huizinga, in his classic study, *Homo Ludens,* play "casts a spell over us; it is 'enchanting,' 'captivating.' It is invested with the noblest qualities we are capable of perceiving in things: rhythm and harmony."

That first night back at Tiger Stadium I thought back to a peculiar moment with my well-meaning but sports-hating Uncle Lou during my senior year in high school, just after my parents divorced. "Why do you have to still play those games, Phil?" he asked, derisively, referring to my basketball career. "You have to grow up now. Be a man. You should get a job after school to help out your mom."

"I don't know," I mumbled, like most high school kids when asked to explain themselves. Inside, I was dying to say, "It's fun. I love it." Instead, I muttered, "I just have to."

I was angry with him, but knew I couldn't show it. He was dying of Hodgkin's disease, and at least was trying to help out my mom. He was part of a family that believed wholeheartedly in the deeply entrenched American Myth of Work, and disdained all frivolous activities, including music, movies, the arts, and sports.

What neither my uncle nor I knew back then was that play is incalculably important in the entire evolution of human beings. But then again, being a good Catholic, he may have been suspicious about evolution, too.

The Myth of Play

On a blistering hot afternoon several years ago, in the central plains of Greece, I rode into the ancient town of Olympia on the back of a wily old peasant's watermelon cart. He had picked me up a few miles out of town after my last hitchhiking ride had left me on the side of the dusty road, and dropped me at the door of a small hostel, but not before offering me one last drink of *retsina* from his old wine bag.

After checking in, I shambled out to the ruins of the ancient sanctuary. The moment I crossed the threshold entrance into the ancient grounds I could feel the silence of the ages. Twilight flickered on the ancient stones. The air smelled of sweet pine and oleander. Even the birds seemed reverent as they swooped through the gnarled olive trees and evergreen oaks. The wild flowers scattered among the tumbled ruins looked like bright red and yellow asterisks, as if footnotes to the serene beauty.

As if in a trance, I drifted among the tumbled columns of the Temple of Zeus in Olympia, one of the Seven Wonders of the Ancient World, then ambled past the site of the sculptor Phidias' workshop, where he created the colossal chryselephantine sculpture of Zeus and the temple of Hera where the Olympic torch is lit every four years. Then with my heart pounding wildly, I crossed under the single arch of stones that once was part of the vaulted entrance tunnel, and crossed into the stadium.

Stretching out ahead of me lay the Ur-track for all runners. It was laid out, according to tradition, by Hercules himself, who walked off six hundred paces, about 210 yards (the *stadia*) to establish the dimensions of a sacred precinct for his father Zeus. The track was flanked on both sides by an earthen embankment that once held more than twenty thousand spectators. When German archaeologists excavated the stadium, which had lay hidden under thirteen feet of mud for a thousand years, they found votive offerings that had been intentionally buried in the seating banks, an attempt perhaps to gain the favor of the fates.

Walking off a few of my own paces, I was startled to find one of the last intact pieces of the long-revered stadium. Still embedded in the ground after almost three thousand years was the starting slab for the foot racers. It ran the width of the dirt track and could accommodate twenty barefoot, usually nude, runners at a time.

I couldn't resist. Remembering the proper form from four years of running high school track, I knelt down on one knee, and slipped my right shoe into the groove cut into the weather-worn stone. Trying to conjure up the classical Greek equivalent of "On your mark, get set...."

I slowly rose into starting position, counted to three, then pushed off and sprinted for a hundred yards or so down the hallowed ground, before slowing down to a jog for the last few yards.

When I reached the *terma*, the traditional end line of the track, I was huffing and puffing in the still-searing heat. I felt exhausted but exultant as sweat ran down my face and chest and I bent over to catch my breath. The stillness was shattered by the sound of a shrill whistle. Reluctantly, I turned and saw a guard windmilling his arm to signal me to come over to where he was sitting under small copse of olive trees. Hands on hips and red-faced in embarrassment that the short run had winded me, I walked slowly toward him. At first I thought I had committed some grievous error. Perhaps it was sacrilegious to run here? Maybe I had forgotten to make some kind of offering? But to my amazement, he reached up into the tree and broke off a couple of sprigs. Deftly, he fashioned them into a crown. I took a few steps toward him, and playing along, leaned over and was awarded a crown of laurels.

We said nothing, not knowing each other's language, but just smiled in that dream of the common language that is sports.

After thanking him profusely I wandered around the grounds and found a restful spot under a gnarled olive tree. In the dappled light of late afternoon I read my well-thumbed edition of Pausanius' *Guide to Greece*, dwelling for a few minutes on his description of the revered statue of Zeus "made of gold and ivory…seated on a throne here; he wears a wreath of olive leaves and holds a gold-and-ivory Victory." An hour later, I found another spot among the ruins of the Temple of Zeus, and lazily opened up a history of Greece by Alexander Eliot that my father had given me years before. Out tumbled two photocopied pages of historian Will Durant's description of the Games, from *The Life of Greece*.

For years my father had been tucking notes and hiding messages into books and magazines, but this was an unexpected surprise. Eagerly, I read Durant's description of the Olympics: "We must not think of the average Greek as a student and lover of Aeschylus or Plato, rather, like the typical Briton or American, he was interested in sport, and his favored athletes were his earthly gods." The real religion of the Greeks, he surmised, was the worship of health, beauty, and strength. After all, hadn't Socrates himself said, "What a disgrace it is for a man to grow old without ever seeing the beauty and strength of which his body is capable"? Of all the competitions around Greece, the Olympiad was considered the most sacred, held as they were in the sacred grove of Gaia and Kronos, the goddess and god of the earth and sky, and rounded out by music performances, poetry readings, historical lectures, and great flights of oratory by the most respected philosophers and playwrights of the day.

As I read, the words turned luminous, reminding me of the poet Ezra Pound's definition of poetry being words that glow like a ball of light in your hand. In that moment I thought I had found not only the birthplace of modern sports, but the origins of the romantic ideal of the fully rounded life that has come down through the Western traditions for the last twenty-seven centuries, right into my own dreams.

The afternoon turned crepuscular while I lazed among the ruins. It slowly occurred to me that I may have stumbled upon my father's secret source for his ideal of the well-lived life. As the sun warmed the huge stones of the temple I was leaning against, my mind meandered back to a recollection about the English traveler who was wandering these parts in the eighteenth century. By a fortunate twist of fate he saw a glimmer of marble in the ground somewhere near where I lay musing over the past. Using his fingers he dug for a few minutes and discovered the base of a fluted column. Tantalized by his discovery, he spent the rest of the day rooting around the peaceful grove and found traces of once-mighty walls and a scattering of enormous stones overgrown with vegetation. Knowing his history, the traveler realized in a rapture that the column was part of the ancient Temple of Zeus, and that he had stumbled upon the long lost grounds of the sanctuary of Olympia, the mythic birthplace of sports.

My own discovery wasn't as dramatic, but it was just as meaningful to me, which is the secret strength of personal mythmaking.

It is always a revelation to discover the guiding images of your life.

The Sacred Grove

Deep-browed scholars now say archaeological evidence for the origins of the Games pushes the traditional schoolbook date of 776 B.C.E. back six centuries to around 1370 B.C.E. The reigning theory is that modest gatherings and staged games were held on the banks of the Alpheios River as part of a very old cult of the dead, as evidenced by the foundations of more than sixty-nine altars in the Attis. Other factors include the natural tendency of a warlike people to be in constant training and finding ways to keep its male youths primed for battle.

Many commentators have noted that politics and religion failed to unite Greece, but athletics did, at least for a few weeks every four years. The philosophical underpinning of the Games was that they established the ideal for athletes, soldiers, politicians, emperors, statesmen, peasants, merchants, philosophers, and trainers, who all traveled by roads and rivers from as far away as Africa and Asia Minor to the grassy plain on banks of Alpheios River. They were there to witness the spectacle of the finest athletes in the Greek world competing for the laurels in most prestigious contest of all, the Olympiad. The foundation, however, was just as important. The ancient Greeks dated the origins of the Games to mythical times, as personified by Pelops, who called the Games to celebrate his marriage to Oedamus, and by Hercules, the embodiment of friendship, fealty, and the ambiguous gift of divine strength. The Games strove to be a marriage of mind, body, and soul, as well as an opportunity to forge friendship and loyalty in a world constantly at war. To accomplish that, athletes and spectators vied to learn, as Hercules had to, the appropriate use of their strength.

While pilgrimage to other sacred sites, such as Delphi, situated high in the mountains, demanded an ordeal, the tranquil setting at Olympia in the grassy plains required the almost subversive idea of reconciliation. Among the estimated two hundred thousand spectators from across the far-flung empire were Athenians, Spartans, Dorians, Ionians, Macedonians, Ephesians, and scores of others—as many strangers and enemies as allies and friends. The Greek archaeologist Manolis Andronicos writes that when all were gathered together at the Games they were forced to contemplate their unity and required to act peacefully, as they were in the sacred grove of Zeus. "The supreme significance of Games," Andronicos points out, "demanded that all be present in peaceful assembly in the sacred grove."

An early clue to the mythic vitality of the Games can be found in one of the famous odes written by the poet Pindar. His ode, which would have been sung at an open-air feast, celebrates both fleetness of foot and the fertility of the goddess. In the four opening lines we find the central metaphor for the Games, an echo of the deep relationship between play, competition, the attempt to unite an entire people:

> Single is the race, single,
>
> of men and gods.

From a single mother we both

draw breath.

To the Greeks, existence itself was a race between life and death. At least during the Games they were temporary members of the "single race." Greeks raced or watched as one race. The spectators camped for five days, some in the open air, others in the splendor of the fabulous guesthouse, in a noisy, hot, crowded festival atmosphere. The Olympiad was the site of raucous political talk, treaty and alliance signings, reunions of old friends and allies, as well as a bit of a classic country fair with horse dealing, food vendors, acrobats, jugglers, fire eaters, sword swallowers, and priests who specialized in animal sacrifices on the altars of the Attis. The famous writer Menander's description was laconic: "Crowd, market, acrobats, amusements, thieves."

Olympia also became the first museum of the ancient world, enriched by the devotion and prayers of worshipers and champions, a sanctuary of reminders and records of the past, embellished by dedications of champions and poets of buildings and sculptors. Moreover, to entertain crowds there were music performances and readings by scholars, poets, and playwrights, such as Gorgias, Hippias, Herodotus, and Menander.

Any free Greek male could compete, provided he swore to train for ten months. But the religious conservatism of the time prevented women from either observing or competing in the Olympic Games. As horse owners, however, they could sponsor their own teams in the chariot events. The most notable among them was Kyniska, the daughter of King Archidamos of Sparta, where women *were* encouraged to participate in athletics. According to Pausanius, she won an Olympic victory in her own chariot. A recently discovered inscription at the base of a monument in the sanctuary of Olympia suggests that she erected a statue of herself, as was the custom for the male winners. An ancient writer copied the entire inscription from the monument, which has been modernized by Judith Swaddling of the British Museum:

Sparta's kings were fathers and brothers of mine,

But since with my chariot and storming horses, I, Kyniska,

Have won the prize, I place my effigy here

And proudly proclaim

That of all Grecian women I first bore the crown.

Despite being prevented from the general competition at the Olympic Games, women were allowed to stage their own competition, the Heraia, which was performed for the glory of the goddess. They were organized by the leading women of the nearby town of Elis, a custom that dated back to the wedding of Hippodameia and Pelops. There were three events, all footraces of 160 meters for girls and women of different ages. One of their races was observed by Pausanius, who wrote that "their hair hangs down, a tunic reaches to a little above the knee, and they bare the right shoulder as far as the breast." The winners were crowned with olive crowns and granted the right of hanging a painting or raising a statue of themselves in Hera's temple.

In the main events, discus throwers, javelin hurlers, jumpers, boxers, and wrestlers consulted oracles and swore oaths as they vied to dis-

A sixth-century B.C.E. vase painting of women runners competing in a race in honor of the goddess Hera at Olympia.

play the divine qualities of strength, endurance, honor, and purity that their priests and trainers told them were within them. These attributes were embodied in the earliest tales we have of the Games.

According to Alexander Eliot in *The Timeless Myths,* in the very first games Zeus wrestled Kronos, and Apollo outraced Hermes, who turned around and outboxed Ares. Olympic lore abounds in legendary accounts, such as the Greek sprinter who outran a hare, and a long-distance runner who raced a horse twenty miles from Coronea to Thebes. It is said that the six-time champion wrestler, Milo of Crotona, trained for the Games by carrying a calf every day until it had grown into a bull. But he was most admired for the control he had over his own strength, as he showed one day when he held a pomegranate so tightly in his fist no one could take it away—yet his touch was gentle enough that not a drop of juice fell to the ground. Another popular anecdote tells of a fifth-century winner named Diagoras whose two sons won laurels at the 448 B.C.E. games. The sons celebrated their victories by placing their wreaths on their father's head and carrying him around the stadium on their shoulders. It is said that as the champions passed by, a friend shouted out to their father that he could die a happy man, because he had nothing left to accomplish other than climbing Mount Olympus itself.

The survival of these myths, legends, and actual lists of victors through the centuries reflects the Greek ideal of human accomplishment. The Games weren't just any games, but were considered displays of godlike powers. Rather than grandiosity, this was respect for the numinous dimension of running, jumping, wrestling, and racing, a recognition of the moments when an athlete feels "the god within," which is the very definition of *enthusiasm.*

By custom, many cities awarded great sums of money to their champions, streets were named after them, odes were written in their honor, land was granted to them, free food and tax exemption for the rest of their lives was awarded to them. They were so heralded that the philosophers of the day complained, somewhat like today's artists bemoaning the salaries of modern athletes and the ink awarded them in daily newspapers. As the Associated Press reporter Mort Rosenblum wrote from Sydney in 2000, Pinder would have been amazed at the sight of the Olympics 2,500 years on. But then maybe not. "Along with the glory, there was political appeasement and publicity hype, corruption and commercialism, drug use, big-money prizes, high-tech gear, and everything from traffic jams to ticket scams."

In that light, the striving for perfection, the honoring of the body, the belief in the beauty of competition is idealistic. The games have survived the all too human failings of any group activity, including scurrilous scandals ranging from Nero's cheating in the chariot races of the Games in 66 C.E., to Hitler's barring of two Jewish athletes at the 1936 Berlin Games, and the egregious obsession with achieving the almighty edge in recent Games, including payoffs, cheating, and doping scandals.

Glimmers of the original spirit of the games, the belief that international competition can ennoble human life and bring about solidarity between people who are divided by geography and politics, has reappeared every now and again since the revival of the Games in 1896. The striving for godlike performance can be heard in the words of the usually reserved Roger Bannister, legendary shatterer of the four-minute-mile barrier in 1954, who once said, "Records are ephemeral. The winning of an Olympic title is eternal." The decathlon winner at the 1968 Olympic games in Mexico City, Bill Toomey, said, "It's like being Peter Pan. It's like a window on your soul and you don't feel you will ever die." In response to a question from *Sports Illustrated* about her pursuit of five gold medals at the 2000 Sydney Games, the ethereally calm Marion Jones replied, "That's my goal. To do something no one has ever done before."

The mythic dimension of sports has survived since the beginning of recorded competition, despite today's reality being worlds apart from the original ideal. But as baseball legend Satchel Page once admitted, "I ain't what I used to be, but who is?"

Durant's conclusion continues to inspire: "The Greeks believed that by frequent public competitions they could stimulate not only the ability of the performer but the taste of the public as well. The principle was applied to almost every art—to pottery, poetry, sculpture, painting, choral, singing, oratory, and drama. In this way, the games had a profound influence upon art and literature, and even upon the writing of history; for the chief method of reckoning time, in later Greek historiography was [determined] by Olympiads."

Behind the romantic myth is the real myth, the inner meaning of play and competition, the sacred history of how a few imperfect human beings strive to experience a moment of perfection, a transcendent experience combining mental discipline and physical endurance that defies time and dramatizes destiny. This at least was what the Baron Pierre de Coubertin had in mind when he announced "the splendid and beneficent task of reviving the Olympic Games" in 1896, dreaming as he did of inspiring world peace through sport.

"Let us export our oarsmen, our runners, our fencers to other lands. That is the true free trade of the future; and the day it is introduced into Europe the cause of peace will have received a new and strong ally." By the time of his death in 1937, the Games had returned but had already been suspended by one world war, falling short of the Greek ideal of calling truces during wars. But the baron had also said, "For me, sport is a religion, with church, dogma, ritual."

It is easy to dismiss the statement as hopelessly romantic, but it is worth considering the remarks by the Czechoslovakian runner Emil Zatopek after the 1956 Games: "The revival of the Olympics was as if the sun had come out. The Olympics are the one true time." The Czech hero could have been citing Pausanius, Pindar, or NBA basketball coach Phil Jackson. In his book *Sacred Hoops*, the coach referred to the feverish passion for sports as "the old time religion," and described the worldwide desire for his star Michael Jordan to return to the Chicago Bulls in 1995, after two years away from the game, as "the yearning for the mythic hero who could set us free."

A sentiment worthy of ancient Olympia, but set us free from what?

Perhaps the limits of what we believe we can accomplish on our own.

Or the reluctance to appreciate and praise excellence.

The One True Time

After the umpire's arm shot up to signal, "Play ball," the Tiger's starting pitcher, Don Mliki, wound up and delivered the symbolic first pitch of the ballgame, a ninety-mile-an-hour fastball past the first Kansas City Royal batter. The pitch pounded like a piledriver into the catcher's mitt of the young All-Star Brad Ausmus and the sound resounded across the ballpark. After only a few pitches the game settled into its easygoing pace, which soon reminded me of why I love it. When time slows down, memory rushes in, and there is more of a chance for close observation, easy conversation, or private reverie.

"Within the ballpark," writes the poet laureate of baseball, Roger Angell, "time moves differently, marked by no clock except the events of the game.... Since baseball time is measured only in outs, all you have to do is succeed utterly, keep hitting, keep the rally alive, and you have defeated time. You remain forever young." What drags for some is timeless for others. In our accelerated world, it is trendy to disparage the slow pace of baseball and revel in the fast pace of football, basketball, hockey, and now the X-Games.

That is where the myth of baseball comes in. Its anachronistic pace and images, its retro ballparks designed to evoke nineteenth-century rural life are not empty exercises in nostalgia, but soulful moves that transform glorified playgrounds into "fields of dreams." And the myth says, to paraphrase Yogi Berra, that you can learn a lot about life—*just by watching baseball.*

The magic was even working on our old friend Ed, who didn't grow up as a fan. Looking around the ballpark, all glowing now under the bright lights, he waxed nostalgic about coming to the stadium "a few years back" with some friends of his from his days in the Navy. When I asked him when that might have been, assuming he meant in the last few years, he said, "Oh, 1955," and we both laughed at the thought of forty-four years just slipping past. Of course, his response shouldn't have surprised me. Timelessness is one of the hallmarks of mythic space.

"Did you ever come here with your Dad?" I probed a little more, and he shook his head sadly, saying that his father was always home drinking on his days off, but his mom brought him by streetcar when he was a kid. While Jack worked over his ice cream bar and the crowd around us hooted for the Tigers to put some runs on the board, Ed and I talked about Detroit's decision to replace our beloved ballpark with one more soulless skybox stadium. It was a bitter reminder of the city's seemingly shame-driven moves to destroy its own past during the past few decades.

"The old landmarks, everything that gave Detroit character, they're all going fast," Ed said, uncharacteristically nostalgic. "The Dodge Main Plant, Olympia, where the Red Wings used to play, the Boblo Boats, Stroh's Brewery, the Vernors Ginger Ale plant—did you know it's the oldest soda pop in the world? Hell, I saw them blow up J. L. Hudson's, one of the oldest and most beautiful department stores in the world. Now foreigners own the River Rouge Plant and Motown has moved out West. It's a goddamned shame."

He took a long swig of beer.

"By Monday night," he said, "the stadium will become another abandoned part of Detroit, like those skyscrapers, bungalows, fire stations, bowling alleys, factories, fish stores, tool and die shops, libraries, and Dom Polski Halls."

"At least the game never changes," I ventured. "It reminds me of the Rip Van Winkle theory of baseball. Somebody from the turn of the century should be able to wake up after being asleep for about seventy years, stride into a ballpark, and still understand the game."

Ed smiled and laughed, "Yeah, except I still don't understand it. I don't even know who we're playing tonight!" He downed his beer, and added, "Kinda warm tonight, isn't it?" changing the subject like a pitcher changing his mind about the next pitch.

Three up, three down here at "The Corner," as the ballpark had been recently dubbed. The crowd roared and I was glad to be sitting with the old faithful. The chatter around us was that of folks who'd been to hundreds or thousands of games in their lives. They were there in the late snows of April and through the sweltering afternoons of Indian summer; it's part of the fabric of their life, not a recent yuppie affectation.

Around us was the other side of the pageantry of spectator sports: grown men watching the game while listening to it with radio earplugs, boyfriends teaching their girlfriends how to keep score, other young couples canoodling in the shadowy corner of the bleachers, a Little League team nearby mischievously tossing a pair of binoculars back and forth over the head of the youngest player among them.

The Tigers put two runners on base in the third inning, which inspired somebody to begin the Wave, a ritual I thought had gone out of style with disco music. The stands seemed to undulate like a choppy sea as whole sections of the crowd rose to their feet, a sight that thrilled Jack, though he couldn't sort it all out.

In the fifth inning the Royals took the lead 2-0 on a sweet single by Mark Sweeney, a long advance fly by Joe Randa, and a triple underneath the Tiger right fielder Kimera Bartee's glove deep in "Kaline's Corner." The Tigers cut the lead to 2-1 in the bottom of the inning on a walk to Ausmus, Tony Clark's right field single, and an error by the right fielder on Dean Palmer's long fly ball.

"Papa, do you know why I love baseball?" Jack asked me after he learned to stand and do the Wave with an ice cream cone in one hand and cotton candy in the other. My heart raced; pride surged in my blood. I was certain that the excitement of the evening had finally sunk in.

"Why, little buddy?" I asked, patting his head with paternal pride, and waited for a little boy's insight about the intricacies of the 6-4-3 double play or a question about the infield fly rule.

Instead, Jack said, "Because I love the ice cream."

I almost spilled my beer laughing.

For a couple of innings I tried to convey a few of the wonders of the game to him, but he became more fascinated by the chemistry of cotton candy, and my attention wandered back to the game. As I did, I realized that every game you watch closely is holographic, with each glimpse containing a memory of every other game you've ever watched or played.

In between asides to Ed and the fans around us I thought of the thousands of games I had played, in sandlot ball, high school and competitive ball in my teens, plus images of my father and uncle, old friends and famous players, then murkier images, from old books and musty museums and my own scrapbook memory. The memories kept coming, as if they had been summoned.

They had. By coming to the game I had summoned them. Of course, that is the function of the temple, to encourage contemplation and provide a space for experiencing a sense of awe and wonder about the world. That is what's supposed to happen. The glory of the game is the rustling of memory, which is really the myth in the making.

As the novelist said, the need for mythmaking is great.

We always need the story that will convince us we had sacred origins. Not "noble origins" or "pure origins," the twisted claims that only leads to eugenics or prisons, but sacred origins.

"Papa, where did it come from?" Jack asked me as we stood for the seventh-inning stretch. He asked as innocently as he had recently asked Jo and me where babies and fishes and trains came from. He asked as sweetly as he did the night he asked, "Papa, where did *everything* come from?"

For a second I thought he meant the seventh-inning stretch tradition, which dates all the way back to 1869, according to the purists. For a moment I mulled over the legend about the opening day crowd at Griffith Stadium in Washington, D.C., that stood in deference to President Taft in the seventh inning when he simply stood up to stretch his legs. Then Jack added, "You know, baseball. Where did it come from?"

"Oh, buddy, I'm glad you asked."

The Creation Myth

Once upon a time, in early 1907, actually, A. G. Spalding, one of the game's early star hurlers and co-founder of the sporting goods company that bears his name, formed a "blue ribbon committee to resolve the origins of the game." Later that summer he sent a mysterious letter to the committee from a certain Abner Graves, a mining engineer. The letter claimed that one day back in 1839, Abner Doubleday, a Civil War hero and friend of Abraham Lincoln, barged into a marbles game that

LOS ANGELES DODGERS
OUTFIELD

ST. LOUIS CARDINALS
OUTFIELD

The once and future aspects are playfully revealed in these baseball card collages by the artist and poet Mikhail Horowitz.

was taking place near a tailor's shop in Cooperstown, New York. According to Graves, Doubleday sketched a baseball field on a piece of paper and explained the rules of "base ball" to those who had congregated around him. Eventually, the Doubleday myth goes, he helped convene local players to play a crude but organized version of the game that became our own.

The Doubleday story is "the lie that tells the truth," as Picasso once defined the function of art. Doubleday was a captain in the Union artillery and is credited with giving the orders for the firing of the first responsive volley of the Civil War. By constellating the origin story around a bona fide American hero who had fired the first shot of the recent war with the invention of the national pastime, Hall recounts the legend of blue teams taking on gray teams during lulls in the fighting. Undoubtedly, this helped spread the popularity and the rulemaking of the new game, but it probably also led to the dubious association of a Civil War officer and the invention of the game. Yet the story fulfills every era's need for a defining myth, the story that fills the emotional void for the ineffable.

Apparently, Spalding believed that the country desperately needed an All-American origin story to bind the identity of the wounded nation after the divisive Civil War. In the doubting words of paleontologist and Boston Red Sox fan, Stephen Jay Gould, the Doubleday story supports the "mythology of the phenomenon that had become so quintessentially American." There was plenty of opposition to the tale from people like Henry Chadwick, who expressed certainty that baseball derived from the British stick-and-ball game called "rounders," or "one old cat" during colonial times. But Chadwick was considered less than patriotic for his theory of "evolutionary change," in Gould's memorable phrase.

Why a cry for myth rather than a shout for science? There has long been a far more verifiable story, that of the most significant innovator of the game in those halcyon days—Alexander Joy Cartwright. Why not champion the man who thought of tagging the runner out rather than throwing the ball at him, foul lines so that spectators could come close to the action, and the rule changes that distinguished baseball from rounders? Why not the truth? Why credit a guy who, as historian Donald Honig writes, probably "didn't know a baseball from a kumquat"?

In his indispensable essay, "The Creation Myths of Cooperstown," Gould describes his objection to the public's need for an indigenous creation myth.

> Scientists often lament that so few people understand Darwin and the principles of biological evolution. But the problem goes deeper. Too few people are comfortable with evolutionary modes of explanation in any form. I do not know why we tend to think so fuzzily in this area, but one reason must reside in our social and psychic attraction to creation myths in preference to evolutionary stories—for creation myths, as noted before, identify heroes and sacred places, while evolutionary stories provide no palpable, particular object as a symbol for reverence, worship, or patriotism.... Yes, heroes and shrines are all very well, but is there not grandeur in the sweep of continuity?

Certainly, there is grandeur. But the soul needs to know how everything began. The Algonquin Indians, who some say have the most extensive body of mythology in the world, some three thousand separate myths, say when you have seen seven generations you have the whole picture. To do that you need to know how things began. The mind needs concepts, the soul needs a story. The well-balanced man or woman, as the Greeks knew, needs both.

Take Time for Paradise

At the Cooperstown, New York, Baseball Hall of Fame there is an affectionate exhibit on Abner Doubleday that is surprisingly sympathetic to the humble intentions of the myth: "In the hearts of those who love baseball, he is remembered as the lad in the pasture where the game was invented. Only cynics would need to know more."

The Doubleday origin story fulfilled the universal need for an indigenous creation myth, in this case one of heroic American origins. However, modern sports scholars now credit Cartwright with arranging the first modern baseball game on June 19, 1846, in Hoboken, New Jersey, where he took his Knickerbocker Base Ball Club of New York to play the New York Nine. With splendid serendipity, the first site happened to be called Elysian Field, after the mythical paradise where the gods went to avoid death. It was there, according to the anonymous writers of myth, that heroes were fated to frolic in the golden fields until the end of time.

As if announcing the Pythagorean belief in the divinity of numbers that day in Elysium also lends us the first baseball score. The Knickerbockers lost to the Nine, 23-1.

The problem, as Gould giddily points out, is that the New York Game that Cartwright helped popularize "may be the highlight of a continuum, but it provides no origin myth for baseball." However, there's no need to take origin myths literally, and no call to take historical origins symbolically.

The game as we know it today incorporated Cartwright's rules with features of the Massachusetts Game, along with many subsequent changes. The game evolved, gradually, as did its myths, from the idealistic musings of the early organizer, Henry Chadwick, who emphasized the health and recreation aspects of baseball.

This is not an insignificant aspect of the American Myth, when we stop to consider the surprisingly long road to respectability that play and even exercise has had in this country. The theologian Michael Novak, in *The Joy of Sports*, calls it the "severe Puritan bias." He writes, "America took root in Protestant culture, and as de Tocqueville noted in 1836, Americans did not play, had no sports, centered their lives in work. As America has grown more Catholic, more Jewish, more various, the world of play has acquired intellectual traditions here."

According to baseball historian John Thorn, "America in the mid-1850s was learning how to play, but still viewed sport in terms of salutary effects on commerce; not until the close of the War Between the States would the focus shift to learning how to play well—for its own sake." This suggests that part of the profound social importance of baseball is the way in which it marks the social move from the grim Puritan work ethic to an ethic of play that encouraged exercise, health, and camaraderie, preferably outdoors.

The poet Walt Whitman detected the soul of the game: "I see great things in baseball. It's our game—the American game. It will take our people out-of-doors, fill them with oxygen, give them a larger physical stoicism. Tend to relieve us from being a nervous, dyspeptic set. Repair these losses, and be a blessing to us."

Underscoring the tenacious continuity of the myth of Olympia, these sentiments echo the ancient Greek ideal, as expressed by the philosopher Simonides: "To be in health is the best thing for man; the next best, to be of form and nature beautiful; the third, to enjoy wealth gotten without fraud; and the fourth, to be in youth's bloom among friends." And in the *Odyssey*, Homer wrote, "There is no greater glory for a man as long as he lives, than that which he wins by his own hands and feet."

The echo from Olympia is great. The field is supposed to be the great leveler, the expression of equality, the display of beautiful, hard-wrought gifts. If you were a Greek male, from anywhere in the empire, you could compete, against an athlete of any social class. You just had to sacrifice, respect the games, learn from your trainers, honor the gods. And you had be free. The Greeks believed that the Olympiad separated them from the barbarians, who were defined as those who didn't speak Greek or play games.

The myth is the model, which isn't always the ideal it is supposed to be. When the myth no longer works, it needs changing, which brings up the shadow side of our National Pastime.

The journalist David Halberstam has written:

> It was part of our folklore, basic to our national democratic myth, that sports was the great American equalizer, that money and social status did not matter upon the playing fields. Elsewhere life was assumed to be unfair: those who had privilege passed it on to their children, who in turn had easier, softer lives. Those without privilege were doomed to accept the essential injustices of daily life. But according to the American myth, in sports the poor but honest kid from across the tracks could gain (often in competition with richer, snottier kids) recognition and acclaim for his talents.

In this way, the myth of sports in general reflects the cultural myth at large. Behind the fog of statistics and spoiled sports behavior is the ancient insight that the way we play tells us as much about ourselves as the way we think, that what we *do* with our bodies is as important as what we do with our minds. For instance, the unfulfilled promise of equal rights for one and all under the Constitution was rationalized for nearly two hundred years, from 1776 until 1947. That is a hallmark year for the game and the country. It is the year that the courageous Branch Rickey stifled decades of pernicious opposition to black players in major league baseball, and chose the brilliant and unflappable second baseman Jackie Robinson.

Robinson broke the "color barrier" to play with the Brooklyn Dodgers. Despite intolerable abuse, Robinson proved to be a player and a man of unimpeachable integrity, grace, and courage, and the doors slowly creaked open for others to follow him. Another great player from the "Colored Leagues," Monte Irvin, said, "Baseball has done more to move America in the right direction than all the professional patriots with their billions of cheap words." It did so because it was a mirror for the culture, as all myths are.

The Shape of Life Is Round

The innings passed, gracefully. Reluctantly, I watched the end of the game approach as fast as groundrush to a paratrooper. The Tigers scored on a booming home run by their All-Star catcher Brad Ausmus, but they couldn't catch the Royals, who won 7-3. But the soul of the game for me isn't always to be found in the final score. Rather, the beauty is in the accumulation of details that make the world come alive for me: the great stretch for a low throw by the first baseman, a triple into the gap, elaborate signals by the coaches, the shift of weight in an outfielder's legs to get better position, the lean across the plate to smack an outside pitch, the pleas of the fans for foul balls to be tossed their way, and the sweetest sight of all, the long high fly ball.

After the last out of the game, I noticed for the first time all night a gigantic flip sign in right field that read, "Games Left" with a number 3 that slowly turned over to read 2. Then hundreds of workers streamed into centerfield and within minutes erected a colossal fireworks setup. I was thrilled at the prospect of seeing the rockets bursting over the old ballpark, but Jack was frightened by the noise. So I reluctantly packed up and we left the ballpark, followed by the cries of the crowd resounding through the night as chrysanthemums of fiery lights exploded over the light towers of the stadium.

When we arrived at our rental car, I shifted my little boy in my arms so I could reach for the car keys. That's when I saw the reflection of the fireworks display in the windows of the cars all around us. It was like being in a house of mirrors while swinging sparklers. The windows seemed to laugh in a wild palette of colors that triggered a distant but dazzling memory. Over the next few minutes, the brief length of time it took me to get my son into his car seat, open the passenger door for Ed, plant myself in the driver's seat, and start the car, I was transported back six years to the ballcourts at Chichen Itza, in the sacred city of the Mayans.

The Sacred Ballcourt

It was the summer of 1993 and I was driving around the Yucatan, visiting as many of the archaeological sites as possible. On my last night in the ancient capital of the Mayans I attended the *Son et Lumiere,* the Sound and Light show, in an effort to learn something new about their cryptic culture. Near the end of the performance, I became restless with the tourist gimmickry and left my seat to stretch my legs. Walking around the back of my fellow tourists in their folding chairs, I noticed that the guards were off in a dark corner by themselves, smoking cigarettes. I looked back to the mighty pyramid just as the stroboscopic lights created the illusion of the Mayan sacred serpent crawling down the side of the main pyramid.

Eager for a private moment, I slipped into the shadows of the long I-shaped playing court, the largest in Mexico, where the Classic Maya competed in a religious game called *pok-a-tok,* a game that was played with a hard rubber ball the size of a bowling ball. Ballcourts have recently been discovered in Mexico that date back to 3400 B.C.E., but the courts here at Chichen Itza were built "only" around the twelfth century. The time span made my head reel as I skulked along the sloping wall, running my hands over the strange carvings of broad-hipped ballplayers fighting over the ball, including one of a player swinging a bat at the ball. On both sides of the ballcourt, exactly midway, stone rings were erected high up on the wall, not horizontally like in our basketball, but vertically. The purpose of the game was to butt the ball with their leather-padded hips or buttocks into the basket, an impressive feat from my humble perspective, thirty feet below the ring.

As the Sound and Light show performance came to a thunderous conclusion, representing the victory of the Chichen rulers over rival cities, the two temples at either end of the court flashed with reflected blues and reds, and I tried to imagine the way the court had functioned as a sacred stage where the struggles between life and death, birth and rebirth, were symbolically played out.

Ballgames were usually played for ritual purposes, but were also occasionally played as sporting competition between friends or professionals, and were often bet on. In its most sacred form, the ballgame was a reenactment of the Ances-

A Mayan ballplayer "hips" the hard rubber ball toward the cosmic hoop.

tral Twins' defeat of the Lords of Death in Xibalba, as told in the *Popol Vuh,* the sacred book of Mayan origins, with the notorious consequences that the losing team would be decapitated and their bodies ignominiously rolled down the steps of the nearby pyramid. Mayan scholars Linda Schele and David Freidel coolly refer to this as the "ritual for the disposition of captives."

According to Schele and Freidel, the reliefs along the sides of some courts allude to war and sacrifice. The imagery strongly suggests that the ballgame bore a metaphorical relationship to war.

"The ballgame," they write, "is the fundamental metaphor of life out of death."

During my few minutes alone, hovering in the shadows of the ballcourt, I thought of the relationship of the Mayan ballcourts to the ritual games held throughout ancient Greece. As is well known, there was a thirty-day truce during the Olympiad. Special heralds were sent out across the empire to declare the truce and assure safe travel for athletes and spectators. Any infraction was dealt with severely. During the competition it was advised that peaceful behavior should be adhered to at all times, similar to the sanctuary status accorded churches for centuries. What this signifies is that during the most prestigious years of the Olympics, before the decadence and deterioration set in, there was an early attempt at sublimation of the war instinct. Every four years, for a few months, there was a substitution for war, a substitution for real violence with symbolic acts of aggression. In the drama of these metaphorical struggles, games were first made sacred.

Mythically speaking, the early fragment of story in which the trickster Hermes outraced Ares, the god of war, is metaphorical language for people attempting to transform the death instinct into the life instinct, the symbolic play of turning fate into destiny.

All sports since dramatize that struggle. We never tire of thinking about the transformation of biological and social fate into destiny, which is never granted, only wrestled away from the gods. Gifted athletes, such as Babe Ruth, Jim Thorpe, Babe Didrikson, Michael Jordan, Billie Jean King, Joe Montana, Marion Jones, and Tiger Woods, have an aura of destiny about them. It should come as no surprise that they are often regarded as heroes and described in the press as gods and goddesses. We exaggerate their deeds to add a little panache to our days, but also to provide a measuring stick for our own deeds.

Writers who mythologize athletes hail from a long lineage of wordsmiths struggling to describe the dramatic transfiguration in men and women who have trained with superhuman discipline. Did not Homer find not only justice and necessity in his heroes and wars, but beauty and nobility? But the mythic tenaciousness of the modern world also casts a long shadow when it overemphasizes the life-and-death struggle of competition. As a result we find brawling Little League parents; college coaches throttling their own players, then complaining that young people don't know good manners; players who intentionally injure other players in the name of winning at any cost; players reneging on contracts or refusing the responsibility of being role models; and athletes who take steroids because they feel they need absolutely every edge they can get.

The other side of myth is the madness of mindless rote behavior.

There are myths we are living by, and there are myths we are dying by.

No wonder Emerson said, "Man is a god in ruins."

Memory Is the Mother of Myth

Back in the motel after the game, I watched the local sports report in our room, then called Jo to tell her about the game, and read Jack to sleep. Then I called my mom, and the first thing she asked was, "Is the grass still so green?"

"Impossibly green," I tell her, not wanting to ruin her own fond memories.

The next morning I rose early with Jack and took him to breakfast, drove him past the ballfields where I had played as a boy from dawn till dusk in the closest thing to rapture in my life. After the obligatory reverie, I doubled back to the motel where we met my brother Paul, who had flown in from Louisville, Kentucky, and our old friend, Jack McCaffrey, who arrived with his father Del, whom we always called Mac.

Good old Mac was hobbling around on two bad knees and hunched over with a bad shoulder, but he was overjoyed to see us and as loquacious as ever. Inside the car he proudly announced that it was quite a baseball reunion, referring to the fact that he and I had coached my brother Paul and his son Jack in Little League baseball way back in the early '70s, even winning the city championship one year. Mac promptly began reeling off the names of ex-players—Sheffield, Reid, Barecy, Edmunds, Plungis, Tessane, Workman—names and batting averages and the scores of games of long ago.

From the back seat of Jack's car I watched Mac's face as he shared cherished memories. The stories reminded me of the way he used to coach, emphasizing pride in a pinch-hit double, a good slide, a stinging bunt that advanced a runner. I thought of the legendary sportswriter Heywood Broun describing the power of John McGraw, the manager of the old New York Giants, as being able to "take kids out of the coal mines and out of the wheat fields and make them walk and talk and chatter and play ball with the look of eagles." That splendid phrase captures the look on the faces of those young teams in the photos from that era. Mac's young Yankees had *the look of eagles* that comes from caring, from playing for love of the game.

All the way to the ballpark Mac talked baseball, from our coaching days in Little League to the shift in the Big Leagues from "pure sport" to "sheer entertainment," a complaint that dates back to the 1870s, according to baseball historians. It was a balm to my soul to hear Mac rhapsodize about the games he went to in the '30s, '40s, and '50s, when he saw Babe Ruth hit one over the roof in right field, Hal Newhouser pitch in the World Series, and Hank Greenberg chase the Babe's home run record, only to fall two short with fifty-eight.

Then Mac quizzed us on our own dubious knowledge of baseball lore.

"Okay, what number did Cobb wear?"

"Four—five—one?"

"Gotcha! You bunch of amateurs. *Zero.* They didn't have uniform numbers in Cobb's day! And you call yourselves baseball fans!" He laughs uproariously and cuffs his son Jack on the shoulder as he's driving.

"You old son of a gun," Mac said to my brother with a devilish grin, then to both of us, "God, it's good to see you bastards."

⁂

Outside the entrance to Tiger Stadium, Paul and I incorrigibly snapped photographs of all us in front of the statue of Ty Cobb, the bleacher entrance, the turnstiles, the ramps. As we walked together through the concourse, Mac, of course, was talking a mile a minute, rattling off statistics from the team we coached together almost thirty years before, like Bob Costas on a World Series broadcast. Mac even remembered to razz my brother about missing fly balls three decades ago, and his boy Jack about giving up home runs to kids who now have kids of their own.

We headed up the ramp toward the bleachers, and the moment that the great green outfield came into view our buddy Jack clutched his heart like the comedian Red Foxx faking a heart attack on his old TV show.

"Sorry, Phil, it happens every time," he whispered to me.

I wanted to say, *I know what you mean,* but could only mutter that the sight always got to me as well. Jack was a finesse pitcher up through the American Legion level "until age and hard living caught up with me," as he put it. It seemed hard for him to watch ballgames because it was his boyhood dream to pitch on that mound.

As we came out into the bright sun, he looked positively mournful and turned his back on the field, and as he gazed at my Jack, he uttered his ultimate compliment, "You know, Phil, he *looks* like a ballplayer."

✳

The hot afternoon sun spangled the bleachers. In the light of day I noticed things I had missed at the night game, like how the metal planks had replaced the old wooden green ones, a garish new scoreboard, and the neon advertising boards that were up all over the park. But it was still the same hallowed ground, which was recognized a few minutes later when the loudspeakers announced that the recently voted "Greatest Tiger Team" ever was being honored on the field. Through my binoculars I could identify several of my now-aged boyhood heroes: Al Kaline, Kirk Gibson, Mickey Lolich, Alan Trammell, George Kell, and the granddaughter of Ty Cobb, the son of Charlie Gehringer, and other family members representing Hank Greenberg, Mickey Cochrane, and Hal Newhouser. The names were enough to set spinning the inner newsreels of my baseball memories, like black and white footage.

"Oh, God, what a lot of memories," said Mac, as he glanced over the park. "Over at first, that's where I remember Norm Cash playing. God, what a hitter—and a great sense of humor. Now there was a guy who *loved* to play baseball."

All around us, the fans were galvanized by the ceremonies on the field, and were murmuring like a bunch of grizzled ballplayers:

"Remember back when Greenberg nearly broke Ruth's record—"

"Yeah, he had fifty-eight with five games left to play—"

"All right, wisenheimer, can you name the '68 infield?"

"Cash, McAuliffe, Oyler, and Wert—with Stanley at short in the Series."

"Smartass. Got nothing better to do than memorize trivia? Get a life!"

"Hey, baseball *is* life. Where ya' been?"

"Okay, yous guys, who was the last Tiger to get seven hits in one game?"

"That's a no-brainer, Ty Cobb, the Georgia Peach—"

"No—Chico Fernandez!"

"Chico *who?* Wasn't he one of the Marx Brothers?"

This was baseball nirvana for any baseball fan beguiled by trivia. You couldn't have wiped the smile off my face with a six-foot eraser. The mere names of my boyhood heroes came streaming across like white lettered titles in a television broadcast. I felt like the archaeologist Heinrich Schliemann as a boy sitting in the tavernas of Piraeus listening to the old fisherman tell stories about the ancient heroes of the Trojan War as if it had all happened yesterday. To me, the good-natured baseball banter was sprinkled like stardust over the ballpark. I thought, *This is what it's all about,* a ballpark bringing together family, friends, and community for years. Conversation, that's what makes for continuity, the sharing of memories, that's what forges community.

"Hey, Mac," I said, "do you remember the story about how Lou Gehrig's streak ended? Most people figure it happened at Yankee Stadium, but it really ended right here. They say Gehrig reached out to catch his first baseman's mitt that had been thrown to him by another player—and flubbed the throw. That was the moment he knew, after 2,130 games, that it was over."

One of the great sports photographs of our time is the one of Gehrig leaning forward from his perch in the visitor's dugout at Tiger Stadium as the first Yankee game in seventeen years began without him. His wry smile is for the ages, as if he were already rehearsing the famous line he delivered a few months later at Yankee Stadium: "Today I feel as if I am the luckiest man in the world...."

"Oh, Christ, I'd forgotten about the Iron Horse. He was some player, all right."

I turned to my brother Paul, who was horsing around with my Jack, and asked him if he remembered Sam Bowie, our Uncle Cy's old friend.

"Sure, the guy who played pro, right?"

"Yeah, I remember when I was about twelve or so playing catch with him. He must have been eighty but the old codger still had a good arm. When I complimented him, he said, *Pshaw.* He told me that he played with Walter Johnson in the minor leagues.

"The Big Train?" Paul asked in astonishment. "The strikeout king? The guy who said that baseball was the dramatization of the life struggles of the ordinary joe?

"Yes, sir," I answered, and recalled how Sam had tossed the ball back to me that long-ago day with a little mustard on it. "Fastest man to ever throw a baseball," he said. "Convinced me I'd never get to the majors. Best decision I ever made."

"How fast was he, Sam?" I asked him.

"Well, I remember one old fella who said after striking out against him, 'Ya can't hit what you can't see.'"

⌖

That morning I had read a wonderful line about the effects of Tiger Stadium on its fans in the local newspaper: "And the old are made young again, and the young old...during every visit." The reference made me think of the ancient mystery rites at Eleusis, Thebes, Mecca, or Newgrange. For instance, Walter F. Otto describes the Eleusinian mysteries as a ritual of rebirth and renewal climaxing in a "stupendous moment [when] myth became reality." That is evocative of what happened to us, on a secular level, as the Tiger game moseyed along. We talked. We told stories. Three generations spoke the common language of baseball for two and a half hours.

Meanwhile, the Tigers scored, tallying two runs in the third inning on a homer from their All-Star catcher, Brad Ausmus. Meanwhile, Tiger hurler C. J. Nitkowski was mowing down the Royal batters with a blazing fastball. As the game progressed, I found myself watching Mac and his Jack huddled close to each other on the bleacher bench, murmuring about the clever movement of pitches. "Sure can throw strikes, can't he, Jack?" The ease with which they spoke made me wonder whether I would be able to talk that easily with my own Jack thirty years from now.

As if on cue, I overheard the young father behind me, who had been struggling with a crying newborn baby, say to his wife, who was handling a restless two-year-old, "It's all about memories, babe. That's why we came." I turned around and winked at him, then a woman in a straw hat and a dozen baseball pins in her Tiger T-shirt leaned over and confided to us as if we were long lost friends, "Ya know, I've come here alone for thirty-seven years. I got my own memories. This is the one place in the world I never need no date or gotta get anyone's damned permission to come here. I came here with my dad when I was a kid and got hooked. You know, every time I come back he's still here with me. It's a great thing you're doing for those kids a yours. They got wonderful parents, yes, they do."

In the fifth inning Paul offered to take little Jack for a walk around the bleachers, where he bought him some souvenirs and a bag of peanuts. I took the opportunity to indulge in some more banter with Mac, reminding him of Goose Gossage in the '84 World Series telling his manager Dick Williams, "I can get him," only to have Kirk Gibson clobber the next pitch into the upper deck in right field. The photograph of Gibbie leaping in the air again as he triumphantly circled the bases has become one of the iconic images of baseball history. We talked about the notorious Tiger pitcher Denny McLain grooving one for Mickey Mantle in his last bat at Tiger Stadium, baseball's all-time hot-dog Reggie Jackson swatting a monster blast in the '71 All Star game, and the radio booth so close players could hear the echo of their own actions twenty feet away. Over there was Kaline throwing out a runner at the plate, and there was Harvey Kuenn dragging a bunt and spitting out a chaw of tobacco after legging out the hit. Over there was Ted Williams confessing to a teammate in the dugout that this is a hitter's paradise because of all the green, and there was Rod Carew smiling at the chance to play here because, he said, "you get a buzz here because you can hear the fans; if you can't hear the fans, you can't get a buzz." On the mound I recall Mark Fidyrich patting it smooth before games and talking to the baseball, even tossing one ball back to an umpire after he'd surrendered a hit with it. After the game he explained why: "Well, that ball had a hit in it, so I wanted it to get back in the ball bag and goof around with the other balls there. Maybe it'll learn some sense and come out a pop-up next time."

For such a slow game it sure moved fast, or to be more precise, flowed fast, like fond accounts of memorable plays, books, or movies. In the last few years, the ballpark had been dubbed "The Corner," which was immediately absorbed by the media and marketeers as if had been the nickname for decades. As my eyes kept scanning the field, stands, press box, and dugouts, it occurred to me that Tiger Stadium could have been called the Memory Theater, in honor of the Greek and Roman art of memory. Their system of artificial memory helped orators retain vast tracts of knowledge, speeches, poetry, and information without the help of printed words. Essentially, the one who wished to memorize something would use the architectural details of a library or temple and in some still-mysterious fashion would "attach" a line of a speech to that detail. Socrates assumed that there is a kind of wax in the soul that allows us to recall things. Cicero wrote, "We use places as wax for images." Giotto, Dante, and Petrarch were all influential in medieval times for their *aide-de-memoires* with their technique of grotesque imagery to help their readers' recall.

Likewise, a visit to Madison Square Garden, the Boston Gardens, Lambeau Field, Yankee Stadium, Fenway Park, or Tiger Stadium with a devoted boxing, hockey, basketball, football, or baseball fan is guaranteed to evoke feats of memory as soulful as any ancient orator's. The Greeks believed this capacity was evidence of the "gift of Memory, the mother of the Muses," which means that memory stirs inspiration. Or as Yogi Berra put it, "It's *déjà vu* all over again."

✳

In the eighth inning the Tiger phenom Gabe Kapler belted a pitch into the right center field gap. The Royals center fielder lackadaisically circled under the flyball for a routine catch—but it bounced off his glove when the rightfielder bumped into him.

Mercilessly, the "bleacher bums" around us razzed the poor center

fielder, conveniently forgetting he was the same guy who threw souvenir balls into the stands before the game began. "You suck! You suck!
You suck!" they shouted. The Royal center fielder hung his head in
shame, desperate for a log to crawl under.

Mac and his son were outraged, as only former players and coaches
can be. My brother, who played a stellar center field for us, shouted at
Mac, "Hey coach, you taught me to catch those. You didn't tell me I could
make a million bucks a year if dropped them! Hey, I feel ripped off!"

The razzing didn't let up, and I noticed Big Jack's rather mock out-
rage had turned into the thousand-yard stare of a man who was still
passionate about the beauty and force of the game. I had long wondered how he'd made the transition between a fine Little League player
and American Legion star pitcher, and that look of deep focus afford-
ed me a glimpse of how he had accomplished it.

The intensity of his gaze reminded me of a night back in the early
1990s sitting courtside at a Golden State Warriors game against the
Chicago Bulls. With only a few minutes remaining on the clock,
Michael Jordan dribbled into the corner, a few feet from where I was
sitting, and seemed to just hover for a moment while he stared down
Warrior forward Chris Mullin with a look of such ferocious focus and
intensity that Mullin sagged back—and Jordan shifted into what he
calls his "extra gear," flew by him down the baseline, and soared up for
an easy reverse lay-up.

Sitting there in the bleachers I thought about the power of big Jack's
brooding gaze. It moved me in mysterious ways. I thought of a story I'd
read the year before, where Jim Edmonds, a teammate of the Cardinal
slugger Mark McGwire, was asked to explain the home run hitter's
extraordinary concentration. He remarked that McGwire sat with his
bat on his shoulder for a full half-hour before each game, staring into
the back of his locker, focusing, trying to get into what a lot of ballplayers call "the zone," the near mystic state that happens from being
absolutely, resolutely, in the moment.

This sustained attention can lead to what Michael Murphy has
described as "the essential joy of sports," in his book *In the Zone*. Murphy compares the capacity of the great athletes for supernormal

experiences as being comparable to that of renowned mystics. He cites a Russian weightlifter's expression, "the white moment," to describe the "extraordinary integration and power of the athlete using terrific concentration and discipline." Murphy writes that it is "possible to imagine an historic adventure in human transformation that might arise from the experiments and transformations in athletics."

In the seventh inning we all stood for the ritual singing of "Take Me Out to the Ballgame." My son Jack was thrilled as fifty thousand-plus fans sang raucously, than we sank back in our seats for the last few innings. Shadows spread across the field as the cool evening came on. My Jack was restless from sitting so long in the bleachers, so I hoisted him on my shoulders and we walked around the concourse to the other side of the bleacher section, and walked up the ramp to watch a few more minutes of the game. The Tigers had loaded the bases, and Luis Polonia, their only .300 hitter of the benighted year, hit a ringing triple into the alley in right field—right in front of us—to stretch the Tiger lead to 6-1. The crowd cheered wildly, ecstatically. I found myself locked into my own thousand-yard stare as I gazed around the ballpark, trying to memorize faces, colors, shifts of light and shadow.

In the Royal ninth, the Tiger's reliever Matt Anderson, the young fireballing right-hander, mowed down the heart of their batting order. The final out was a long arching fly ball to left field, a hit I watched with great pleasure: a ball in flight, the suspension of time itself, a kind of extension of the greatest game of catch in the world.

After the game, hundreds of us loitered in the bleachers, unwilling, unable to leave. The field was guarded by policemen on horseback patrolling the warning track while the light towers flickered on. Planes flew overhead with banners advertising the new stadium that will open in April 2000. The "Games Left" number in the upper right field press box flipped from *2* over to *1*. Only one game left and I was nearly sick with grief. Then, engulfed in my anger about the loss of the stadium, I saw my brother lift my son Jack up on his shoulders to see the horses on the field. Paul was misty-eyed, almost as much as the Detroit cops next to him who were wiping tears from their eyes or the weeping woman behind us dressed in a tiger-striped Tiger shirt and wearing

Phil and Jack Cousineau, the bottom of the ninth inning, Tiger Stadium.

tiger stripes across her face who was having her picture taken between the cops and sobbing to them about how the last time she saw her husband was here at the ballpark.

"Hey, bro,' do you think this is what Bart Giamatti meant when he said that the game was meant to break your heart?"

"Yeah, I think so. Didn't think it would get to me like this," he replied. "I keep thinking about coming here with Dad and all my buddies through the years and '68, the year we won the pennant—"

We held Jack between us, cradling him in our arms, and put our arms across each other's shoulders while gazing out over the field. I thought about the startlingly beautiful passage by Giamatti in "The Green Fields of the Mind," the Yale scholar, former commissioner, and official eulogizer of the game:

> It breaks your heart. It is designed to break your heart. The game
> begins in the spring, when everything else begins again, and it blos-
> soms in the summer, filling the afternoons and evenings, and then as
> soon as the chill rains come, it stops and leaves you to face the fall
> alone.

As the guards ushered us toward the exit, Jack gestured that he wanted me to hold him. When my brother transferred him over to me and we began the march out of the ballpark Jack whispered in my ear that he was glad he could come with me to see these last games. Then he cupped his hands and whispered to me, "This is a *great* trip, Papa."

Late in the Season

The brilliant essayist Roger Angell once wrote, "Late season baseball stabs you."

An odd but apt choice of verb. It feels right. I believe he was alluding to the sad splendor of October playoff games, which are played while leaves are falling over the land, trees are turning bare, the weather is going cold, and something that has been part of your daily life, the season itself, is ending. Each pitch of the playoffs pulls the game along but brings the end of the season that much closer.

The bludgeoning line came to mind a couple of weeks after our pilgrimage back to Tiger Stadium. I was home alone with my son, watching one of the 1999 playoff games between the Mets and the Braves, a brilliant, hand-wringing affair. Every few minutes Jack looked up from his wooden train set, as if to make sure I was still around, or rolling a question around in his mind before asking me. While he played I picked up a copy of *Baseball Weekly* and chanced upon a small item about Todd Jones and Brian Moehler, two Tiger pitchers, and pitching coach Dan Warthen, sleeping in the clubhouse after the last game at the stadium.

"We were going to get a tent and sleep on the field," Jones said, "but the stadium operations director caught wind of it and bagged the idea. So we came back about 1 A.M., walked around the stadium and then slept in the clubhouse. It was awesome, sleeping in her lap on the last night."

Softly, Jack's voice pulled me, "Papa, why do you love sports, why do you love baseball?"

The question stymied me, like being asked who is God, why is the sky blue, or where did Grandpa go when he died? How do you explain how you love *anything*? Do I tell him about my own sandlot exploits? Do I describe the unforgettable thrill of sitting on my bike with my friends under a streetlight at the corner of Second Street and Forest listening on a transistor radio when the Tigers won the '68 pennant? Do I regale him with tales of hitting the game-winning shot against Saint Agatha or being called a "cheeky American" by the London papers after scoring at the buzzer to lift my team to the city championship in 1975?

Do I hold off and work on that story about the time I was jogging across the park on my way back to a painting job and had to pass by a basketball court where a pickup game was in motion, and one of the players caught my eye and my grin and tossed a perfect bouncepass to me, hitting me in mid-stride, yelling, "Yo, bro,' *do it!*" and me taking the ball and leaping toward the hoop, corkscrewing in the air, feeling like never before in my life that I was *flying,* and realizing in that one mighty leap why I *loved* playing ball, and then the beauty of it all, pumpfaking, bringing the ball around my back, and lifting it, underhand, off my fingertips, effortlessly, into the basket, before floating back down to the cool asphalt.

Yes, I thought, I better tell him that one someday. Then while he waited for me to reveal to him the secret of our little corner of the universe, a recent story flashed in my mind, a haunting anecdote about our neighborhood's favorite son, Joe DiMaggio, who grew up just blocks from here, playing stickball on the playground next to Jack's preschool.

One cold and foggy Saturday morning in the late 1970s, in a small baseball field near Ocean Beach in San Francisco, a band of media league softball players were loosening up their stiff muscles by tossing the ball around. Suddenly they saw far out in center field the approach of a stately gentleman, a hero from a long-lost era. He was wearing a black suit, white shirt, and tie, and walked with the unmistakable grace of an old-time ballplayer. As he approached, the players stopped playing catch and chatted amiably with him. On a whim one of the local sports columnists invited the hero to throw out the ceremonial first pitch of the media league season, but he never dreamed the legend would accept. But there was the Yankee Clipper motioning for the ball, then calmly tossing it to the catcher, resurrecting memories of the long low ropes he used to throw from deep center field in Yankee Stadium. After a few shy words, the hero turned and walked away, slowly disappearing into San Francisco fog.

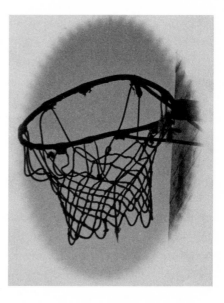

A thing of beauty to peripatetic basketball players: an old bent basketball hoop with a brand-new net floating above an empty court.

Years later, as the reporter said after DiMaggio's funeral, some of them weren't sure if it had actually happened or not.

When I first read about the ghostly encounter I thought I heard a distant echo of DiMaggio's legend-barnacled answer to the question about why he played so hard: "Because there is always some kid who may be seeing me for the first or last time. I owe him my best."

I've told this story to a dozen people since reading the original article by Dwight Chapin, and without exception, baseball fan or not, listeners gasp, as we all do when dropped into mythic time. DiMaggio's surprise appearance and disappearance bears no mean resemblance to one of the legendary cowboy actors. As noted by Robert Lipsyte, he had "ridden into our consciousness just as the myths of the frontier West were receding, one of a posse of cowboys in the outfield who became our new manly heroes, one individual standing just outside the group, our last defense."

Of such resemblances are myths made. Resemblances to a time when we were younger and the world was larger and it's always twilight on the farm and the trains are moaning past the baseball diamond and the boys and girls are waving to the engineer who doffs his hat and waves at the air in a pretend swing of the bat and the radios are playing all across the land in hopes of stopping time.

During his far-flung travels across North America during the 1840s, artist George Catlin encountered an early form of lacrosse commonly played by all forty-eight tribes of American Indians. In this lithograph, *Ball-players: Choctaw and Sioux,* he immortalized three of them: Tul-lock-Chish-Ko (He Who Drinks the Juice of the Stone), Wee-Chush-Ta-Doo-Ta (The Red Man), and Ah-No-Je-Nahge (He Who Stands on Both Sides).

"When the truth becomes legend, print the legend," barked the newspaper editor in *The Man Who Shot Liberty Valance*. Because we can't handle the truth about our heroes or the real news of the world?

On the contrary.

We know only too well the truth of Achilles' heel and DiMaggio's tortured personal life, much as we are aware of our own shortcomings. What we don't know is how anyone can find the "grace under pressure," as Hemingway called it, to transcend their all-too-human limitations—for a moment, a game, a season. That is the power of the myth, the epiphany, the "shining forth" of human courage and excellence.

It's All in the Game

In my travels I have watched cricket in London, rugby in Wales, hurling in Dublin, boules in Paris, cockfights in Bangkok, hockey in Montreal and lacrosse in Sudbury, soccer on Easter Island, jai alai in Manila, and baseball in an Osento, a public bathhouse in Japan—on a steamed-up television. I have actively sought out some kind of sporting activity virtually everywhere I've gone, in the belief that the way we play tells us who we are—and who we long to be. As Wilfred Sheed wrote in a brilliant essay, "Why Sports Matter," athletic competition is, despite the corruption, greed, obsession, and narcissism, not "the devil's work," as believed in nineteenth-century England, but a "window into the soul."

How a nation *plays* often reveals more than we care to admit—witness the joylessness in the athletes from the Eastern block countries during their last years of competition, or the savagery of the hooligans disrupting soccer leagues in Western Europe, in dramatic contrast to Brandi Chastain's exultant celebration at the end of the 1999 World Cup Final, or the ethereal grace of Cathy Freeman after she won the 400 meters in Sydney.

Games are games, and more. As the Portuguese poet Ferdinand Pessoa said, "Everything is something else, *besides*." Every sport, every game, every form of play is a metaphor for the aspirations and anxieties of a people.

America is a land of mythic metaphors of play and competition.

Baseball is one of the last vestiges of pastoral America, a game that was established while the country slowly and often reluctantly shifted from farms to cities. Its myth is firmly rooted in a romantic and harmonious vision of turn-of-the-nineteenth-century rural America. In contrast, the myth of football tends toward martial metaphors for corporate and bureaucratic takeover, an aggressively twentieth-century vision of ritualized violence in urban America. The myth of basketball is a self-styled twenty-first century vision of the emerging world culture of hip-hop, blues, and jazz, as well as a metaphor world for the urge to "get off" the streets, soar out of the inner city, and dance in and out of trouble, away from defenders, and score to the jazzed-up tempo of the city. We need all these games, and more, in order to reflect the ever-changing protean face—and body—of our culture.

The myth of the Olympics reveals a surprisingly fathomless depth of belief that it is sacred to compete for something greater than yourself, the sanctity of the homeland, as illustrated the opening night of the Sydney Olympics in 2000. There were a record 199 countries participating in the Games, involving some ten thousand atheletes, 40 percent of whom were women, more than double the previous Games in Atlanta. The American television crew numbered more than three thousand. It was the most comprehensive coverage of a sporting event in history. Despite the proposed overhauling of the International Olympic Committee that is in the works because of the bribery scandals surrounding the 2002 Salt Lake City Games, and the sniping about ever-creeping nationalism, there was more interest than ever before in the athletic competition.

Overcoming the corrosive cynicism that marks our times, the Sydney Games were a display of grace, courage, will, strength, endurance, and, as was apparent in the opening night pageantry, a profound celebration of the love of home that transcends borders. Times change, but ideals remain the same, since human character has not changed since Milo won his first laurels some thirty-seven centuries ago. Money threatens to overwhelm all sporting events, but the choice is still up to the individual athlete to perform in the pursuit of utter excellence, and for the spectator to watch for the telling details that give us a glimpse of human possibility in a moment of action.

For me, the mythic moment of the Sydney Games came seconds after Cathy Freeman crossed the finish line and fell to her knees. She closed her eyes as a mixture of exhaustion and relief overcame her, and seemed to utter a prayer. When she opened her eyes and glanced around the stadium she seemed genuinely astonished at the near-delirium of joy and national pride. Then a look of astonishment swept across her face as she seemed to realize for the first time the immensity of the hunger that people have for great athletes to achieve the impossible, but with grace, even love of the game.

Of all people, it was the poet T. S. Eliot who said, however ironically, "It would be worthwhile to squeeze the universe into a ball and roll it toward some overwhelming question...."

I believe him. If we squeeze life into the shape of a ball and roll it, toss it, hit it, pass it, catch it, and listen closely to it, we might hear the sound of our own pulse, the beat of wild joy coming from our own hearts as we formulate the question that is aching in our hearts: How will *I* play at the meaning of life?

ACKNOWLEDGMENTS

I wish to express my gratitude toward the many generous souls who shared their time and attention during the course of this book project. First and foremost I would like to acknowledge everyone at Conari Press who showed patience with the once and future manuscript, and helped guide it between the Clashing Rocks of Art and Commerce, especially Mary Jane Ryan, who first saw the mythic potential for the book, my editor Leslie Berriman for her muse-like advice, and Brenda Knight for her "beat-ific" marketing skills. I would also like to extend my hearty thanks to the design team of Suzanne Albertson and Claudia Smelser, who lavished the book with mythic beauty, Pam Suwinsky for her lynx-eyed copyediting, and Heather McArthur for her protean skills in bringing the book home.

I also wish to convey my incalculable debt to my old friend and mentor, the late Joseph Campbell, who recognized my passion for what he was fond of calling "this great stuff of myth," and to his wife Jean Erdman-Campbell, for her encouragement and friendship through the years. Special thanks are due, as well, as to Stuart Brown, executive producer of the film *The Hero's Journey,* with whom I have shared many hours of discussion about the wide-ranging importance of the origins of creativity; to Stephen Larsen for our animated discussions about the mythic imagination; to Alexander and Jane Eliot for my initiation into the "mythosphere"; to Keith Thompson for seventeen years of soulful talk about the power of myth; to Richard Beban and Kaaren Kitchell for their friendship and for sharing with me the vision of their ground-breaking work, *Living Mythically;* and to the late Rollo May, for our numerous lunchtime talks about the cry for meaning in modern times. My gratitude also goes out to all those I interviewed for this work, including James Botsford, Gary Rhine, Joan Marler, P. J. Curtis, John O'Donoghue, Rebecca Armstrong, Edwin Bernbaum, Huston Smith, Sam Keen, Michael Grosso, Connie Martinez, Bob and Lynda Schnekenburger, Ed Fallon, Penny McCann, and Valerie Andrews.

Thanks to Robert A. Johnson for "the holy time" of our many collaborations and discussions on the nature of the symbolic life; to Lauren Artress and Alan Jones at Grace Cathedral in San Francisco; and to Annette and Jim Cullipher at Journey into Wholeness, in Asheville, North Carolina, for the opportunity to stage early forums on "The Myth of Mentorship"; to Michael Murphy and Nancy Lunney at Esalen Institute in Big Sur, for the chance over the last seventeen years to teach a far-ranging series of courses on the mythic imagination.

For their guidance during my sabbaticals in Paris I want to thank Mort Rosenblum, Jeannette Hermann, George Whitman, Jean-Francois Pasquilini, Sarita Beraha, Noel Riley-Fitch, William Wiser, and Glen Myrent. For making possible the film shoots in Brazil, Chile, and Easter Island, I want to express my appreciation to film producer and publisher Chris Zelov at the Knossus Project in Durham, Pennsylvania, and to our colleague Henrique Kopke for his trenchant translation during filming. Thanks also to Roberto Takaoka in São Paulo, Brazil, Juan Purcell in Ritoque, Chile, and Jaime Lerner in Curitiba, Brazil, for their hospitality while we were filming in their countries.

Thanks also to my brother Paul Cousineau for helping me put the shoulder to the boulder with the Sisyphus material, to Del McCaffrey and Jack McCaffrey for their generosity in helping to arrange our pilgrimage back to Tiger Stadium in Detroit, and to Ruth Ross for her generous help in researching the archives of the history museum in Wayne, Michigan. *Mille grazie* to Antonio Anteleri of Caffé Puccini for his poignant insights into the ever-changing face of café life in San Francisco, and to Herb Gold for his reflections into the phenomenon of Bohemia around the world.

Finally, my boundless thanks go out again to my companion, Jo Beaton, for her consummate patience on this once and future book, and to our five-year-old son, Jack, a born *flâneur*, lover of rock and roll, and Tiger fan, thanks for the way you light my way through dark times.

PERMISSIONS

For permission to quote material here, I am indebted to Harcourt, Inc., for an excerpt from "The Rock," in *Four Quartets,* copyright 1942 by T. S. Eliot, renewed 1970 by Esmer Valerie Eliot, reprinted by permission of Harcourt, Inc.; to Coleman Barks for an excerpt from *Unseen Rain: Quatrains of Rumi,* by John Moyne and Coleman Barks, Threshold Books, 1986, used with permission by Coleman Barks; to U Sam Oeur for permission to quote from "The Kingdom of Hell," in *Scared Vows,* Coffee House Press, 1998.

I want to extend my gratitude for the use of the illustrations in this book to H. Roger-Viollet for use of the photograph of Paris café life; to Art Resource for permission to use *Delphica* from the Vatican Museum and *Women Runners* from the Vatican Museum; to the Mansell/TimePix Collection for permission to reprint *Orpheus and the Animals;* to Mikhail Horowitz for permission to reprint two of his baseball card collages previously published in *The Temple of Baseball,* North Atlantic Books, 1985; and to Robin Eschner for the use of her mythic woodcut, "The Saxophone Player," from the book *Deadlines.*

A lengthy and exhaustive effort has been made to locate all the copyright holders and to clear permission rights to the text and illustrations in this book. If any acknowledgements have been omitted, or any rights overlooked, it is unintentional. If the publishers are notified, any omissions will be rectified in future editions of this book.

LIST OF ILLUSTRATIONS

RECOMMENDED READING

Bahn, Peter, and John Flenley. *Easter Island, Earth Island*. London: Thames & Hudson, 1992.

Berry, Thomas. *The Great Work: Our Way into the Future*. New York: Bell Tower, 1999.

Bierlein, J. F. *Living Myths: How Myths Give Meaning to Human Experience*. New York: Ballantine, 1999.

Brand, Stewart. *The Clock of the Long Now*. New York: Basic Books, 1999.

Calasso, Roberto. *The Marriage of Cadmus and Harmony*. New York: Alfred A. Knopf, Inc., 1993.

Campbell, Joseph. *Creative Mythology*. New York and London: Penguin Books, 1968.
———. *The Inner Reaches of Outer Space: Metaphor as Myth and as Religion*. New York: Alfred van der Marck Editions, 1986.

Chatwin, Bruce. *The Songlines*. London and New York: Penguin Books, 1987.

Cleary, Thomas, translater. *Unlocking the Zen Koan*. Berkeley, CA: North Atlantic Books, 1993.

Cousineau, Phil. *The Book of Roads: Travel Stories*. San Francisco: Sisyphus Press, 2000.
———. *The Art of Pilgrimage*. Berkeley, CA: Conari Press, 1998.

Cousineau, Phil, and Christopher Zelov, editors. *Design Outlaws: On the Frontier*. Durham, PA: The Knossus Project and White River, CT: Chelsea Green Publications, 1997.

Daumal, Rene. *Mount Analogue.* Translated and introduction by Roger Shattuck. London: Penguin Books, 1959.

Dubos, Rene. *A God Within.* New York: Charles Scribner's Sons, Inc., 1972.

Eco, Umberto. *Serendipities: Language and Lunacy.* Translated by William Weaver. New York: Columbia University Press, 1999.

Eliade, Mircea. *Images and Symbols: Studies in Religious Symbolism.* Translated by Philip Mariet. New York: Harvill Press, 1961.
———. *Myths, Rites, Symbols: A Mircea Eliade Reader.* Vol. I. Edited by Wendell C. Beane and William G. Doty. New York: Harper Colophon, 1975.
———. *Ordeal by Labyrinth: Conversations with Claude-Henri Rocquet.* Translated by Derek Coltman. Chicago: University of Chicago Press, 1982.

Eliot, Alexander. *The Universal Myths: Heroes, Gods, Tricksters and Others.* New York: Meridian Books, 1990.
———. *The Timeless Myths: How Ancient Legends Influence the Modern World.* New York: Meridian Books, 1997.

Eliot, T. S. "The Rock," *Four Quartets.* New York: Harcourt Brace Jovanovich, 1968.

Emerson, Ralph Waldo. *The Essays of Ralph Waldo Emerson.* New York: Heritage Club Editions, 1949.

Epictetus. *The Art of Living: The Classical Manual on Virtue, Happiness, and Effectiveness.* A New Interpretation by Sharon Lobell. San Francisco: HarperSanFrancisco, 1995.

Feinstein, David, and Stanley Krippner. *Personal Mythology: The Psychology of Your Evolving Self.* Los Angeles: Jeremy Tarcher Press, 1988.

Frankl, Victor E. *Man's Search for Meaning.* Translated by Ilse Lasch. New York: Pocket Books, 1949.

Frye, Northrup. *The Educated Imagination.* Bloomington, IL and London: Indiana University Press, 1964.

Giamatti, A. Bartlett. *A Great and Glorious Game: Baseball Writings.* Edited by Kenneth S. Robson. Chapel Hill, NC: Algonquin Books, 1998.

Gleick, James. *Faster: The Acceleration of Just about Everything.* New York: Pantheon Books, 1999.

Gold, Herbert. *Bohemia: Where Art, Angst, Love and Strong Coffee Meet.* New York: Simon & Schuster, 1993.

Gould, Stephen Jay. *Bully for Brontosaurus: Reflections in Natural History.* New York: W. W. Norton & Co., 1990.

Graves, Robert. *The Greek Myths.* London: Penguin Books, 1955.

Grudin, Robert. *Time and the Art of Living.* New York: Ticknor & Fields, 1982.

Guillevic, Eugene. *Carnac.* Paris: Gallimard, 1961.

Hall, Donald. *Fathers Playing Catch with Sons: Essays on Sport (Mostly Baseball).* San Francisco: North Point Press, 1985.

Hawkings, Stephen. *A Brief History of Time.* Prepared by Gene Stone. New York: Bantam Books, 1992.

Herbert, Zbigniew. *The King of the Ants: Mythological Essays.* Translated by John Carpenter and Bogdana Carpenter. Hopewell, NJ: The Ecco Press, 1999.

Hillman, James. *City and Soul.* Irving, TX: Center for Civic Leadership, University of Dallas, 1978.

Houston, Jean. *The Hero and the Goddess.* New York: Ballantine Books, 1992.

Kazantzakis, Nikos. *Zorba the Greek.* New York: Penguin, 1958.

Keen, Sam. *Your Mythic Journey.* New York: J. P. Tarcher, 1989.

Kinsella, W. B. *Shoeless Joe.* New York: Ballantine Books, 1982.

Larsen, Stephen. *The Mythic Imagination: Your Quest for Meaning through Personal Mythology.* New York: Bantam Books, 1990.

Leeming, David, and Jake Page. *Myths, Legends & Folktales of America: An Anthology.* New York: Oxford University Press, 1999.

Lightman, Alan. *Einstein's Dreams.* New York: Pantheon Books, 1993.

Lippincott, Kristen. *The Story of Time.* London: Merrill-Holberton, 1999.

Lipsey, Roger. *An Art of Our Own: The Spiritual in Twentieth-Century Art.* Boston and Shaftesbury: Shambhala Books, 1988.

Lorca, Federico García. *In Search of Duende.* Edited and translated by Christopher Maurer. New York: New Directions Books, 1998.

Macaulay, Rose. *Pleasure of Ruins*. New York: Walker and Company, 1953.

Meade, Michael. *Men and the Water of Life*. San Francisco: HarperSanFrancisco, 1993.

Mellen, Joan. *Big Bad Wolves: Masculinity in the American Film*. New York: Pantheon, 1977.

Michener, James A. *On Sport*. New York: Random House, 1976.

Murphy, Michael, and Rhea A. White. *In the Zone: Transcendent Experiences in Sport*. New York: Penguin Books, 1995.

Murray, Henry A., editor. *Myths and Mythmaking*. New York: George Braziller, 1959.

Needleman, Jacob. *Time and the Soul*. New York: Currency/Doubleday Books, 1998.

Novak, Michael. *The Joy of Sports: End Zones, Bases, Baskets, Balls, and the Consecration of the American Spirit*. New York: Basic Book Publishers, Inc., 1976.

Oeur, U Sam. *Sacred Vows*. Minneapolis MN: Coffee House Press, 1998.

Packard, David. *Imagining the Universe: A Visual Journey*. New York: The Berkley Publishing Group, 1994.

Pausanius. *Guide to Greece*. London: Penguin Books, 1950.

Peary, Danny. *Cult Movies*. New York: Dell Publishing Company, 1981.

Pendleton-Julian, Ann M. *The Road That Is Not a Road: And the Open City, Ritoque, Chile*. Cambridge, MA: Massachusetts Institute of Technology, 1996.

Pritchard, Evan. T. *No Word for Time: The Way of the Algonquin People*. Tulsa, OK: Council Oak Books, 1997.

Rosenblum, Mort. *Mission to Civilize: The French Way*. New York: Harcourt Brace Jovanovich, 1986.

Rubin, Robert Alden. *Poetry Out Loud*. Chapel Hill: Algonquin Books, 1993.

Sautet, Marc. *Un Café pour Socrates*. Paris: Editions Robert Laffront, 1995.

Sheed, Wilfred. "Can the Joy of Sports Be Saved?" *Wilson Quarterly*, Winter 1995.

Singer, Thomas, ed. *The Vision Thing: Myth, Politics and Psyche in the World.* London and New York: Routledge Press, 2000.

Soleri, Paolo. *Omega Seed.* New York: Anchor Press, 1981.

Sphinx 4: The Mythology of Everyday Life. A Journal for the Archetypal Psychology and the Arts. Edited by Noel Cobb with Eva Loewe. London: London Convivium for Archetypal Studies, 1992.

Theroux, Paul. *The Happy Isles of Oceania.* New York: Simon & Schuster, 1997.

Thomas, Lewis. *Late Night Thoughts on Mahler's Ninth Symphony.* New York: Viking Press, 1983.

Thorn, John. *Baseball: Our Game.* New York: Penguin Books, 1995.

Toynbee, Arnold, editor. *Cities of Destiny.* New York: McGraw-Hill Book Company, 1967.

Van der Post, Laurens. *The Lost World of the Kalahri.* San Diego, New York, and London: Harcourt Brace and Company, 1958.

von Franz, Marie-Louise. *On Divination and Synchronicity.* Toronto: Inner City Books, 1980.
———. *Time: Rhythm and Repose.* New York and London: Thames and Hudson, 1984.

Warner, Marina. *Six Myths of Our Time.* New York: Vintage, 1996.

Watts, Alan. *Myth and Ritual in Christianity.* Boston: Beacon Press, 1968.

Whitrow, Gerald J. *The Nature of Time.* New York: Penguin Books, 1972.

INDEX

ABOUT THE AUTHOR

Phil Cousineau is an author, editor, teacher, adventure travel leader, photographer, and documentary filmmaker. His life-long fascination with the art, literature, and history of culture has taken him on journeys across the globe. He lectures around the world on a wide range of topics from creativity, mythology, mentorship, and soul to travel and community work.

Born at an army hospital in Columbia, South Carolina, in 1952, Cousineau grew up in Wayne, Michigan, just outside of Detroit. While moonlighting in an automotive parts factory he studied journalism at the University of Detroit. Before turning to writing full-time in 1984, his peripatetic career included stints as a sportswriter and photographer, playing basketball in Europe, harvesting date trees on an Israeli kibbutz, and painting forty-four Victorian houses in San Francisco.

His numerous books include the bestselling *The Art of Pilgrimage; Riddle Me This; Soul Moments: Marvelous Stories of Synchronicity; Soul: An Archaeology. Readings from Socrates to Ray Charles; The Soul of the World; The Hero's Journey: Joseph Campbell on His Life and Work;* and *Deadlines: A Rhapsody on a Theme of Famous Last Words,* which won the 1991 Fallot Literary Award. His books have been translated into seven languages, and he is a contributor to twelve other books, including a collaboration with John Densmore on his bestselling autobiography, *Riders on the Storm: My Life with Jim Morrison and the Doors.*

His screenwriting credits in documentary films, which have won more than twenty-five international awards, include *Ecological Design:*

Inventing the Future; Wayfinders: A Pacific Odyssey; The Peyote Road; The Red Road to Sobriety; Your Humble Serpent: The Life of Reuben Snake; Wiping the Tears of Seven Generations; Eritrea: March to Freedom; The Presence of the Goddess; The Hero's Journey: The World of Joseph Campbell; and the 1991 Academy Award-nominated *Forever Activists: Stories from the Abraham Lincoln Brigade.*

Currently, Cousineau lives in San Francisco, California, with his companion, Jo Beaton, and their five-year-old son, Jack.

TO OUR READERS

CONARI PRESS publishes books on topics ranging from spirituality, personal growth, and relationships to women's issues, parenting, and social issues. Our mission is to publish quality books that will make a difference in people's lives—how we feel about ourselves and how we relate to one another. We value integrity, compassion, and receptivity, both in the books we publish and in the way we do business.

As a member of the community, we donate our damaged books to nonprofit organizations, dedicate a portion of our proceeds from certain books to charitable causes, and continually look for new ways to use natural resources as wisely as possible.

Our readers are our most important resource, and we value your input, suggestions, and ideas about what you would like to see published. Please feel free to contact us, to request our latest book catalog, or to be added to our mailing list.

2550 Ninth Street, Suite 101
Berkeley, California 94710-2551
800-685-9595 · 510-649-7175
fax: 510-649-7190 · e-mail: conari@conari.com
www.conari.com